AARON T.
Beck

Key Figures in Counselling and Psychotherapy

Series editor: Windy Dryden

The *Key Figures in Counselling and Psychotherapy* series of books provides a concise, accessible introduction to the lives, contributions and influence of the leading innovators whose theoretical and practical work has had a profound impact on counselling and psychotherapy. The series includes comprehensive overviews of:

AARON T. Beck

MARJORIE E. WEISHAAR

SAGE Publications

London • Thousand Oaks • New Delhi

SAGE Publications Ltd
6 Bonhill Street
London EC2A 4PU

SAGE Publications Inc
2455 Teller Road
Thousand Oaks, California 91320

SAGE Publications India Pvt Ltd
32, M-Block Market
Greater Kailash – I
New Delhi 110 048

British Library Cataloguing in Publication Data

Weishaar, Marjorie E.
  Aaron T. Beck – (Key Figures in Counselling
  & Psychotherapy Series)
  I. Title II. Series
  616.8914092

ISBN 0–8039–8564–9
ISBN 0–8039–8565–7 (pbk)

Library of Congress catalog card number 93–085097

Typeset by Mayhew Typesetting, Rhayader, Powys
Printed in Great Britain by Biddles Ltd, Guildford, Surrey

This book is dedicated to the supervisors
and post-doctoral fellows at the
Center for Cognitive Therapy, Philadelphia
and to
Stephen, Annie and Evan McGarvey

Contents

Acknowledgments

Many people helped me with this book and I gratefully acknowledge their valuable contributions. I was overwhelmed by a wealth of interview information, not all of which appears in this volume. In the text, quotations not attributed to published sources are from interviews I conducted.

Aaron T. Beck endorsed and encouraged this project. He allowed me to interview him from coast to coast; at conferences, workshops, and award ceremonies; in coffee shops and in taxi cabs. He answered my questions with directness, self-disclosure and good humor. He also introduced me to his family, whose acquaintance has been a source of pleasure for me as well as a fount of biographical information. I wish to thank Aaron Beck's brother, Maurice, for his recollections and for sharing the poems of his father, Harry Beck. Dr Irving Beck and his wife, Edith, provided and confirmed much family information. Throughout my research, 'Ask Irving' became a familiar refrain. Dr Judith Beck allowed me to interview her several times and provided a unique perspective on her father. Minna Saxe, Aaron Beck's cousin, provided family writings, photos, and historical information. Joan Temkin Slafsky, also a cousin, drew a Temkin genealogy. The part of the genealogy which appears in this book was designed by graphic artist Jill Brody.

Barbara Marinelli, executive director of the Center for Cognitive Therapy in Philadelphia, supported this endeavor and pointed me in the right direction. She introduced me to several people who provided information and made accessible archival material at the Center. Karen Quinn, assistant to Dr Beck, responded to all my requests for publications, checked facts, and verified information with professional efficiency. Ann L. McGarvey assisted with research at the Pennsylvania State University. Eleanor F. Horvitz, librarian and archivist of the Rhode Island Jewish Historical Society, directed me to the Temkin family archives. Her own article on Harry Beck was an invaluable resource as well. I am thankful for all this help.

Many people were interviewed or consulted for this book. I wish to thank Drs David M. Clark, W. Edward Craighead, Gary

Emery, Arthur Freeman, Ruth Greenberg, Steven Hollon, Maria Kovacs, Michael Mahoney, Donald Meichenbaum, Christine Padesky, James Pretzer, A. John Rush, Brian Shaw, Mark Whisman, Jesse Wright, Jeffrey Young, and Albert Ellis. Dr Ellis made available, as did Dr Beck, their 30 years' correspondence with each other. In addition to my own interviews, I drew from interviews with Dr Beck conducted by journalists Ann Diffily and Peter Ross and by Drs Paul Salkovskis and Michael Yapko.

Finally, I am indebted to Sandra Kopel, who transcribed, with accuracy and discretion, hours of tape recorded interviews, typed the references, and corrected the final manuscript. I also thank Dr Windy Dryden, the series editor, for his careful reading of the manuscript and his determination to keep me on target.

1

The Life of Aaron T. Beck

Overview

Aaron Temkin Beck, MD is the founder of Cognitive Therapy, a form of psychotherapy based on an information-processing, rather than a motivational or instinctual, model of human behavior and psychopathology. Beck's Cognitive Therapy was developed during a period of great and rapid change in psychology and psychiatry and was innovative in its emphasis on the role of cognition in emotional distress and behavioral dysfunction. Beck's work is a major stride in our understanding and treatment of psychological problems, for he presents a coherent and unified theory of psychopathology, strategies which are congruent with the theory, and research which tests and further elaborates his hypotheses. Beck's scrutiny of his own work helped set a precedent within the psychotherapeutic world, and his manuals of how to practice Cognitive Therapy similarly challenged other theorists to codify what is actually done in psychotherapy.

Beck established his expertise and early renown in the field of depression, reconceptualizing it, developing diagnostic tools such as the Beck Depression Inventory, and creating an effective therapy for its treatment. His 1967 textbook on depression (Beck, 1967) has been described by reviewers as the 'principal work in this area' and his 1979 book *Cognitive Therapy of Depression*, written collaboratively with some of his students, is a landmark text on the subject. More than 50 published studies of clinical depression have supported descriptive aspects of the cognitive model (Haaga, Dyck and Ernst, 1991). Over 25 outcome studies have supported the efficacy of Cognitive Therapy for depression (Dobson, 1989). Its inclusion in the National Institute of Mental Health's multisite collaborative study on depression confirms it as a viable treatment for depression.

Because of early research comparing Beck's Cognitive Therapy with antidepressant medication in the treatment of unipolar depression (Rush et al., 1977), Cognitive Therapy was initially viewed as a challenge to pharmacotherapy. However, this is an over-simplification of the purpose and treatment applications of Cognitive Therapy. Cognitive Therapy has grown in scope to address a number of disorders, health problems, and clinical populations. Future directions appear to include nonclinical populations (for example, in educational settings) and prophylactic treatments for depression among the never depressed.

Beck's Cognitive Therapy is one of a number of cognitive therapies, all of which assume that psychological distress is, at least in part, a function of how the individual constructs his or her experience. Mahoney (1988) lists 17 current cognitive therapies which differ from one another in terms of basic assumptions about (1) the nature of reality, (2) theories of knowledge or knowing, and (3) theories of causation. The field of cognitive therapy is so broad that two scholarly journals are devoted to it, *Cognitive Therapy and Research* and the *Journal of Cognitive Psychotherapy: An International Quarterly*. In this book, Cognitive Therapy refers specifically to Beck's model; 'cognitive therapy' or 'cognitive therapies' refers to the general category of cognitive psychotherapy.

As director of the Center for Cognitive Therapy in Philadelphia, Beck has designed and supervised the training of hundreds of psychiatry residents, as well as postdoctoral fellows in psychology, many of whom have gone on to establish their own Cognitive Therapy centers throughout the United States and other countries, particularly in Europe.

Beck's accomplishments have been recognized by both fields of psychiatry and psychology. Since 1983, he has been University Professor of Psychiatry at the University of Pennsylvania in Philadelphia. (There are 14 University Professorships within the entire University.) He has received the Foundations Fund Prize for Research in Psychiatry of the American Psychiatric Association, the Paul Hoch Award of the American Psychopathological Association, the Distinguished Scientific Award for the Applications of Psychology from the American Psychological Association, and the Louis Dublin Award of the American Association of Suicidology. In 1982, he received an Honorary Doctor of Medical Science degree from his alma mater, Brown University, and in 1987 he was elected a Fellow of the Royal College of Psychiatrists.

Aaron T. Beck is a prolific writer, a careful researcher, and a skillful promoter of Cognitive Therapy. He is an intensely creative yet extremely pragmatic individual who has been able to stimulate a generation of researchers. He is also a voracious reader, well-versed in many subjects from Darwinian evolution to American films and entertainment. With his shock of white hair and red bow tie he is immediately recognizable. His warm and genuine manner often cause acquaintances to describe him in fatherly terms. He is, however, shrewd, for he knows exactly what he wants to accomplish and is quite determined to achieve his goals. Moreover, Beck emits a vitality that one associate describes as contradicting any fatherly impression.

Aaron Beck is the third surviving son and youngest child of Harry and Elizabeth Temkin Beck. Both his parents were Russian Jewish immigrants to the United States. Beck was born, raised and educated in New England and has academic and familial ties to Providence, Rhode Island. He was raised by principled and politically active parents in a family which revered literature and learning. His career interests, shaped by both science and the humanities, didn't coalesce until he had nearly completed college. Throughout medical school he maintained wide-ranging interests and he entered psychiatry, not by design, but by serendipity.

Beck has been married for more than forty years to Phyllis Whitman Beck, a Superior Court judge in Pennsylvania. They have four adult children and eight grandchildren. Dr. Judith Beck, his daughter, is the director of professional services at the Center for Cognitive Therapy, and trains Cognitive Therapists.

Family Background

Elizabeth Esther Temkin migrated from Russia to the United States in 1905, at age 16, with her father, Noah Temkin, her older brother Max and another brother. The passport issued indicates that one particular brother was to travel with them, but there is some speculation in the family that he was ill and so another son went in his place. They left behind in Lubitsch, near Chernobyl, Elizabeth's mother, Basha Devorah (later called Deborah), and younger siblings Charles, Nathan, Louis, Sarah, Bella (who later changed to Belle), and Samuel. (A partial Temkin genealogy appears in Figure 1.1.) They were soon to follow on the *Rotterdam*, destined for New York. Basha Devorah, pregnant with her youngest child, Jacob, accompanied her children on the voyage, but travelled in a different class because of her pregnancy. On board ship, the young children were separated from their mother by wire mesh and pressed their bodies against the wire to see her, to be closer. The family did not travel by steerage and did not disembark through Ellis Island in New York. Instead, immigration officials came on board the ship to process their immigration. Basha Devorah and her children departed New York immediately to join her husband and three other children in Providence, Rhode

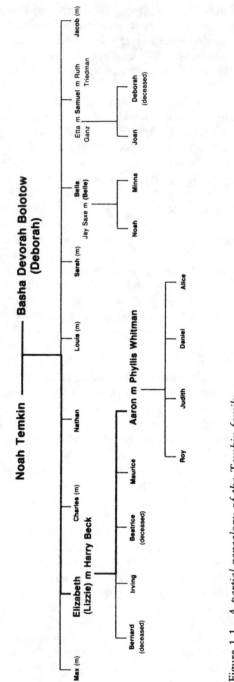

Figure 1.1   *A partial genealogy of the Temkin family*

Source: 'The Noah Gluskin Temkin and Basha Deborah Bolotow Temkin Families', compiled by Nathan Temkin, Temkin Family Archives, RI Jewish Historical Society; Joan Temkin Slafsky; Irving Beck.

Island. Her brother, Louis Bolotow (né Bolotowski) was a physician in Providence and, thus, the community was chosen as their new home.

Lizzie Temkin, as she was known, was the oldest daughter among nine children. Two of her brothers eventually were to graduate from Brown University and one from Harvard Law School. She herself aspired to be a physician, according to her son, Aaron Beck. However, that type of education was not available to her. Instead, she cared for her younger siblings, worked in a sweat shop assembling jewelry, and helped run the family grocery store. She learned English by waiting on store customers.

Within four years of migrating to the United States, Basha Devorah Temkin died of influenza and Lizzie assumed even more responsibility for her brothers and sisters. This role continued throughout her life. She made sure, for instance, that the youngest boys in the family were educated. While her own formal education was not to be, her quest for intellectual life continued, including the study of Hebrew, traditionally reserved for men. She was also involved in women's suffrage and spoke up about social issues. Aaron Beck says his mother 'was a rather dominant person, very outspoken, and did not know the anguish of self-doubt. Occasionally she was wrong, and it was problematic. But she was a good manager and she kind of arranged the relationships in the family. While they were all close, there were certain problems that would arise. She had a philosophy that you had to forgive and forget. She would put out all the little brush fires. In the Jewish community, she was highly respected because she was president of organizations and had this superb self-confidence. If there was a public meeting and the governor was there, she would get up and talk.'

Aaron Beck's oldest brother, Irving, says that his mother was 'the boss of the brothers and sisters. She liked to have her way. She liked to, as she put it, "dictate things". If she had an objective in mind, she kept to it.' Lizzie remained the family matriarch throughout her life, directing many family decisions, including approval of intended spouses and naming babies.

The Temkins played an extremely active role in the intellectual and religious life of their community. Noah Temkin was involved in the Zionist Organization of Rhode Island, the Jewish Home for the Aged, the Miriam Hospital, the Jewish Publication Society of America, and the Jewish Community Center. He was an Orthodox Jew and quite involved in a synagogue called Howell Street Shul. His children all belonged to it, but later his sons Max and Charles split off from the Shul and helped to found a Conservative temple,

Temple Emanu-El. Belle Temkin's daughter, Minna Saxe, says that at one point Temple Emanu-El was referred to as 'Temkin Emanu-El' because the family was so active in it.

All the Temkin brothers were members and leaders (often directors or trustees) of the Hebrew Free Loan, the General Jewish Committee, the Zionist Organization of America, the Jewish Home for the Aged, the Jewish Community Center, the Hebrew Day School, the Rhode Island Jewish Historical Society, the Miriam Hospital, and Temple Emanu-El. During her life, Lizzie Temkin held membership in the sisterhood of Temple Emanu-El, Pioneer Women of Providence, the Providence chapter of Hadassah, the Ladies Association of the Jewish Home for the Aged, the Ladies Union Aid Society, the Miriam Hospital Women's Association, the Ladies Montefiore Association, Workmen's Circle (a labor organization with social, educational and community goals), and the Providence Hebrew Day School Association.

The newspaper report of Lizzie's wedding to Harry Beck in 1909 reflects the importance of the Temkin family in Providence. It reads:

Beck–Temkin

Fully 1000 persons gathered in the Jewish Synagogue on Howell street yesterday afternoon to witness the wedding of Harry Beck to Miss Elizabeth Temkin, a well-known young couple of the city, both members of prominent Jewish families. The synagogue has a seating capacity of 800, and in addition to the seats being taken, all standing room was occupied during the ceremony.

The wedding was to have taken place two months ago, but because of the death of the bride's mother it was postponed. Owing to that fact yesterday's ceremony was tinged with sadness, the absence of the mother being noted during the ceremony.

Rabbi Bachrach, assisted by Rev. Michael Wechsler, performed the marriage ceremony. The bridesmaids were Miss Eva A. Izenberg of this city, Miss Bella Ettenberg of New York, Miss Emma Riskin of Central Falls and Miss Sophia Surdutow of this city. The witnesses for the bridegroom were Louis Bolotow of Lonsdale and Simon Horenstein of this city. The music was furnished by Prof. Bender.

The bride was given away by her father, Noah Temkin. The marriage ceremony was then performed, the usual customs being followed. Following the ceremony a wedding banquet was served at the home of the bride's father, 49 Benefit street, at which about 200 relatives and invited friends of the family were present.

Mr. and Mrs. Beck will spend their honeymoon in New York sightseeing, and upon their return will make their home on Clorane street.

(*Providence Journal*, May 10, 1909)

Harry Beck was born in the Ukraine in 1884 and migrated to the United States in 1902. After arriving in New York, he settled in Providence, Rhode Island because his uncle, who had taken the name Horenstein, lived there. In Russia, Harry Beck had apprenticed with a commercial printer and had learned to set type in Ukranian, Hebrew, Russian, German, and Yiddish. In Providence, again by working in printing shops, he taught himself English. In 1907, he started his own printing business, H. Beck and Company.

It is not known whether Noah Temkin, described as 'quite autocratic,' fully approved of his daughter's marriage to Harry Beck, for Beck was not as religious as Noah Temkin. Moreover, Beck was a 'free thinker.' Having been an anti-Bolshevik in Russia, he was an active Socialist and strong supporter of the labor union movement in the United States. In fact, throughout his career he had continuous union membership. Being both a member of the Typographical Union and owner of the business was a unique labor–management arrangement, one worked out by the International Union with printers who were shop owners (Horvitz, 1990).

Being a Socialist may have been disadvantageous for Harry Beck in some respects, for Aaron Beck's brother Maurice remembers his father being referred to scornfully as 'Beck the Socialist.' Nevertheless, he was a man of quiet conviction who once became angry with his wife for buying a loaf of bread from a bakery at which the workers were striking.

Harry Beck also had a vibrant intellectual life which included regularly hosting a group of men in his home to exchange philosophical, political, and literary opinions. Later in life, he took both psychology and literature courses through the Brown University extension program. Beck was keenly interested in literature and the theatre. He first became interested in the theatre as an adolescent. As part of his printing apprenticeship, he would deliver playbills to the theatre attended by Russian officers. He would stay to see the plays and thus learned of Shakespeare and the great Russian playwrights. His interest in literature extended to poetry, which he both read and wrote. He also translated from Yiddish the autobiography of his mother, Etta Beck.

By his sons' accounts, Harry Beck loved to write. He had wanted to be an editor of a small town newspaper, according to Maurice. After Lizzie Beck died, Harry began to write poetry. Those close to him describe this late blossoming as his emergence from his wife's shadow. He wrote of childhood experiences in Russia, reworked Yiddish folktales, and addressed current events such as the racial bombing of a Birmingham Sunday School during the

American civil rights struggle. Harry Beck dedicated many of these poems to his grandchildren and sent them to the grandchildren for their comments. A young Judy Beck received poems from her grandfather and corresponded with him, sending her own poetry in return.

Harry Beck taught his sons to love literature, writing, and ideas. Maurice Beck was on the staff of the *Brown Daily Herald* newspaper during college and has a Master's degree in psychology. He describes his relationship to literature today as that of a 'consumer.' Irving Beck, in addition to being a renowned physician, former Chief of Medical Service of the Miriam Hospital and author of numerous scientific articles, is a James Joyce scholar and a member of the John Russell Bartlett Society of bibliophiles in Providence. He has served on the boards of libraries devoted to science and rare books and used to have a very large personal library on the history of science. Aaron Beck is a prolific and eclectic reader, subscribing to more than 25 journals and magazines in addition to his professional subscriptions. His preparation for workshops and lectures is extensive and his students may see a similarity between Harry Beck's solicitation of feedback on his poetry and Aaron Beck's solicitation of feedback on his ideas. In anticipation of weekly seminars and meetings at the Center for Cognitive Therapy, Aaron Beck sends trainees and fellows memos outlining his ideas to be presented, requesting their written reactions. He also sends manuscripts to colleagues for criticism and articles from assorted journals to associates with a particular interest in the topic. Part of the format of Cognitive Therapy itself is the elicitation of feedback from the client at the end of each session. Perhaps this is a natural response for Aaron Beck, for he believes criticism to be generally helpful. He also believes that scholarship is not solitary, and finds the exchange of ideas exciting. This may be the legacy of Harry Beck.

Harry and Elizabeth Beck had five children, two of whom died in childhood. Their first child, a son named Bernard, died in infancy. Irving Addison Beck's birth on November 4, 1911 was followed by the birth of the only daughter, Beatrice. Beatrice died in the influenza epidemic of 1919. This plunged Lizzie into a deep depression which was to last, at some level, for the rest of her life. Maurice Peretz, born on September 2, 1917, was significantly affected by his mother's depression, Aaron Beck believes. Although he was too young to know his mother was depressed, Maurice Beck remembers, 'Mother Beck was quite distraught. If I made reference to it [Beatrice's death] she would moan. There wasn't anything I could do about it.' One imagines a young child trying to help an inconsolable mother.

Lizzie's sister Belle tried to distract Lizzie from her loss by taking her to the movies. Minna Saxe, Belle's daughter, believes they spent a week at the movies following Beatrice's death. Saxe is not sure whether their movie going actually started prior to Beatrice's death, but family members attest to its importance in Lizzie Beck's life at that time of grieving. Maurice Beck says it was common understanding that his mother was depressed but only recently, he says, did he realize why he had a thorough knowledge of vaudeville songs from the 1920s. 'I saw a lot of movies at the Albee Theatre. I remember vaudeville and an awful lot of movies. I must have tagged along every time she went to a movie.' Movie going became a lifelong diversion for Lizzie Beck, as it was to be for her son, Aaron.

Childhood

Lizzie Beck's depression apparently remained fairly constant for a few years. According to what Irving and Harry Beck told Aaron, Lizzie's depression remitted with the birth of her youngest child, Aaron Temkin Beck, on July 18, 1921. Aaron Beck believes he was a replacement child for the beloved Beatrice and that his mother was somewhat disappointed that he was not a girl, although he never heard her say so. On the positive side, he smiles at the notion that he was able to cure his mother's depression at such an early age. He jokes that this illustrates his need for control in all situations!

Due to the losses of two of her children, Lizzie Beck was overprotective of her youngest son, Aaron. An accident and life-threatening illness when he was seven compounded her concern with his well-being. Maurice Beck remembers the accident, for he had accompanied his brother to the neighborhood playground where it happened. Aaron 'was apparently on top of a slide, and I was around playing with some other people. Someone pushed him and he broke his arm. He contracted an infection and later it became life-threatening. I remember seeing him in bed with his arm stretched out. He had it in a cast.' At the time, Maurice did not know how serious his brother's injury was because the information was kept from him.

What had happened was that Aaron Beck's broken bone had developed an infection. The osteomyelitis then developed into septicemia, a generalized infection in the blood. Irving Beck recently told Aaron that there was no type of treatment for such an infection at the time and, thus, the condition was 90 per cent fatal. Irving overheard the surgeon telling Lizzie that Aaron would likely die. Irving heard his mother urgently reply, 'He will *not* die! My son will *not* die!'

'She was very determined,' says Irving. Aaron vividly remembers being ill, but had no idea that his illness could be fatal. 'I had my eighth birthday in the hospital,' he says. 'I remember the day my mother was so happy because I was off the danger list.' He had been on the danger list for two months. During this time of tremendous strain and worry, Lizzie Beck would frequent the movies. Lizzie Beck's overprotectiveness of Aaron did not seem to thwart his autonomy. However, he says, 'Being autonomous doesn't prevent me from being hypochondriacal.'

The effects of his illness were manifested primarily as anxieties and phobias and in missing school, which, in turn, created his beliefs that he was inept and stupid. In addition, his first grade teacher that year was harsh and rigid and once screamed at him for coloring the sky the 'wrong' color (he used blue). Although this was just one incident, he recalls he felt very stupid as a consequence. 'It hurt a lot,' he says. 'It probably made a strong schema because I never forgot it.'

'I was held back in the first grade and I always thought it was because I was dumb. Many years later I asked my mother and she said I'd been sick a great deal. That meant I fell behind my peer group, so that all my friends were in a different grade. That stamped me as genetically and unalterably inferior.

'I didn't like being behind my friends. When I was in third grade I was already out of synch [by half a year]. It was possible to skip [ahead], so I spoke to my mother and she spoke to the teacher. The idea was that my brother Irving could tutor me and my brother Maurice could help him.'

Through self-help, Beck actually ended up a year ahead of his peer group. For him, 'psychologically it did show some evidence that I could do things, that if I got into a hole I could dig myself out. I could do it on my own. The experience had a significant influence on me. Psychologically, the idea that I was being put down really mobilized me. It was a challenge, that "never say die" [attitude], turning a disadvantage into an advantage.'

These efforts to overcome beliefs that he was stupid or inept were reinforced by disconfirmatory evidence, for Aaron continued to excel in school. Maurice, incidentally, relished his younger brother's success. He found Aaron's report cards and gleefully saw that Aaron's grades were even better than Irving's.

Beck's childhood memories reveal parents with very different temperaments. While his father was tranquil, his mother was mercurial. Beck says she had a lot of common sense and was encouraging of positive steps, such as his decision to skip a grade in school. However, 'she wasn't the perfect parent. She was terribly inconsistent. When she was in a bad mood, she'd scream. That was kind of troublesome. I'm not sure it affected my character, but it has been a great source of sensitivity. I couldn't explain it. For certain periods of time, she would be irrational and have tremendous tears. She'd be fine for a few weeks and then go off again. I couldn't understand it, so we just decided she was excitable. I still didn't like it.' Beck believes he is still very sensitive to others' unexpected mood changes because of experiences with his mother and the unanticipated fury of his first grade teacher.

Harry Beck encouraged Aaron's interests in science and nature. Aaron joined the Audubon Society, enjoying the observation of birds and plants, and later assisted Maurice as a camp counselor. He also joined the Boy Scouts and became, at age 15, the youngest Eagle Scout in his troop.

At Hope High School, Beck was editor of the school paper, contributing a column and poems. During his high school years, a friend dubbed him with the nickname Tim, from Temkin. No one in the Temkin and Beck extended families calls him Tim; to them he is Aaron. However, his wife and close associates use the nickname.

Aaron's career interests varied, but what he 'really wanted to do was make a living.' The Becks weren't poor, but lived frugally. While Harry Beck had his own shop and always had accounts, the family never had a car and all three sons worked their way through college.

Aaron Beck graduated first in his class at Hope High School (noted anthropologist Stanley Garn was a schoolmate) and followed his brothers to Brown University. Irving became a doctor of internal medicine and Maurice, obtaining Bachelor's and Master's degrees in psychology, entered social work. While at Brown, Aaron was desk editor for the school paper, the *Brown Daily Herald*. His financial aid scholarship paid a fraction of his expenses, so he earned the remainder by delivering the paper, working in the library, assisting an urban planner with a survey of Providence, and selling Fuller brushes door-to-door, an enterprise he continued into the first semester of medical school at Yale.

Beck majored in English and Political Science at Brown, but took courses in art, music, accounting, and other disciplines: all fields, in fact, except engineering. His sense of mastery and strong curiosity dictated his choices. Unsure of a career direction, he sought the advice of a career counselor. After testing it was recommended that Beck become a YMCA counselor. That advice didn't sit right with him and he began to inquire about a career in medicine, for he was as intrigued by organic chemistry as he was by English literature. At that time, a dean at Brown discouraged him from applying to medical school because of the quota system enforced against Jews. They could fill medical schools with qualified Jews, he was told. Nevertheless, Beck pursued pre-med coursework, taking more courses after graduation to complete the required curriculum to apply to medical school.

Beck graduated *magna cum laude* from Brown in 1942, having been elected to Phi Beta Kappa, an association which honors academic excellence in the humanities. At graduation, he won awards for oratory and essay writing. Having the minimum requirements for medical school, Beck applied to only three or four. He credits Aldous Huxley with his admission to Yale School of Medicine. During his admission interview with a professor of pediatrics, Beck was asked what books he'd read. Beck revealed he'd read all of Huxley's published works and found the interviewer was also a Huxley devotee.

Beck's own Anxieties

Aaron Beck's bout with a near fatal illness resulted in anxieties and phobias. The surgery experience at age seven was horrific. He was separated from his mother and told he would be reunited with her following a brief x-ray procedure. Instead, he was taken off to surgery. He suffered a terrible nightmare while being anesthetized and the surgeons began cutting before he was fully unconscious. He thought he was going to die. Consequently, he developed long lasting fears of abandonment and surgery.

'First of all,' he says, 'I had a blood/injury phobia, which I didn't really understand at all until I started working on *Anxiety Disorders and Phobias* [Beck, Emery and Greenberg, 1985]. It wasn't until I started thinking clinically about it and looking in the literature that I realized there was such a thing as a blood/injury phobia.' (A conversation with behavior therapist and anxiety expert David Barlow apparently clarified the diagnosis and removed the stigma.) 'Up until then I thought I was very neurotic. Nonetheless, I still managed. I had a lot of phobias. I simply would not let anxiety get the best of me. I had a tremendous fear of surgery. I would even feel faint if I smelled ether. Then I saw a movie, I think I was about twelve, called *Men in White*, which was about interns. It showed hospital scenes and I fainted. I didn't find out until decades later that this was a typical blood/injury phobia. That was one of the reasons for going into medicine: to defeat this.

I remember it did come to the fore when I was assisting at operations. I would stand there gripping forceps, retractors, trying to hold back, be there. I'd be sweating and they had one nurse just wiping my forehead. But I stayed with it and ultimately that aspect diminished until it went away. I learned systematic desensitization not through working in a laboratory, but through experience. In anticipation of Surgery [rotation], I started to expose myself in gradual ways so by the time I got into the operating room I was still able to proceed although I was very uncomfortable. Later on, I became an internist doing surgery myself. I wasn't fazed at all as long as I was in the act of doing something. I learned an awful lot from my own experience. As long as you're actively involved in something, anxiety tends to hold back. When I was in a passive position, unable to do something, it would come to the fore.'

Another fear established in childhood was the fear of suffocation. Maurice Beck, by both brothers' accounts, treated Aaron as a 'kid brother,' looking after him and bedeviling him. He would let Aaron tag along with him and, routinely, he would try to smother him with a pillow. 'I think that might have been conditioned until I worked it through cognitively,' Aaron Beck says now with admirable objectivity. At the time, of course, he was far less objective. 'My brother used to put this pillow over my face and I never knew if he was going to take it off in time. I didn't know till he asked if I'd stopped breathing.' A bad case of whooping cough at age three and chronic asthma compounded the fears of suffocation.

One expression of this anxiety became tunnel phobia. 'It wasn't a complete phobia that developed later, but I'd feel really anxious going through tunnels.' He'd feel a constriction in his chest and begin to breathe shallowly. One day, approaching the Holland Tunnel in New York he realized that he was interpreting the tightness in his chest as a sign he was suffocating. 'After I worked that through cognitively,' he says, 'I never had it again. I could go through tunnels and I'd still get tightness, somehow it's kind of a defensive action, but I would be amused by it because I'd see it as a kind of residue.'

Beck admits to having fears of abandonment, public speaking, and heights, which he attempted to cure by climbing the Leaning Tower of Pisa. He isn't sure of the origin of the abandonment schema, but he has an image of himself, recalled from a photograph taken at age two, alone on the beach, looking terribly lost. A few years later he actually was abandoned by accident. He was taken by another family to Roger Williams Park, a vast park outside the city of Providence. While there with this family, he ran into two of his uncles. It seems that the family he accompanied and his uncles each assumed the other would take Aaron home, but both groups left without him. Aaron remained alone in the Park for several hours until his family came to retrieve him.

Medical Training

Although Beck began medical school with some interest in psychiatry, he soon lost it. He found the Kraeplinian approaches to be nihilistic and unrewarding. As an alternative, psychodynamic formulations seemed esoteric and 'soft,' with little evidence to support the theories, especially compared to internal medicine. He remembers that for a course assignment, teams of students had to see a patient and write up their case according to a psychodynamic formulation just given them. Beck found himself unable to get involved in the assignment, for 'it seemed I'd have to make up so much' (Ross, 1990: 35). Fortunately, his partner, interested in psychoanalysis, wrote the report for both of them to sign.

In an interview with psychologist Paul Salkovskis (1990: 3), Beck explained his resistance to psychoanalytic formulations in medical school. 'I thought it was nonsense. I could not see that it really fitted. I always had a kind of rebellious thing, there was a rebellious aspect I just couldn't control. I just could not do it. This was the first time I really became aware of it. Being the youngest son probably had something to do with it.' While his rebellion was not expressed in overt behavior, it found expression in unconventional thinking, according to his teachers.

Beck had enlisted in the Army after his first semester of medical school and had an accelerated pace of training during wartime. What was usually taught in 48 months was done in 31 months, with no time off for vacations and with school held five or six days a week. To cope with the physical exhaustion, he learned to take cat naps. To deal with the strain, he went to the movies once a week. He believes he discovered the diversionary powers of the movies independently and did not learn them from his mother, for although his mother sought solace from worry at the cinema during his illness, he learned of it only years later. As long as Aaron could tolerate the story line, he loved sitting in the dark watching the big screen. Today it is difficult to have a movie date with him, for he has seen almost everything.

Irving Beck wanted his youngest brother to join his practice in internal medicine, but did not want his brother perceived as his assistant. Lizzie Beck also thought it preferable for Aaron to have his own specialty. Still undecided after graduation from medical school in 1946, Beck did a rotating internship at Rhode Island

Hospital in order to get as broad a background as possible. From 1946 to 1948 he was trained in a range of specializations including surgery, dermatology, obstetrics, infectious disease, and neurology. He also completed a residency in pathology. He settled on neurology as a specialization, attracted to the discipline and precision required.

Beck got into psychiatry by circumstance. He was set for a residency in neurology at Massachusetts General Hospital. It turned out that he'd have to wait a year before that residency could start because of all the veterans returning from World War II. So instead, in 1949, he began a neurology residency at the Cushing Veterans Administration Hospital in Framingham, Massachusetts. At the end of the year, the chief of neuropsychiatry found there was a shortage of psychiatry residents and thus required all neurology residents to complete a six-month rotation in psychiatry. Against his wishes, Beck began the rotation.

Psychiatry at Cushing was dominated by the influence of the Boston Psychoanalytic Institute. 'Everything that we would see in patients would be interpreted in terms of some deep, dark invisible forces' (Yapko, 1991: 8). When Beck expressed his opinion that the formulations were far-fetched and not substantiated, his friends convinced him that he wasn't relating to the material because of his own resistances. 'I thought maybe my mind is really blind to this,' he has said (Salkovskis, 1990:4). He thought his pragmatic nature might be in his way, making psychoanalysis counterintuitive. He decided to suspend his disbelief and make a serious attempt to understand analysis. When his six months were up, Beck decided to remain in psychiatry, believing that the longer he stayed in it, the better his insight would be. He was also taken by the ease with which psychoanalysts 'had answers for everything. They could understand psychosis, schizophrenia, neuroses, and every single condition that came in, you could get a good, sound – apparently sound – psychoanalytic interpretation for. And psychoanalysis also held out the promise that it could cure most people's conditions, so I found that very provocative' (Ross, 1990: 35).

While an intern, Beck had met Phyllis Whitman at the Hillel Foundation at Brown University. She was a student at Pembroke, the women's college at Brown. Beck recalls, 'The room sort of lit up when I saw her, but it took me a long time. I had to find out her name, whom she associated with, whether she was going out on dates. It wasn't easy to do this.'

Beck finally introduced himself by way of conveying greetings from a mutual acquaintance and she agreed to have coffee with him. He says they had a formal courtship, but that he made the mistake of taking her to a wild party of interns which really turned her off for about a year. However, Beck confides, he knew from the beginning that he would marry her.

After graduating from Pembroke, Phyllis became a journalist for *Time Magazine* and moved to New York. The courtship continued and they were married on June 4, 1950 at Temple Emanu-El in Providence. After they married, she became a reporter for the *Berkshire Eagle*, published in Pittsfield, Massachusetts. Later she obtained a Master's degree in social work and ultimately she went to law school while raising four children. Today she is a Superior Court judge in Pennsylvania. Irving Beck describes his sister-in-law as a 'remarkable and very determined individual.'

In 1950 Beck began a two-year fellowship in psychiatry at the Austin Riggs Center in Stockbridge, Massachusetts, a psychoanalytically oriented hospital. He became very involved with psychoanalytic approaches (Erik Erickson was a supervisor) and continued to be intrigued by the 'unitary explanations for everything from incest taboos to war and peace' (Yapko, 1991: 8). 'It was interesting seeing how, now I became much more accepting, when cases were formulated in psychoanalytic terms, there was a certain logic to the presentation. Once you buy the model, everything follows perfectly' (Salkovskis, 1990: 4).

One benefit of the Riggs Center was that the staff was very pragmatic, a style which probably appealed to Beck's own practicality. Despite the more abstract supervision he was getting, he was also encouraged in working with staff to be an active problem-solver.

After two years at Riggs, he decided to go into psychoanalytic training and get his diploma. This was during the Korean War and Beck, realizing that he was likely to be called up from the reserves, volunteered to serve at the Valley Forge Army Hospital outside Philadelphia. He served there from 1952 to 1954 as chief of outpatient psychiatry, assistant chief of neuropsychiatry, and, eventually, chief of the division of psychiatry. During that time, he developed the outpatient service. He also assessed the return-to-duty rate while he was in charge and found it to be three times greater than it had been prior to his direction.

Among the disorders treated was posttraumatic stress disorder. He says the Army

> had a very enlightened system. They used to try to treat them as soon as possible, often on the battlefield itself, at the battalion aid station. They would use amytal or hypnosis [to have the patient relive the experience according to Freud's notion of abreaction]. I found, by the time they came to us, these traumatic neuroses were more structuralized,

so it took longer. I used hypnosis for a while with a lot of patients, but I found that you could almost accomplish the same thing without hypnosis, by just having them relive the battle scenes. (Salkovskis, 1990: 6).

Thus, Beck used imagery within a psychoanalytic framework.

Early Research

Beck was board-certified in psychiatry in 1953 and became an instructor in psychiatry at the University of Pennsylvania Medical School in 1954. He completed his analytic training at the Philadelphia Psychoanalytic Institute, graduating in 1958. He became an assistant professor of psychiatry at Penn in 1959, and received his first grant, to begin dream research, in the same year. His academic interest was to design and run studies that would confirm psychoanalytic hypotheses. His brother Irving recalls how restless and dissatisfied Aaron had been with the lack of scientific basis for psychoanalysis. 'I remember when he was in analysis and that analysis was not scientifically provable and perhaps not really with scientific foundation.' Indeed, Beck believed it was important that psychology respect the major contributions of psychoanalysis, for 'It was very obvious to me that here was a whole body of people who were very influential who did not believe in analysis' (Salkovskis, 1990: 7). He also recognized that empirical evidence was necessary to convince 'hard-headed psychologists.'

Beck had a lot of contact with the psychology department at Penn and his early collaborators, Seymour Feshbach and Marvin Hurvich, were psychologists. These colleagues were well-skilled in research methodology and thus could provide research tools, statistics and research methodology from experimental psychology as well as be honest critics.

Thus, he embarked on a research path to substantiate psychoanalytic principles and instead founded Cognitive Therapy.

These early studies on the dreams of depressed patients were designed to test the psychoanalytic hypothesis that depression was caused by inverted hostility. He chose to study depression through Freudian dream analysis for two reasons: (1) he had an available population of depressed patients in his private practice and (2) he believed that psychoanalytic theories of depression were concrete, well elucidated, and highly researchable. Beck's dream research was influenced by his association with Leon Saul, a 'progressive' psychoanalyst who wrote about conscious processes, conducted dream research himself, and was Beck's second analyst. (His first had been Catherine Bacon.)

The initial studies seemed to fit the hypothesis of retroflected hostility, for the dreams did show the dreamer as a loser. Such a finding could arise from the subject's motivation to degrade himself or herself. However, borrowing some procedures from experimental psychology, Beck then did some verbal conditioning experiments and the results were the opposite of what the theory would have predicted. Next he devised a card-sorting test for depressed and nondepressed subjects. Subjects were predetermined to succeed or fail. If, as Freudian theory stated, a depressed person had a need to suffer, depressed subjects in the experiment should react negatively to success. However, contrary to Freud's theory, subjects who succeeded on initial card-sorting tasks both gained in self-esteem and performed better on subsequent tasks, with depressed subjects showing positive changes to an even greater extent than nondepressed subjects. Beck interpreted these collective findings to mean that depressed persons did not seek failure, but distorted reality by adopting negative views of themselves and of their potential for happiness.

Beck recalls how these experiments changed his thinking:

'When the other studies did not fit in, I went back to my dream studies and I thought, "Maybe there is a simpler explanation and that is that the person sees himself as a loser in the dream because he ordinarily sees himself as a loser." Since I was doing therapy at the same time, it became clear to me as I went into it that the dream themes were consistent with the waking themes. It seemed to me a simpler notion about the dreams was that they simply incorporated the person's self-concept. Well, if it is just a question of the person's self-concept, you don't have to invoke the notion of dreams being motivated. Dreams could simply be a reflection of the person's thinking. If you take motivation and wish fulfillment out of the dream, this undermines the whole motivational model of psychoanalysis. I started looking at the motivational model all the way through, and its manifestations in behaviors, everyday slips and so on. It seemed to me that the motivational model did not hold. Once that collapsed and I inserted the cognitive model, I saw no need for the rest of the superstructure of psychoanalytic thinking.' (Salkovskis, 1990: 7–8)

From Psychoanalysis to Cognitive Theory

Beck's research had heightened his earlier skepticism about psychoanalysis. He says, 'It re-emerged because I attempted to apply pragmatic approaches and rules to the data of psychoanalytic research. It simply did not pan out. The psychoanalytic theses did not bear up under the harsh scrutiny of what you call academic analytic investigation.'

However, his colleague Ruth Greenberg believes Beck's break with traditional Freudian analysis had its roots in his personality. She says, 'I think there is some rebelliousness to him. I always had the sense, and this is a complete guess, that he must have hated it [going through analysis]. He has an aggressive edge to him. I just can't imagine he would have taken well to it. I just picture him tolerating this with tremendous restiveness, and resisting efforts to really change his personality, and really developing a determination to tackle the problems presented to psychiatry in a different way. He would have much preferred something he could control himself. He's extremely goal-directed. He wants to be the authority. On the other hand, he is anxious to equip patients to be their own authority. He made this explicit in the form of a collaborative model. As a clinician he is absolutely nonauthoritarian. He'll very often be seen on tapes to be almost humble with patients. It [being the authority] is not what he practices as a clinician. So maybe he was, in effect, sensitized from the outset to what the patient experiences.'

Aaron Beck acknowledges his wife's influence on his thinking at many points in his career, including her pragmatic skepticism toward psychoanalysis. Just as he was completing his analysis, they attended a meeting of the American Psychoanalytic Association where they spotted a sign outside a lecture hall reading, 'Symposium #15: Problems of Reanalysis.' Beck recalls Phyllis' reaction. 'What?!', she exclaimed, 'reanalysis? You mean you have to go back and get reanalyzed? That's crazy!' Beck claims that her opinion helped crystallize his own thoughts, for after two and a half years of analysis, he hadn't noticed any changes.

Beck's clinical observations from his private practice helped him formulate his theory of psychopathology. A session with a patient helped him conceptualize levels of cognition and sensitized him to the patient's 'automatic thoughts' (Diffily, 1991). In 1959, he was working with a depressed young man. While free-associating in session, the patient began criticizing Beck angrily. Beck then asked the patient what he was feeling. 'I feel guilty,' said the patient, for while he was yelling at Beck, he was simultaneously having self-critical thoughts, such as, 'I shouldn't have said that. I'm wrong to criticize him. I'm bad. He won't like me.' Beck was impressed that the patient had this second train of thought accompanying his verbalized thoughts. Instead of the patient's anger leading directly to guilt feelings, the secondary train of thought acted as an intermediary between the outward emotion and the guilty feeling.

Beck investigated this phenomenon of internal monologue with other patients and learned that they also had thoughts during therapy sessions which they had not reported. Many patients were less aware of these thoughts until Beck specifically asked about them. Although less accessible than voluntary thoughts, these other thoughts appeared as if they had lives of their own. They were 'automatic thoughts.' They were immediate and plausible, and went unchallenged by the individual. They provided running commentary on the person's experience. In the case of depressed persons, these automatic thoughts, as they were labeled, were negatively biased.

Thus the combination of his experimental work and clinical observations led to an abandonment of the psychoanalytic model. Breaking with psychoanalysis may have also appealed to him personally. He has remarked, 'One of the things that got me out of the whole psychoanalytic framework is the notion that authorities don't have to be taken at their face value. My own data can be trusted rather than the authorities.' Beck has continued to enjoy the challenge of opposition because, he says, he likes the unexpected, like proving authorities wrong.

Marvin Hurvich and Seymour Feshbach introduced him not only to research methodology, but to theories which helped him conceptualize and shape his own theory. While reading a review of George Kelly's (1955) work in *Contemporary Psychology*, Beck discovered the congruence between his nascent ideas and Kelly's. Kelly's work provided terminology for Beck's concepts and validation for a nonmotivational theory of psychopathology. Beck initially used and then abandoned Kelly's term 'constructs,' substituting the word 'schemas' for cognitive structures because he felt that these structures were not necessarily bipolar (good–bad) like constructs, but rather categorical. Beck discovered Kelly's work just as he was formulating his own theory. 'I was already structural at that point,' he says, 'and started talking about personal constructs, later called schemas. As I got into Piaget and other structural developmental psychologists, I preferred the term schemas. Within the period of a month, I latched on to the whole body of developmental and cognitive psychology.'

While the discovery of Kelly's work catalyzed the development of Beck's theory, there were other formative influences on his thinking. Most important was the work of Karen Horney and thus, indirectly, Alfred Adler. Beck had read all of Horney's works before he went into analysis and found her 'right on target.' He was also personally influenced by his teacher and analyst, Leon Saul, whose own dream research was a source for Beck's research.

The break with psychoanalysis was not as abrupt as it might sound. Temporarily, Beck professionally identified himself as a neo-analyst of the Adler, Horney and Harry Stack Sullivan mode. He met with little opposition to his ideas of a nonmotivational model because he mostly worked with experimental psychologists and simply did not tell the psychoanalysts what he was up to. 'I had my own private practice, and the psychoanalysts thought I was still doing psychoanalysis and short-term psychodynamic psychotherapy, so they would send me cases. I did not make an issue of it within the establishment; I saw no point to it' (Salkovskis, 1990: 9).

The period from 1960 to 1963 was the most important for him professionally. 'I started to re-examine psychoanalytic theory,' he recalls, 'and was doing research. The whole thing seemed to cave in. Then Cognitive Therapy started to come up. Within a couple of years, I really laid the framework for everything that's happened since then. There's nothing that I've been associated with since 1963 the seeds of which were not in the 1962 to 1964 articles. That was the critical period: changing from psychoanalysis and developing a new theory of therapy. It was very exciting. I even had trouble sleeping sometimes, I was so excited about this thing.'

One imagines that establishing a new form of psychotherapy might be a lonely endeavor, but Beck doesn't remember it that way. 'If you had talked to me then,' he says, 'I might have told you a different story, but in retrospect I don't feel as though the isolation was an unpleasant one. It would have been nice to share it with other people, but then again I did feel as though I was a pathfinder, beating my way through the woods. I must have an autonomous streak that doesn't depend on immediate feedback. Getting my papers published, there was some sense that I was registering someplace.'

During this time, he shared ideas with his brothers and with Phyllis. Irving Beck, who sees his brother as a highly creative person, urged him to publish his work quickly, but Aaron held off, further refining his ideas. He was very deliberate in his work, according to Irving, who also denies that his brother was professionally lonely. Once, says Irving, 'he came to talk to this analytic group and they got up and walked out. He joked about it.' Phyllis Beck may have been her husband's closest ally. In fact, he credits her with labeling cognitive structures 'schemas,' a decision she helped him reach while driving in the car one day.

Judy Beck thinks her father probably felt isolated for a long time and adds that her mother is the one 'that he shared his work with absolutely the most throughout the years.' Later, when Judy was an adolescent, her father presented her with the notion of automatic thoughts and how the way one feels is influenced by what's going through one's mind. After her father gave her a few examples of this phenomenon, Judy responded to him, 'Yeah, that makes sense,' but meanwhile she was saying to herself, 'What's the big deal?'

The Use of Self-observation

One clue to Beck's success as a fairly solitary researcher in the early years is the way he develops his ideas. He begins with observations, often as much about himself as his patients. Jerome Frank (1985: 54) writes, 'Most innovative psychotherapeutic procedures are really derived from clinical experience and the discoverer then seeks to support them by laboratory analogies.' Beck describes the formulations of his theories thusly: he begins with observations of patients, develops ways of measuring these observations, formulates a theory if the observations are validated by a number of cases, designs interventions that are congruent with the theory, and continues to assess whether the theory is confirmed or disconfirmed over time and through further experimentation.

Beck readily admits that he often begins with self-observation in the conceptualization of theories. He denies that he was ever severely depressed, but says he's experienced a moderate depression which he was able to use in understanding the illness. When he was an intern at Framingham, he had a bout of hepatitis during which he became depressed. His mind was full of negative thoughts – his job was no good, his relationship with Phyllis would not last. He even thought of quitting medicine. While visiting Providence during this time he saw Irving who diagnosed his hepatitis at a glance, saying, 'How long have you been yellow?' This diagnosis gave him perspective on his mood and he found that, with the correct attribution, his negativity remitted. Beck's understanding of the cognitive and physiological components of anxiety come firsthand and his ability to view them dispassionately allows him to teach patients how to deal with anxiety in a manageable way. He uses his own experience for heuristic as well as therapeutic goals, generating hypotheses based on his clinical work and personal experience which he subsequently validates with a larger sample and with further experimentation.

Cognitive therapist Christine Padesky, PhD speaks admiringly of Beck's ability to build from personal experience to a more general level. She remarks that George Kelly stated that a psychological theory is no good as long as it is about other people. Rather, a psychological theory should be judged by whether it describes the behavior and functioning of psychologists. A good deal of psychological theory, says Padesky, is about the 'person as patient,' about a pathological process. In contrast, Beck's theory of anxiety describes it as an exaggeration or hyperactivity of a normal process.

Beck has been able to review, with considerable objectivity, his own blood/injury phobia, his speech anxiety, and his deeper fear of abandonment to describe both physiological and cognitive processes accompanying anxiety. Beck's public speaking anxiety has ameliorated, he says, with continued practice and challenging his automatic thoughts. He once consulted Albert Ellis, PhD for treatment of this anxiety, but neither one thinks the single session of Rational-Emotive Therapy was curative. Some of his students say that he is much more anxious in videotaped demonstrations than alone with a client, and what may appear as a constrained, businesslike manner on tape is actually his anxiety. His anxiety also manifests itself as irritability and, as he admits, a need for a sense of control.

Cognitive Therapy of Depression

When Beck got his first research grant at the University of Pennsylvania, he established the Depression Research Unit at Philadelphia General Hospital and a Depression Clinic, which provided a source of outpatients.

In 1961, the Beck Depression Inventory was published. It is a 21-item inventory which assesses the severity of depressive symptomatology by asking respondents to rate their symptoms on Likert-type scales. The BDI has been used in more than 200 research studies and its utility and validity are well-established (Beck and Steer, 1987). At the time of its development, however, it was received rather neutrally by the department of psychiatry at Penn. Beck remembers a lack of interest on the part of the chairman when Beck suggested that the BDI might be a money-maker for the department.

Dr Greenberg, who has worked with Beck since she was 16, recalls that in psychiatry at Penn in the 1960s, there 'were a lot of people who had strong research agendas,' so there was not particular support for the innovations of Cognitive Therapy. Beck says that as long as his grants continued to be funded, he could proceed with his work autonomously. While Beck remembers the atmosphere at the time rather benignly, Greenberg, as a member of staff in Beck's clinic, remembers the environment as more hostile. 'We felt,' she says, 'very much on our own, that there was a need to kind of fight for our place in the department and fight for prerogatives in the department, fight for fair treatment in the department. I don't have the sense that anybody necessarily discouraged him, but I don't think there was a lot of support.'

In 1963, Albert Ellis read Beck's article on thinking and depression in the *Archives of General Psychiatry* and, recognizing the overlap in their formulations, contacted him and sent him reprints of his work in Rational-Emotive Therapy. Ellis's journal, *Rational Living*, also reprinted Beck's article. Beck and Ellis continued corresponding and Beck invited Ellis to give a lecture to the psychiatry residents at Penn as part of a course Beck taught on various approaches to psychotherapy. Ellis continued to lecture at Penn for several years. As their professional relationship continued, Ellis included Beck's pamphlet on depression and *Cognitive Therapy and the Emotional Disorders* (Beck, 1976) in the catalogue of materials offered by the Institute for Rational-Emotive Therapy and the Institute for Rational Living.

Ellis recalls that Beck had an effect on the first year residents he taught, for they became enthusiastic about Cognitive Therapy. Then, as part of their residency training, they had to undergo analysis. Many of them became attached to their analysts, says Ellis, and thus endorsed psychoanalysis. Others, however, maintained interests in both Cognitive Therapy and RET; some entered brief therapy with Ellis and others sought further training with Beck.

Beck and Ellis continue to exchange ideas, mostly in print, and respect their professional differences. They maintain cordial relations and are appreciative of each other's unique personal qualities. Beck credits Ellis' voracity in persuading or attracting skeptics to the cognitive model. People, says Beck, who otherwise dismissed the role of cognitions in psychopathology paid attention when Ellis spoke. He also credits Ellis with introducing the fundamental concept that people's beliefs are accessible. Ellis, in turn, sees Beck as very persistent and an extremely clear thinker. He views Beck's research as a major contribution to psychotherapy. Ellis adds, 'He, unlike myself, seems to be sort of noncontroversial. He doesn't get into personal kinds of difficulties in the sense that I have mostly told people exactly what I think is good and what I think is bad! But Tim, as far as I can tell, is much more tactful and, consequently, has aroused, probably, a lot less opposition than I have. He's not as forceful or anything like that, but that has its advantages because in a sense it's more objective and sometimes more persuasive.'

Beck and Ellis, along with Donald Meichenbaum, PhD are often identified as the founding fathers of what became cognitive-behavior therapy (Mahoney and Arnkoff, 1978). Recently, the three of them appeared, along with other noted psychotherapists, at the second Evolution of Psychotherapy conference. Since the first such conference, several famous psychotherapists who had participated had died. Meichenbaum recalls that as he, Beck and Ellis proceeded into the huge arena filled with thousands of conference attendees, they saw overhead large cardboard cutouts of the psychotherapists who had died. Meichenbaum overheard Beck say to Ellis, 'Don't look up, Al. It's bad luck!'

Beck continued his research and teaching at Penn, becoming an associate professor in 1967. He got only a one-year renewal on his depression research grant and lost his office on campus. Thus, he decided to work from his home and write up his formulation of depression. This became the book *Depression: Clinical, Experimental and Theoretical Aspects* (Beck, 1967), later published as *Depression: Causes and Treatment.* Beck believes he was mildly depressed when he wrote the book, but also views the writing as therapeutic.

By this time, both Hurvich and Feshbach had left the University of Pennsylvania and, although Phyllis Beck remained a sounding board for his ideas, he had few people in his immediate environment with whom to discuss ideas about Cognitive Therapy. In the late 1960s or early 1970s he would travel to the State University of New York at Stony Brook to discuss his ideas with Gerald Davison (Salkovskis, 1990).

In 1970, the journal *Behavior Therapy* published an article by Beck on Cognitive Therapy and its relation to behavior therapy (Beck, 1970a). Allen Bergin and Gerald Davison were discussants and Leonard Ullman wrote a negative reply, arguing, as have radical behaviorists since, that private events could be treated just like public ones. Beck modestly admits that his article 'had some impact'. Dr Michael Mahoney believes it is one of Beck's landmark articles. With the article, Beck was initiated into the cognitive revolution in psychology which was a major paradigm shift within the field and which coincided and interacted with Beck's formulations.

In 1971 Beck became a full professor of psychiatry and began integrating training, research and clinical service. He hired Maria Kovacs, PhD to work on his suicide research grant. She had met Beck while finishing her psychology graduate work at Penn. In addition to her work in psychology, she had been involved in the training of second year psychiatry residents. Joining Beck also was A. John Rush, MD who was a psychiatry resident at the University of Pennsylvania Medical School from 1972 to 1975.

Beck provided supervision to Rush and others at the 'Mood Clinic,' an outpatient service housed at Philadelphia General Hospital, and taught an outpatient psychotherapy course. One of the first patients the residents presented to Dr Beck was a severely depressed man who had been hospitalized many times, tried on several medications, and treated with ECT without success. Rush says the patient was on his way to the state hospital because treatment up until that point had failed. However, Beck provided them with techniques such as scheduling activities and cognitive restructuring which they tried on the patient. They measured the patient's depression over the course of treatment with Cognitive Therapy and found, to their surprise, that the patient recovered fairly quickly, as did the next several patients receiving Cognitive Therapy.

Psychiatry at the time was moving ever more toward biological factors in psychopathology and pharmacologic treatments. If psychotherapy was done, it was exploratory, psychodynamic psychotherapy, conducted intensively up to four times a week, says Rush. The success of Cognitive Therapy, a short-term treatment, was even more dramatic in contrast to the existing models.

Rush continued to be supervised by Beck and they decided to investigate, in a more scientific manner, whether Cognitive Therapy worked. They designed a randomized, controlled trial in which depressed outpatients received either antidepressant medication or Cognitive Therapy. The research team of Beck, Kovacs and Rush was joined over time by Drs Brian Shaw, Steven Hollon and Gary Emery. Notes were kept assiduously, with therapists writing down the techniques used in each case in order to provide a manual for training therapists. The first 'manual' of how to do Cognitive Therapy was about 12 pages in length, recalls Rush. It then grew to 85 pages, then to 150 pages, then to 200 pages. Ultimately, it became Cognitive Therapy of Depression (Beck et al., 1979). By September of 1973, according to Rush, the manual was complete enough to begin running research subjects. Patients were recruited and randomly assigned to either pharmacotherapy with imipramine or Cognitive Therapy. Psychiatry residents were the therapists and received weekly supervision from Beck based on audiotapes of sessions. The study was conducted for a couple of years and was published as 'Comparative efficacy of cognitive therapy and pharmacotherapy in the treatment of depressed outpatients' (Rush et al., 1977). A follow-up report (Kovacs et al., 1981) provided information on what happened to these patients over time. The success of Cognitive Therapy demonstrated that it was effective in reducing the symptoms of major depression in moderately ill nonpsychotic outpatients. Rush states that the study had a very low dropout rate and attributes this to the appeal of Cogntive Therapy. He says the patients liked it, for they had a way to deal with their depression that wasn't hard to learn. Rush adds that, for therapists, it was a way to treat depression without getting depressed themselves, for there were tools to teach the patient.

In the early 1970s there was tremendous excitement and optimism about creating something new that was efficacious. Brian Shaw says, 'It was an exciting time because the whole approach was being assaulted or challenged from so many different quarters, so there was the excitement of being the underdog and coming up with something that was really challenging the establishment, both psychoanalysis and drug therapies.'

In looking back, Ruth Greenberg says, 'I think there's been maturity in 25 years. We are one school and we don't have to keep insisting that we're new and unique and totally ourselves. A lot of phenomena are more complicated than we wanted to think. We wanted to feel like we had this technique which, applied skillfully, was really going to knock these things out. I think the reality is it's a very useful approach, but many problems persist, and we have to recognize that there are things beyond the scope of these immediate techniques.' Greenberg speaks not only about the fervor and eventual maturity of young researchers doing original research, but of how Cognitive Therapy has expanded as it has gone beyond the treatment of unipolar depression. Cognitive Therapy, viewed as a set of techniques, is not likely to be successful in treating the range of disorders confronting clinicians. Yet, Cognitive Therapy based in a theoretical framework, grounded in psychological literature, and presented within a sustaining therapeutic relationship has wide-ranging utility. How it relates to other therapeutic modalities has implications for the integrationist movement in psychotherapy.

The Cognitive Revolution in Psychology

The early 1970s was a time of ferment in psychology, for several individuals were independently researching and theorizing about the role of cognitions in psychopathology and psychological functioning. Beck's work received some notice, but it was the culmination of a number of events and the work of many individuals that ultimately led to the flourishing of what was to be called the cognitive revolution in psychology.

In the early 1970s, Beck's work was not widely known in

psychology. His introduction to the circle of behavior therapists who were exploring cognition came in 1973 when he attended the annual meeting of the Association for Advancement of Behavior Therapy (AABT). Beck had been asked by Dr Peter MacLean to participate in a workshop on depression. Beck recalls, 'Peter had asked me to do it. I wouldn't have done it on my own because I wouldn't have expected that the workshop would be accepted. Peter presented his behavioral approach and I presented my cognitive approach. After that there was a very active question and answer period. Dozens of questions were asked, but not a single one was on Cognitive Therapy. They were all directed towards him. Around the same time, the Society for Psychotherapy Research had a meeting in New York. Alan Bergin sponsored this. They had some type of Existential psychologist present his stuff and I was on next. After he presented his material, half the audience walked out. That was just before the dawn. When I started making public appearances, there was not much interest. I was unable to stir up interest although I had already presented preliminary data showing some efficacy.'

The following year, a symposium was organized featuring Ellis, Mahoney, Meichenbaum, Goldfried and Beck. Several hundred people attended. Beck, anticipating the usual response, brought 25 handouts. His reaction to the turnout was, 'I thought it was due to Ellis.' Beck was seated next to Mahoney, whom he had just met. Mahoney remembers Beck asking him, 'What are all these people doing here?' Mahoney replied, 'Dr Beck, they've come to see you.' Beck said, 'That's not possible. I've never gotten this kind of turnout before,' to which Mahoney replied, 'Well, perhaps the time has arrived.'

Beck's bonds with Mahoney and with Dr W. Edward Craighead, both then at the Pennsylvania State University, continued through correspondence and visits. Craighead and Mahoney invited Beck, Steve Hollon and Brian Shaw to come to Penn State to discuss the similarities and differences of the cognitive work being done at Penn and Penn State. Beck says that in the 1970s Penn State was doing more teaching about cognitive therapies than many other graduate programs.

Meanwhile, Marvin Goldfried and Gerald Davison were speaking about cognitive processes from, in Craighead's words, 'the den of behaviorism,' the State University of New York at Stony Brook. Goldfried has described the move towards cognitive interventions in psychotherapy as being driven by clinical need and the inadequacy of existing models to address the patients' internal dialogues (Arnkoff and Glass, 1992).

Craighead states that psychiatry identifies cognitive therapy or cognitive behavior therapy with Beck's work, but psychology tends to see his work as one of the approaches to dealing with cognitive variables, along with several others. Like behavior therapy, the cognitive movement in psychology initially grew from experimental psychology. Problem-solving, self-control strategies, and Meichenbaum's work on the verbal control of behaviors were early applications. Beck's model dealt more with underlying constructs than did the models of many behavioral psychologists, but there was enough of a shift in behavior therapy at the time, says Craighead, for many to be receptive to Beck's work.

Of his acceptance by psychology, particularly behavior therapy, Beck says, 'Psychology has been much more sensitive to paradigmatic change. Psychotherapists, the clinical psychologists, were more wedded to the psychodynamic model, but academic psychologists went through various phases, and the behavioral phase gradually gave way to the cognitive phase.' In addition, the empirical support for Beck's theory was persuasive to these psychologists. 'Psychology, because it has such a powerful academic base, is far more influenced by the empirical data than psychiatry is. Psychiatry is much more likely to go by the consensus of senior experienced clinicians,' says Beck. He remarks that he moved into what was becoming the mainstream of psychology at a time 'when mainstream psychiatry was moving away from phenomenology into biological causes and treatments and toward the present emphasis on drug therapies' (Diffily, 1991: 26).

The 'cognitive revolution' in psychology has been well documented in a number of sources (Arnkoff and Glass, 1992; Baars, 1986; Dember, 1974; Dobson and Block, 1988; Mahoney 1977, 1981, 1988; Mahoney and Gabriel, 1987). It signified a paradigm shift in behavior therapy from primarily operant models to ones acknowledging and emphasizing the role of information processing in human behavior and behavior change. Conceptually, opinions differ on whether to view cognitive therapies as part of the natural evolution of behavior therapies (Wilson, 1978) or to see them as a radical departure from existing models (Mahoney, 1977). Mahoney and Arnkoff (1978: 689) describe the change, whether evolution or revolution, as the 'emergence of fundamentally cognitive therapies within the boundaries of behavior therapy.' What may be revolutionary is that they combined a return to the patient's internal world with empirically-based interventions.

Meyers and Craighead (1984) identify three central factors precipitating this paradigm shift in behavior therapy to the cognitive domain: developments in cognitive psychology; the emergence of self-control procedures; and the formulations of cognitive therapies, notably the independent contributions of Albert Ellis, Aaron Beck, and Donald Meichenbaum.

The Influence of Cognitive Psychology

In the 1970s, cognitive psychology itself was undergoing changes precipitated by developments in the neurosciences and computer sciences which focused psychology on issues such as the nature of perception and the mechanisms of memory (Shaw and Segal, 1988). A number of findings from cognitive psychology had an impact on behavior therapy including modeling, problem-solving, language control of behavior, and self-control (Craighead, 1990). The information-processing, or cognitive mediational, perspective assumed that humans were 'active and selective seekers, creators and users of information' (Shaw and Segal, 1988: 538). Previous nonmediational models emphasized historical or environmental control over behavior.

The information-processing model of cognitive psychology is apparent in the work of Albert Bandura, whose research on modeling offered a cognitive explanation of observational learning (Bandura, 1969). Bandura's investigations identified the cognitive processes of attention and retention, along with motor reproduction, incentive and motivation, as major factors in observational learning, thus emphasizing cognitive processes as never before within the purview of behavior therapy. Bandura's work 'legitimized the study of such intra-individual cognitive variables as expectancies, self-verbalizations, predictions, and other covert processes that had heretofore been excluded from accounts of human learning and behavior' (Shaw and Segal, 1988: 538).

The contributions of Donald Meichenbaum also relied on applications of findings from cognitive psychology. Like Bandura's work, Meichenbaum's Self-Instructional Training (SIT) (1974, 1975a, 1977) grew out of laboratory observations. He found that schizophrenics operantly conditioned to speak 'healthy talk' were repeating the experimental instructions aloud before giving the trained responses. He thus speculated that individuals could be taught to produce internally generated 'self-statements' and talk to themselves in a self-guiding fashion. Meichenbaum's formulation also drew from the language branch of cognitive developmental psychology, especially the works of Luria (1961) and Vygotsky (1962), which described how a child's behavior was initially under the verbal control of adults, gradually coming under the child's control, first by overt speech and then by covert speech. An early application of SIT was a program teaching impulsive children to control their behavior, first by imitating a model who performed the behavior accompanied by overt self-instructions, then by whispering the self-instructions and finally covertly rehearsing the self-instructions (Arnkoff and Glass, 1992; Dobson and Block, 1988; Meyers and Craighead, 1984). SIT has since found wide-ranging applicability for both childhood and adult disorders, including management of anxiety, aggression and pain, and social skills training.

A third area derived from cognitive psychology and influential in the rise of cognitive behavior therapy was problem-solving, notably the work of D'Zurilla and Goldfried (1971). They argued that what we may interpret as 'abnormal behavior' may actually be in-effective behavior, generated by an inability to solve certain problems and leading to emotional distress. These researchers iden-tified the steps in resolving problems and devised ways to teach people to master each step. The growth of problem-solving therapies is also attributable to Spivak and his colleagues, who identified differences in the problem-solving skills of normal and clinical populations (Spivack, Platt and Shure, 1976). Problem-solving training has continued to be an important therapeutic approach, becoming a major type of cognitive therapy itself (Mahoney, 1988). Its applications are numerous, with recent interest devoted to the problem-solving deficits of depressed (Nezu, Nezu and Perri, 1989) and suicidal individuals (Weishaar and Beck, 1990).

The work of Arnold Lazarus also relied on the concept of cognitive mediation and thus drew on cognitive psychology (Dobson and Block, 1988). Lazarus and his associates conducted studies in the late 1960s and early 1970s which documented the role of cognitive processes in anxiety. The presence of cognitive components in anxiety challenged behavioral models of the etiology of anxiety and further fermented the cognitive revolution. At about the same time, Goldfried (1971) proposed that systematic desensitization he conceptualized in terms of a general mediational model. Clients would be taught, within a coping skills orientation, to relax themselves in the face of distressing imagery rather than terminate the image. Goldfried's approach directly challenged Wolpe's (1958) counterconditioning model, then the standard conceptualization of how desensitization worked.

The Development of Self-Control Strategies
In addition to the general category of cognitive psychology, a second factor which gave rise to the cognitive revolution was the

development of self-control stategies and a consequent debate over the roles of internal and external factors influencing self-control responses. Cognitive explanations of self-control procedures began to appear with Homme's (1965) definition of coverants as operants of the mind (Meyers and Craighead, 1984; Mahoney and Arnkoff, 1978). Although he suggested operant procedures to modify thoughts, Homme's work stimulated further investigations of self-control programs designed to change behaviors by modifying cognitions.

The importance of internal controlling mechanisms was further elucidated by Kanfer (1970, 1971; Kanfer and Karoly, 1972), whose classification of self-control components – self-monitoring, self-evaluation, and self-reinforcement – is still used. At the same time, Bandura and Mischel at Stanford were conducting clinical laboratory research to assess the effect of self-control on modeling and delay of gratification (Bandura, 1971; Mischel, 1974). Applications of self-control strategies proliferated throughout the 1970s, particularly in such areas as overeating and smoking cessation.

Partly in response to the issue of the roles of internal and external factors on self-control responses, Bandura presented the idea of reciprocal determinism, the notion that individuals (including their cognitive processes) and environments interact and affect each other. His groundbreaking book, *Social Learning Theory* (1977b), and the concept of reciprocal determinism did much to foster the paradigm shift, for they moved the explanation of behavior away from strictly environmental control. Bandura also introduced the notion of learning by vicarious experience rather than direct reinforcement. Central to the notion of vicarious learning is expectancy of reinforcement, a cognitive concept. As Wessler (1986: 5) writes, 'This important shift in emphasis led to a legitimation of cognition within a scientific behavioural theory of human action.'

By the time *Social Learning Theory* was published, Beck had published *Cognitive Therapy and the Emotional Disorders* (1976), outlining his theory, as well as the first clinical outcome study comparing cognitive therapy to pharmacotherapy in the treatment of unipolar depression (Rush et al., 1977). Although Beck and Bandura had met when Beck visited Stanford, they were working so independently of one another that Bandura's influence came only later in Beck's career, as part of the general movement of cognitive behavior therapy.

The Influences of Meichenbaum and Ellis
While Beck was developing his theory and model of psychotherapy within psychiatry, two psychologists, Albert Ellis and Donald

Meichenbaum, were similarly developing therapies based on the primacy of cognition in behavioral and affective change. Despite the differences among the three approaches, they share common assumptions: (1) a collaborative relationship between client and therapist, (2) the premise that psychological distress is, at least in part, a function of disturbances in cognitive processes, (3) a focus on changing cognitions in order to produce desired changes in affect and behavior, and (4) a time-limited and educative treatment focusing on specific target problems (Dobson and Block, 1988; Kendall and Bemis, 1983).

In addition to Self-Instructional Training (SIT), Meichenbaum developed a multi-component coping skills therapy, Stress Inoculation Training. It teaches such skills as relaxation, problem-solving, and self-instructions, and then exposes the client to difficult situations in which to practice the skills (Meichenbaum, 1975b, 1985). It is used as a broad coping skills treatment.

While Meichenbaum derived SIT from clinical laboratory research and cognitive psychology, Ellis, like Beck, developed his brand of cognitive therapy, Rational-Emotive Therapy (RET), from clinical observations and in reaction to his analytic training. Arnkoff and Glass (1992) state that the time was right for the emergence of cognitive therapies in the late 1960s and early 1970s because of a general dissatisfaction with existing models. Behavior therapists were finding nonmediational models, which ignored covert phenomena and private events, to have limited utility. Many trained in psychoanalysis, including Beck and Ellis, were coincidentally dissatisfied with the analytic model of psychopathology and long-term psychotherapy.

Ellis based much of RET in philosophy as well as in behavior therapy (Ellis, 1989). Both Beck and Ellis were influenced by Greek Stoic philosophy; Ellis also credits the works of Popper, Reichenbach, Kant, and Russell. Neo-Freudians Karen Horney (1950) and Alfred Adler (1927) helped shape RET (Dryden and Ellis, 1988) and Cognitive Therapy. Ellis says that the 'thought management' programs of such writers as Carnegie (1948), Coue (1922), DuBois (1905) and Peale (1960), which asserted the importance of what people say to themselves, were also important to the development of cognitive therapies in general and RET in particular (A. Ellis, 1989; Arnkoff and Glass, 1992).

Ellis' work predates Beck's by several years. His 'New Approaches to Psychotherapy Techniques' was published in 1955, with his *Guide to Rational Living* appearing in 1961 and his landmark book, *Reason and Emotion in Psychotherapy*, in 1962.

The similarities and differences between RET and Cognitive

Therapy have been extensively discussed and updated in the literature (Beck and Weishaar, 1989a; Ellis, Young and Lockwood, 1987; Weishaar and Beck, 1986). Both approaches emphasize the role of maladaptive cognitive processes in psychological disorders and the importance of interventions aimed at modifying those cognitive processes. Ellis was the first to argue, in the psychological literature, that it is not events *per se*, but people's interpretations of events, that create distress (Ellis, 1962). 'Irrational thinking,' a biological tendency (Dryden and Ellis, 1986), is thus considered the driving force behind maladaptive behavior. In his early work, Ellis identified a number of specific irrational beliefs underlying psychopathology. In RET, these beliefs are disputed logically to create attitude change. Ellis recently wrote, 'Most of my actual treatment process in RET consists of active–directive cognitive debating – with emotional and behavioral homework always integrally included but with a strong emphasis on helping clients achieve a profound – and preferably quite conscious – philosophic or attitudinal change' (Ellis, 1989: 8).

The popularity of RET grew without benefit of research. Ellis quite singlehandedly promoted his therapy through writing and workshops. He is credited with being a founding father (or grandfather, as he has said) of cognitive behavior therapy. Beck states that it was Ellis who first promoted the notion that assumptions and beliefs were much more accessible to patients than psychoanalysts believed, thus challenging the concept that behaviors were driven by unconscious motivation which had to be interpreted by the therapist. Ellis' focus on here-and-now problem-solving also signified a shift in psychotherapy to current events (both internal and external).

Several differences exist between RET and Cognitive Therapy. It has been argued that Cognitive Therapy places greater emphasis on the modification of fundamental beliefs or schemas, rather than on specific self-statements (Meyers and Craighead, 1984). Therefore, it emphasizes change in the structural aspects of personality. Moreover, Beck's focus on errors in logic or 'cognitive distortions' also intervenes at the level of cognitive processing or how the individual perceives, categorizes, and interprets data. Thus, a goal of treatment is to correct this systematic bias in cognitive processing as well as to examine and modify the content of dysfunctional beliefs. In addition, Cognitive Therapy does not maintain that the same set of 'irrational beliefs' operates for everyone; rather, it emphasizes the idiosyncratic nature of thoughts and assumptions. The therapeutic styles of Cognitive Therapists and Rational-Emotive Therapists probably overlap, but Cognitive Therapy is based on the empirical testing of beliefs, not on rational disputation alone. Ellis states that irrational thinking is biologically-based; people have a tendency toward it. Beck emphasizes the impact of life events on the development of psychological disorders (Beck, 1967). Beck eschews the word 'irrational' in reference to beliefs, for at the time these beliefs were established in the person's life they made sense, even though they aren't helpful at present.

Debates between Cognitive Therapy and Rational-Emotive Therapy continue, for Ellis has recently written that a single imperative, absolutistic or 'mustabatory' thinking, underlies psychological distress in general and depression in particular (Ellis 1987, 1989: 14). Beck has empirically challenged this hypothesis (Brown and Beck, 1989). In addition, both Beck and Ellis have been drawn into the current 'rationalist' versus 'constructivist' debate in cognitive psychotherapy, each describing his own approach as constructivist, with Beck emphasizing the influence of George Kelly's personal construct theory on Cognitive Therapy.

The Politics of the Cognitive Revolution
The interest in cognitive processes in human behavior grew rapidly in the early 1970s with the appearance of articles and books about clinical interventions from a cognitive perspective. Mahoney's (1974) seminal work, *Cognition and Behavior Modification*, provided a scholarly rationale for cognitive models and procedures. Yet, the fervor in favor of cognitive therapies was met by a strong reaction on the part of radical behaviorists, who either espoused the view that thoughts *are* behavior (Wolpe, 1976b) or held that thoughts could only be speculated about and not demonstrated, and certainly not within the realm of behavior therapy (Skinner, 1977). The place of cognition in the philosophical and political lives of behavior therapy has been debated ever since (Thyer, 1992; Wolpe, 1985).

By the mid 1970s, the acceptability of cognitive therapies within behavior therapy was hotly debated. Following the publication of *Cognition and Behavior Modification*, Mahoney was warned to 'cease and desist' from pursuing that direction by some behavioral colleagues (Arnkoff and Glass, 1992). Readings in cognition and 'cognitive behavior modification' were prohibited in some graduate programs in psychology (Mahoney, 1985b; Mahoney and Gabriel, 1990). The board of the Association for Advancement of Behavior Therapy (AABT) debated whether cognitive presentations should be allowed on the annual conference program, whether researchers with cognitive interests could head a program committee, and whether cognitivists would be better to leave AABT entirely

(Mahoney, 1984). The development within AABT of a Special Interest Group on cognitive–behavioral approaches caused a group of conditioning theorists to secede from AABT and join the Midwest Association for Behavior Analysis, renaming itself the Association for Behavioral Analysis (Mahoney, 1988).

One of the foremost opponents of the cognitive movement has been Joseph Wolpe, whose articles, 'Behavior Therapy and Its Malcontents,' Parts 1 and 2 (1976a, 1976b), present his beliefs that critics of behavior therapy, such as his former student Arnold Lazarus, as well as Ellis, Meichenbaum, and Isaac Marks, misunderstand the principles of behavior therapy. 'Cognitive behavior,' writes Wolpe, 'is a subclass of behavior, obeying the same rules of acquisition and extinction, no matter how complex the contents may be or how subtle the contingencies of reinforcement, internal or external, physical or social; and cognitive therapy is a subclass of behavior therapy' (Wolpe, 1976b: 114). Despite this inclusive view of cognitive therapies, cognitive models were not embraced by radical behavior theorists; rather, they were treated as heresy (Mahoney, 1988).

During this period of turmoil, Donald Meichenbaum's column was pulled from the AABT newsletter because, he remembers, it was seen as too cognitive. In 1975, he began publishing his own newsletter, called *Cognitive Behavior Modification*. The newsletter was initially mailed to 100 clinicians and researchers for the purpose of communicating with one another. The subscription list eventually grew to nearly 300 people in 20 countries (Arnkoff and Glass, 1992). At the same time, the *Journal of Applied Behavioral Analysis* would not accept any article that used the word 'cognitive.' Thus, cognitivists were having trouble getting their works published. There was discussion among the cognitively oriented members of AABT whether to withdraw from AABT and form their own organization. Meichenbaum, Goldfried, Beck and Mahoney met and decided to remain in AABT, for it was important that cognitive therapies be identified with empirical research. However, as a result of their discussions and the response to Meichenbaum's newsletter, the journal *Cognitive Therapy and Research* was founded in 1977, with Beck nominating Mahoney as the first editor. In the first issue appeared the article by Rush, Beck, Kovacs and Hollon comparing Cognitive Therapy and imipramine in the treatment of unipolar depression and finding Cognitive Therapy superior to pharmacotherapy. This outcome study helped establish the credibility of Cognitive Therapy as well as give impetus to further research. As research in Cognitive Therapy flourished, so did the growth of cognitivism within

AABT, so that by 1990 69 per cent of the membership identified themselves as cognitive–behavioral, while 27 per cent called themselves behavioral (Craighead, 1990).

Writing *Cognitive Therapy of Depression*

Cognitive Therapy of Depression, developed from the training manual for the Rush et al. study, was published in 1979. The book has become a classic in the field of depression research and treatment. It was important for another reason, as Donald Meichenbaum has said, for 'it became a prototype for people to go public with what they think they do in therapy. Beck was the first person to lead a team who fully explicated a therapist's manual.' Even with multiple collaborators, the final product, says Brian Shaw, had a 'significant impact from Beck's thinking. He pulled the different chapters together and wrote his own conceptual framework for the book,' including the role of emotions in psychopathology.

Beck's early students describe him as a tremendously creative, innovative and optimistic teacher and researcher. When he wasn't at the research offices, he would be at home working on ideas and phoning students to share ideas. (He still phones the Center and his students daily.) Rush remarks on Beck's ability to let him run a research project. Beck acted as Rush's mentor and supervised the residents who were providing treatment in the outcome study. At one point, Beck got anxious and told Rush, 'I'd better call these residents just to tighten up their methods, make sure they're doing the therapy correctly.' Rush responded, 'You can't call these residents up. You're the senior professor with gray hair and the bow tie. You'll get them so rattled and afraid that they'll quit the study. You have to just stay in your office and not interfere with the study. Just come once a week, do the supervision, and that's it.' Beck agreed. Rush says, 'He was good enough to contain it and let the study run without meddling in it. I don't know any originator of a therapy up to that time who was willing to put the whole package on the line in a test of efficacy and keep his nose out of it. That takes a lot of guts.'

The NIMH Treatment of Depression Collaborative Research Program

In 1979, the American Psychiatric Association awarded Beck the Foundation Fund Prize for Research in Psychiatry for his research on depression and the development of Cognitive Therapy. In the same year, planning began for what was to become the National Institute of Mental Health Treatment of Depression Collaborative Research Program, a multisite outcome study designed to test the efficacy of two short-term therapies, Interpersonal Psychotherapy and Cognitive Therapy, in the treatment of unipolar depression. Beck had sought funding to do research on Cognitive Therapy, designing a study that would compare three cells: Cognitive Therapy alone, drug therapy alone, and the combination of the two. NIMH funded the study, but cut the budget in half, resulting in a two-cell study comparing Cognitive Therapy alone with Cognitive Therapy in combination with pharmacotherapy, which were found to be equivalent. Beck then asked for additional funding to conduct further small studies with well-trained Cognitive Therapists. However, NIMH planned a multisite study and added Interpersonal Psychotherapy, developed by Gerald Klerman and Myrna Weissman at Yale from a psychodynamic model. The initial planning was done without Beck's input, and he was skeptical of attaining clear results from multisite studies. In his experience of multisite drug studies, differences between sites precluded clear conclusions. Nevertheless, Beck agreed to go along with the plan for a period of time, and he and Dr Jeffrey Young were awarded a small grant to study how well they could train Cognitive Therapists over a three-month period.

The psychologists and psychiatrists in the study started off poorly, according to both Beck and Young, but improved somewhat. Rating the therapists at the end of a year, however, indicated that most failed the competency ratings for Cognitive Therapists. Beck and Young concluded that (1) unless therapists are 'wired to the Cognitive way,' they will not do well with brief training, and (2) regression will occur unless supervision is maintained for a year. They stated that it took at least a year to train motivated therapists to an adequate standard of Cognitive Therapy. Both of these conclusions were ignored by the NIMH Collaborative Study. Plans to supervise therapists closely were vetoed by the NIMH planners. The project became more expansive and, at one point, Beck argued that the study would end up with inadequate therapists. The study planners responded that they wanted to test the way Cognitive Therapy was probably practiced 'in the marketplace,' not by skilled Cognitive Therapists. Beck replied with dismay, pointing out that, if one is testing open heart surgery, one doesn't get an inexperienced surgeon to perform it. Other decisions, such as having equal numbers of psychiatrists in each treatment condition, were spurious, for few psychiatrists at that point had been trained in Cognitive Therapy. In contrast,

Interpersonal Psychotherapy is derived from analytic therapy and thus had a larger pool of skilled therapists to draw upon. According to Dr Young, who trained and rated Cognitive Therapists for the study, the Interpersonal Psychotherapists were all analytic therapists to begin with, so it took very little additional change to get them all to be quite competent on their own rating scale. The Cognitive Therapists, however, were barely adequate, but none could be dropped from the study because there were so few of them. Moreover, says Young, trying to teach Cognitive Therapy in a short time yielded 'technical Cognitive Therapists,' who were not really attuned to the interpersonal component of therapy, just with delivering a technique. Beck himself, says Young, 'is not that technical; he's not that structured. It's a shame that some of it got lost; some of the beauty of the way he does therapy got lost in the translation into a manualized therapy.'

Young worked closely with Beck to design the training for the Cognitive Therapists in the NIMH study. He recalls that the study was very important to Beck 'because he saw it as a chance to achieve a level of acceptance for Cognitive Therapy at a time when Cognitive Therapy had very low recognition. Beck was pretty adamant that if the study was going to work, the therapists had to be people who were already experienced in Cognitive Therapy and were committed to it. He wanted to get the best Cognitive Therapists to provide the therapy. NIMH was taking the position quite strongly that this should be therapy as would be provided by the average practitioner using Cognitive Therapy. So, that would have involved taking novice therapists and training them in Cognitive Therapy.'

Although Beck and Young presented the initial didactic training to the therapists in the study, they relinquished further responsibility for the project. At that point, Brian Shaw agreed to oversee the Cognitive Therapy training and administration. Jeffrey Young, Maria Kovacs and John Rush rated therapy tapes for the study. Beck resigned because he didn't believe the study was being done right and predicted, says Young, that Cognitive Therapy would not be adequately represented. Young says, 'I think his underlying feeling was "this won't come out that well," which is what did happen.'

The NIMH collaborative study of 250 depressed outpatients found no significant differences in mean scores and recovery rates among patients receiving imipramine plus clinical management, placebo plus clinical management, Interpersonal Psychotherapy or Cognitive Therapy. Patients in all treatments showed improvements. Significant differences were found only among a subgroup

of severely depressed patients for whom Interpersonal Psychotherapy and imipramine plus clinical management were more effective. Site differences were found for both Cognitive Therapy and
Interpersonal Psychotherapy (Elkin et al., 1989).

These results are considered a setback by Beck, who believes this
single study is viewed by many as proof that Cognitive Therapy is
not as efficacious as has been demonstrated in other studies. Young
sees the collaborative study as 'a test of the therapist rather than
the therapy.' Other Cognitive Therapists have more heartened
views. Brian Shaw views the collaborative study as 'a landmark
study. It's an exceptional study in what it attempted to do. I think
there's no taking away from the fact it has set the field on a new
course with respect to issues like adherence and competence, using
treatment manuals and really finding out what therapists actually
do.' Yet, Shaw adds, 'It's unfortunate that we didn't have therapists .
with very extensive experience in Cognitive Therapy. There was
much more variablity than ever hoped for in the therapists' performance. Therapists would be struggling [to meet competency
standards] both during training and the actual protocol.' The site
differences, Shaw explains, could be due to therapist, patient, or
teacher differences. He believes that the therapist differences were
important. Shaw finds the overall results 'disappointing compared
to what you would hope or what even past studies have found.'
However, at the point of one-year follow-up, those treated
successfully with Cognitive Therapy had the lowest relapse rates
(Shea et al., 1992).

Steven Hollon thinks the collaborative study is a 'strong study,'
but adds that he doesn't 'think they got an adequate representation
of Cognitive Therapy in there. The supervision was too infrequent
for fairly recently trained therapists. Recently trained Cognitive
Therapists don't get the system as well or as rapidly as they need
to. It shows up most obviously with more severe patients, and I
think the poor showing of Cognitive Therapy with the more severe
depressives in that sample is a reflection of that rather than any
real limitation of Cognitive Therapy.'

Hollon and his associates themselves conducted a study looking
at the combined effects of Cognitive Therapy and pharmacotherapy along with each modality separately (Evans et al., 1992;
Hollon et al., 1992). The treatment phase lasted three months with
a two-year follow-up. Results indicate that pharmacotherapy and
Cognitive Therapy were virtually interchangeable in terms of their
effect over the three-month acute treatment phase, even among
severely depressed patients. Moreover, among those patients who
responded to treatment, the people who received Cognitive

Therapy in the acute treatment phase had about half the relapse rate following the end of treatment as did the people who were treated with medication.

In general, Hollon thinks that Cognitive Therapy is likely to provide a long-term reduction of risk for depression. He says, 'I think Cognitive Therapy is likely to compare quite nicely with other existing interventions like pharmacotherapy in terms of short-term effects. But I think it's in the long-term effects – the prevention of relapse, the prevention of recurrence, and possibly the prevention of the initial onset in the first place – that's Cognitive Therapy's major contribution.'

Recognition at Home and in Europe

In 1982 Beck received an Honorary Doctor of Medical Science degree from his alma mater, Brown University, and was also named one of the 'Ten Most Influential Psychotherapists' in a survey of clinical and counseling psychologists published by the *American Psychologist*.

In the same year, Beck attended the meeting of the European Association of Behaviour Therapy (EABT) in Rome. At that meeting, he met British researcher Dr David M. Clark. 'He had never met me before, but greeted me warmly, and invited me to stay for dinner and spent several hours going over the experiments [on depression] I'd been doing.' Clark is quick to point out that at conferences Beck can usually be found talking with young researchers. 'Tim has personally been very good at spotting young, enthusiastic research people and then really encouraging them enormously and helping them.' Many colleagues remark on Beck's ability to identify and cultivate talented researchers and clinicians. Clark and Beck continued to correspond. In 1983, Clark was appointed to a permanent post at Oxford University and began conducting research on the cognitive treatment of anxiety. In 1984, he visited at the Center for Cognitive Therapy in Philadelphia for four months in order to collaborate more closely with Beck.

In 1985, Beck published, with Gary Emery and Ruth Greenberg, *Anxiety Disorders and Phobias: A Cognitive Perspective*, which combined Beck's theoretical model of anxiety disorders, based in evolutionary theory, and practical, therapeutic techniques to treat various anxiety disorders.

In 1987, Beck took sabbatical leave to write a book on Cognitive Therapy for couples called *Love is Never Enough* (1988b). During this time, he went to England to work and conducted a number of workshops with David M. Clark and his associates at Oxford, who had distinguished themselves in the area of anxiety and panic disorder. Beck remembers his time in England very fondly and Clark hypothesizes why. 'He gets much more recognition often in Europe, particularly in England, than he does in the States. He was very, very warmly received, and everyone was just delighted to have him. The other thing, presumably, was that he was away from the day-to-day running of the Center and so felt free to develop his own ideas. There's quite a large group of young people who are very keen on Cognitive Therapy, cognitive research, and with whom he spent a lot of time batting around ideas. He also probably did more actual therapy than he does when he's in Philadelphia, in the sense that he did demonstration sessions and trained on the wards. In England, he's the outstanding figure in this field [cognitive therapy]. RET hasn't had much influence in Europe. He's seen as someone with phenomenal intuition, but also people think that Cognitive Therapy has developed as well as it has because it has been linked with a strong research base. He's managed to stimulate a lot of research in England.' In 1987, Beck was elected a Fellow of the Royal College of Psychiatrists. He has endeavored to establish Cognitive Therapy as part of psychiatric training in the United Kingdom.

Beck himself is very optimistic about the future of Cognitive Therapy in Britain. 'In other countries, such as Britain, there's been a large trend towards getting Cognitive Therapy introduced into training programs, and I think within a few years, it will be introduced. I think the young British psychiatrists are much more likely to pick it up because they haven't been indoctrinated with psychodynamic concepts as have the young psychiatrists in this country. I understand, though, that psychology in Britain, contrary to psychiatry, already is strongly cognitive–behavioral and all of the training programs in clinical psychology have a very important cognitive–behavioral orientation.'

With the publication of Love is Never Enough in 1988, Beck introduced Cognitive Therapy to couples' therapy within the format of a book for the general public. In 1990, Cognitive Therapists Drs Frank Dattilio and Christine Padesky published Cognitive Therapy with Couples, describing for mental health professionals how to do Cognitive Therapy with couples. Chris Padesky and Aaron Beck have presented more than 25 workshops together on various applications of Cognitive Therapy, including couples' therapy.

In 1989, Beck received the Alumni Recognition Award from Brown, which acknowledged his recent work on Cognitive Therapy for couples as well as his earlier work on depression and

anxiety disorders. In 1989 he also received a particularly meaningful award: the Distinguished Scientific Award for the Applications of Psychology from the American Psychological Association.
The citation reads in part,

> His pioneering work on depression has profoundly altered the way the
> disorder is conceptualized, assessed, diagnosed, and treated. His
> influential book *Cognitive Therapy of Depression* is a widely cited,
> definitive text on the subject. The systematic extension of his approach
> to conditions as diverse as anxiety and phobias, personality disorders,
> and marital discord demonstrates that his model is as comprehensive as
> it is rigorously empirical. He has provided alternative psychological
> treatment for a variety of conditions that had largely been treated by
> medication. (*American Psychologist*, 1990: 458)

Beck was very moved to have his work recognized by psychology
and is the only psychiatrist to have won the highest research
awards from both the American Psychiatric and the American
Psychological Associations.

Theory of Personality

In 1990, Beck published, in collaboration with some of his former
students, *Cognitive Therapy of Personality Disorders*. With this
work, Cognitive Therapy expanded to longer-term therapy and
became focused on underlying schemas in ways more obvious than
ever before. Beck defines schemas as cognitive structures that
organize experience and behavior, whereas beliefs and rules are the
content of schemas (Beck, Freeman and Associates, 1990).
Schemas can be inferred from behavior or assessed through interview and history taking. In personality disorders, schemas are
firmly held by cognition, affect and behavior. Thus, therapeutic
interventions must address all three channels. In working with
personality disorders it is insufficient only to examine the logic or
reasonableness of cognitions, promote emotional catharsis, or set
behavioral contingencies. Beck and associates describe Cognitive
Therapy of personality disorders as a modification of Cognitive
Therapy with less complex disorders. In work with personality
disorders, there is greater emphasis on imagery and reliving past
experiences to activate schemas and make them more accessible,
particularly when they have been cognitively avoided by the
patient. The use of childhood material becomes more important as
the development and function of the schema are explored and then
challenged.

Suicide Research

In 1991, Beck received the Research Award from the American Suicide Foundation in honor of a body of research begun in the early 1970s. Suicide research was a natural outgrowth of his work on depression, for he had written early on about his observed association between hopelessness and suicidality.

In the early 1970s, Dr Harvey Resnik, a former psychiatry resident of Beck's, asked him to head a task force on suicide. The product of that task force is the NIMH tripartite classification on suicidal behaviors which is still used in research (Beck et al., 1973). Dr Maria Kovacs was initially hired by Beck to work on one of his suicide grants, and since the 1970s, Beck has collaborated with Dr Robert Steer on numerous publications examining the cognitive features of suicidal individuals.

Research in Cognitive Therapy has yielded a taxonomy of suicidal behaviors; assessment scales for measuring suicidal ideation and intent, hopelessness, and self-concept; and a model of suicidality with hopelessness as the key psychological variable. Chief among Beck's research findings is that, among suicide ideators, the degree of hopelessness at the time of index admission or contact with outpatient therapist is predictive of eventual suicide (Beck et al., 1990a; Beck et al., 1985).

Current Interests

Beck's current interests focus on new applications of the cognitive model; psychotherapy integration; and the use of Darwinian theory, ethology, evolutionary models to develop Cognitive Therapy further. The most recent applications of the cognitive model by Beck and his associates include books on inpatient treatment with Cognitive Therapy, and Cognitive Therapy of drug abuse. Beck continues to encourage other researchers in further applications of the model with both clinical and nonclinical populations.

As Cognitive Therapy moves into the treatment of personality disorders, it becomes longer-term and incorporates experiential or emotive techniques and psychodynamic considerations of the therapeutic relationship. These changes add impetus to the possibility of psychotherapy integration. Beck sees Cognitive Therapy as *the* integrative therapy, for it combines strategies from various modalities under one cohesive theory (Beck, 1991b).

Finally, Beck is currently drawn to evolutionary theory and primate ethology as well as to social and cognitive psychology as sources to explain human behavior and the role of cognition in human experience. He believes these fields provide information which standard psychotherapy research is, necessarily, slow to yield. Thus, he is incorporating data from various fields to refine his model while seeking new applications for it.

Personal Qualities

Beck has always been more creative than ambitious, say family members and colleagues. This creativity has often led Beck to prescient notions. Beck and Steven Hollon both tell of how Beck would present ideas to a skeptical Hollon and ask how much, in terms of percentage, Hollon believed Beck was correct. Hollon says, 'The thing that keeps intriguing me is that he'll come up with some new idea. The first time I hear it, it sounds kind of odd and strange and offbeat. I think he's clearly wrong, out of step with current thinking. Then in about six months or so, I realize, the more I think about it, the more I trust the idea. By the time people start paying attention to it empirically, it's starting to work out better with most other people, too. So, I'd have to say that it stands out for me the way he's been able to repeatedly come up with novel, interesting, creative ideas that have moved the clinical area forward.'

David M. Clark sees similarities between the theoretical stance of Cognitive Therapy and Beck's personal style. Specifically, Beck has a highly developed ability to see the world from another person's point of view. 'It's very noticeable in his professional interactions with people that he's very much thinking about how the person perceives what he is presenting – research or when he's doing the politicking of getting Cognitive Therapy recognized. That skill, obviously, serves him very well.'

The ability to view a disadvantage as an advantage has buoyed Beck through an academic career, an arena in which funding is precarious and at the mercy of unpredictable reversals and windfalls. In most instances, he has viewed disagreements or criticisms as challenges rather than defeats, particularly when there has been an active exchange of ideas. For example, when someone in an audience disagrees with him, 'I feel as though I have an opportunity to directly address the issue, and at least the other people in the audience can weigh what I have to say and what they have to say.' He is more frustrated when in a position that precludes responding to critics; for example, 'when somebody publishes his own journal and an *ad hominem* type of attack on the theory and just keeps with it. He will have some influence over which you

don't really have control.' Other frustrations include misinterpretations of Cognitive Therapy and the failure of some mental health
professionals to acknowledge the empirical evidence supporting the
efficacy of Cognitive Therapy. It appears to be narrowness of
clinical perspective and not simply rejection of Cognitive Therapy
that troubles him. A great frustration for him, due to his lack of
control over the situation, was the handling of the NIMH
Collaborative Study.

Beck's autonomy and goal-orientation have certainly helped him
pursue his scientific goals. There is another side of him which some
speculate has aided him. Says Michael Mahoney, 'I think he's a
very strong individual in some complex ways, and by that I mean
he's resilient and he's a man of integrity. He's not afraid to be on
the outside of the group majority if he believes that the evidence
or the theory or the logic is in the direction he's moving. I think
also that there's a warmth and a human sensitivity there that has
helped him. My hunch is that he has friendships and family relations that have helped him cope. He's certainly been a friend to me
at times when I was struggling. My hunch is that has happened in
his life, too, and he has wisely used his social network or friends
and family to support him.'

Aaron T. Beck's approach to psychotherapy combines the
pragmatism and intellectual curiosity of his parents with a reaction
to authority which was acceptably channeled into scholarship and
research. Even as a child, says Beck, teachers told him he rebelled
by being an original thinker. Beck's experience with moderate
depression and, especially, his history of anxieties gave him
firsthand knowledge of these syndromes. His self- and clinical
observations allowed him to note and articulate the roles of perceptions, appraisals, and interpretations in the development of symptoms. His use of patient populations to test his hypotheses gave
viability to his theories and credibility to the cognitive movement
in psychology.

Beck rejected much of psychoanalytic theory, but maintained an
emphasis on the person's internal world and on the meanings a
person ascribes to events. Beck combined this focus on how an
individual constructs experience with an active and pragmatic
stance, creating a therapy which gives much control to the client
in a collaborative endeavor of examining and testing his or her
beliefs. These aspects of Cognitive Therapy will become apparent
as we examine Beck's theoretical and practical contributions to
counseling and psychotherapy.

2
Theoretical Contributions

Overview

Beck's Cognitive Therapy is a system of psychotherapy which provides (1) a comprehensive theory of psychopathology that drives the structure of psychotherapy, (2) a body of knowledge and empirical findings which support the theory, and (3) research findings which demonstrate its effectiveness (Beck, 1976, 1991a). Thus, it offers both a conceptual model and therapeutic techniques which are logically derived from the model. This, in itself, is a contribution to psychotherapy, for neither theory nor techniques are presented without the other. In the history of psychotherapy, techniques have been offered without theoretical rationale and, conversely, elaborate, even convoluted, theories have been maintained without guidelines as to how to intervene in human behavior. Beck says, 'A lot of my contributions have to do with a conceptual model. The methods apply the theory.' One of the appeals of Cognitive Therapy has been its armamentarium of therapeutic techniques. However, application of the techniques without the conceptual model yields what some have called 'technical cognitive therapy', which misses the fundamental aspects of effective Cognitive Therapy, most particularly the therapeutic relationship.

Beck's theoretical contributions are a conceptualization of human behavior based on a phenomenological perspective and an information-processing model; tools to effectuate cognitive, behavioral, and affective change; and an approach to psychotherapy which is testable. He has provided these within the context of treating the patient as a collaborative partner, or co-investigator, and within a period of history which has yielded basic research in experimental social and cognitive psychology with which Beck's theories are compatible (Hollon and Garber, 1990). By seeing human behavior on a continuum, he has not divided it into 'normal' versus 'pathological' categories, and thus benefits from using an evolutionary framework, placing behaviors, including syndromes, within the context of adaptive processes (Beck, 1976, 1991a).

Phenomenological Perspective

For many, Beck's greatest theoretical contribution is that he brought private experience back into the realm of legitimate scientific inquiry. This was a theoretical revision from both the analysts' motivational model and the behaviorists' conditioning model. It shifted the theoretical focus from the environmental determinism of behaviorism to an internal determinism or phenomenological approach. Unlike the analytic model, this determinism was not based on biological drives or unconscious motivations, but on how the individual constructed his or her experience. An implication of this persepctive is that the patient's beliefs are assumed to be accessible, an assumption held by Kelly (1955) and promoted by Albert Ellis (1962). In addition, these beliefs can be approached in a direct way, using questions rather than interpretations to gain full understanding of the patient's point of view.

Brian Shaw describes it thusly: 'There are data or information that can come from the patient which are amenable to an inquiry which doesn't depend on constructs like the unconscious or defense mechanisms. You have a way of using the patient's actual self-reports as they occur and can do something with them. It has the benefit of simplicity.'

John Rush points out that Beck develops the theory to fit the patient's behavior rather than taking the theory and making the patient's behavior fit the theory. 'He's much more likely to change the theory to fit reality,' says Rush. In Beck's research as well, the data drive the theory, creating a pragmatic, empirical approach.

Information-Processing Model

Beck's model of psychological functioning and of psychopathology is based on an information-processing model. Human beings are always taking in cues from the environment and responding to them in ways to enhance survival. Thus, we perceive, interpret and assign meanings to events as well as formulate response strategies in order to adapt to our environments. Affective and behavioral responses are largely influenced by the cognitive appraisals made.

The information-processing paradigm involves a cognitive organization that is hierarchically structured and cognitive mechanisms which may selectively take in or screen out relevant information. The information processing is usually flexible, so that initial impressions or primary appraisals may be checked for verification or clarification.

Cognitive Organization

The cognitive organization includes levels of thought or imagery which differ from each other in terms of accessibility and stability. The most accessible cognitions are voluntary thoughts, which appear in stream of consciousness. Less accessible, and more important to cognitive theory, are automatic thoughts, which seem to arise without awareness and may be difficult to inhibit, particularly at times of distress. Deeper still are an individual's assumptions and values, and at the deepest level, out of an individual's awareness, are schemas. Schemas are conceptualized as organizing principles (Safran et al., 1986) on which the person bases such things as a world view, beliefs about the self, and relatedness to others. Schemas are also defined as cognitive structures containing a network of core beliefs (Segal, 1988) and operationalized as the tacit beliefs themselves (Beck, 1987a). The cognitive model proposes that these beliefs are latent until activated by particularly relevant life events.

Model of Psychopathology

When schemas are triggered, they emerge full-blown, accompanied by strong affect. Automatic thoughts, which are expressions of schema content, proliferate one's consciousness. Cognitive distortions, which bias the selection and integration of environmental information, operate to maintain and reinforce the schema. Thinking becomes more rigid and judgments more absolute. Cognitive deficits such as difficulties with memory and recall interfere with reasoning.

Schemas are established by early learning experiences. They may be highly personalized, but may be common to a diagnosis. For example, depressogenic schemas often contain themes of deprivation, defeat, loss, or worthlessness. Schemas common to anxiety disorders reflect danger or threat. Features of Beck's model of psychopathology will be further discussed in terms of his model of depression.

Continuity Hypothesis

Beck's theory maintains that various psychopathological syndromes are exaggerated forms of normal emotional responses (Beck, 1976). This is what he calls the continuity hypothesis, for there is continuity between the content of 'normal' reactions and the excessive responses seen in psychopathology. In depression, a sense of defeat and deprivation becomes pervasive and, thus, sadness increases. In mania, there is an increase in expansion and goal-directed activity and, thus, euphoria increases. In anxiety, a sense of increased vulnerability leads to an increased desire to escape and defend oneself (Beck, 1991a).

This theoretical perspective has several implications. First, it removes some stigma from psychological distress and makes it comprehensible. Second, it allows investigation of the functions of various disorders in an evolutionary sense, for they are somehow linked to adaptive behavior. Third, it gives us information on the 'more subtle biases in normal everyday reactions' (Beck, 1991a: p. 370) such as the positive bias apparent in many nondepressed individuals (Alloy and Abramson, 1979; DeMonbreun and Craighead, 1977).

Theoretical Differences from Psychoanalysis

Beck's conceptualization of an information-processing model as the basis for human adaptation and psychopathology broke from both traditions of the time: psychoanalytic theory and behavior modification. Cognitive Therapy, in contrast with psychoanalysis, places greater validity in the conscious or preconscious experiences of the individual. That is, people are usually regarded as reliable communicators of their experience rather than obfuscating it with layers of unconscious motivations. For the Cognitive Therapist, the client's experience is accessible in a rather straightforward manner, rather than requiring interpretation.

Ericksonian therapist Dr Michael Yapko asked Beck to distinguish between the Freudian concept of the unconscious and Beck's concept of automatic thoughts. Beck responded,

> Freud had a particular construction of the unconscious. His idea was that underneath the surface of one's thinking and feeling was a cauldron of taboo drives and wishes and motivational patterns. Then there was a thick concrete wall of repression. The 'unconscious', according to Freud, consisted of the compartment of the mind that is completely isolated from the conscious mind and kept in isolation through repression and defense mechanisms. Now my own notion is that consciousness is on a continuum. Some things are more conscious than others and some are less conscious than others. When you drive your car, you're not conscious of every single move you're making, but if you're focusing on it, then you do become aware of what you're doing. Automatic thoughts are brief signals at the periphery of consciousness. It's only when people train themselves to concentrate on the periphery that they become aware of their automatic thoughts. They are the most significant messages going through the brain in terms of emotions and

psychopathology. These little signals don't have to be at the forefront of your consciousness. However, it's interesting that when people get into a psychopathological state, this internal communication system becomes dominant. (Yapko, 1991: 10)

Despite his differences with Freudian theory, Beck maintains an appreciation of his analytic training.

'Even though I'm often identified with psychologists, I had no training in psychology. But the traditional psychiatry that I learned in medical school focused a great deal on phenomenology, on what actually goes on inside patients. The clinical descriptions we learned in psychiatry are just as good today as they were in my medical school days. The second aspect of my psychiatric training that helps me was psychoanalysis. That was when I really started to ask a lot of questions and probe for meaning. As it turned out, the meanings that were most important to me in developing my theories were not the deep subconscious ones, but accessible ones.' (Diffily, 1991: 25)

Differences from psychoanalysis are also explained by psychiatrist John Rush, who says, 'It isn't always the case that the patient wants the outcome of the pathology to occur, [as in] the idea of unconscious motivation. It isn't that they want to feel bad; they just don't see ways to feel better. I think that shifts the burden off the patient. You're not miserable because you want to suffer and cause problems for other people. You're a miserable person because you have a funny way of looking at things that you may have learned in the past, but you can certainly change your views. If you can change your views, you can change your behavior and, therefore, change the outcome. So, it takes the blame off the patient, and gives the patient a sense of choice, of freedom. That introduces a lot of optimism for both the patient and the therapist.'

Theoretical Differences from Behavior Therapy

This notion of freedom of choice contrasts with the perspective of radical behaviorism. Joseph Wolpe writes (1980: 198), 'Delightful as it is to regard ourselves as partially free agents, and not entirely under the domination of the causal sequences that relentlessly channel the course of events for everything else in nature, this freedom is, alas, only an illusion.' In contrast, Beck has stated that (1) people have free will and can change, (2) people have a responsibility to change, and (3) people will change. Thus, this perspective on individual freedom is a theoretical perspective which differs from a reductionistic or an environmentally deterministic view.

Differences between Cognitive Therapy and behavior therapy

have been discussed in Chapter 1 and will be further analyzed in Chapter 4. Cognitive Therapy focuses on the person's internal world, how individuals perceive and organize information, and how these formulations affect emotion and behavior. Cognitive Therapy sees humans as highly interactive with and evaluative of their environments.

While Cognitive Therapy employs behavioral techniques, it is for the purpose of cognitive change. Moreover, it is assumed both that cognitive change is necessary for new behaviors to be successfully maintained and that behavior change may spur cognitive change.

Cognitive Therapy attempts to integrate several channels – affective, behavioral, and cognitive – in explaining human functioning. Cognitive Therapy emphasizes the cognitive channel as an entry point into this constellation and as a prime mover in effecting change, but maintains that all channels must be addressed.

'Until cognitive therapy,' says Michael Mahoney, 'you were either an insight person, that is an analyst, or a behaviorist or a humanist, and none of the twain shall meet. There was just no respect for the possibility, let alone the promise, of studying the relationships among thoughts and feeling and behavior patterns.'

Differences from other Cognitive Therapies

Along with Meichenbaum and Ellis, Beck demonstrated the importance of what people say to themselves. The theoretical concept that people's internal dialogues were constant and interacted with emotions and behavior was important for many reasons, not the least of which is that this dialogue is accessible and modifiable. Beck's unique contributions to cognitive theory are: (1) the notion of cognitive organization and the importance of modifying deeper cognitive structures; and (2) the principle that a cognitive bias operates in psychopathology that affects all level of cognitive processing.

According to Beck's model, in psychopathology there is a shift in cognitive processing. It's not simply that people have unrealistic thoughts; it's that the mechanics of cognitive processing change. Thus, Beck introduces the idea of *cognitive deficits*, meaning that normal cognitive functions of perception, recall, inference and long-term memory are affected by activated schemas.

A number of these changes in cognitive functioning have been documented in depression (Blackburn et al., 1990; Bradley and Mathews, 1988; D.M. Clark and Teasdale, 1982; DeMonbreun and Craighead, 1977; Dunbar and Lishman, 1984; Gilson, 1983; Krantz and Hammen, 1979; Powell and Hemsley, 1984).

Cognitive deficits such as poor problem-solving, cognitive rigidity, and an inability to foresee consequences of various courses of action have been noted among suicidal patients (Weishaar and Beck, 1992). In high anxiety there appears to be an inability to access higher cognitive powers in order to reason with oneself. Individuals have trouble with concentration, directed thinking, and recall (Beck, Emery and Greenberg, 1984). Thus, the cognitive model focuses on how information processing is biased by the activation of schemas. Beck states that dysfunctional beliefs are problematic 'because they interfere with normal cognitive processing, not because they are irrational' (Beck and Weishaar, 1989a: 288). In this way, Beck takes a more functional view of negative or biased beliefs as opposed to seeing them as philosophically incongruent with reality, the position of RET.

Beck has also made contributions to the theory of psychotherapy which distinguish him from other cognitive therapists. They are: (1) the emphasis on structural change rather than focusing on more superficial cognitions; (2) the presumed mechanisms of change; and (3) the nature of the therapeutic relationship.

Structural Change
Beck's schema concept is cited by many as his unique contribution to cognitive psychotherapies. Like Freud and Kelly, Beck views cognitions as hierarchically arranged. In Beck's model, schemas are deeper-level cognitive structures, the content of which is latent or out of the person's awareness until a relevant life event potentiates the schema. Beck's focus on the necessity of modifying these deeper-level structures goes beyond the work of several other theorists who focus only on responding to self-statements or, in Beck's terminology, automatic thoughts. Moreover, it is important, according to Beck's cognitive model, that clients themselves arrive at alternative interpretations rather than having them supplied by the therapist. The client is trained in examining his beliefs and arriving at more adaptive responses, making those responses more likely to be believable and significant for that individual.

Finally, modifying an underlying assumption, or making structural change at a schema level, is presumed to change a multitude of automatic thoughts. Such changes are most likely to occur when cognitive changes are paired with behaviors congruent with new beliefs.

Mechanisms of Change
According to Beck's model, change is achieved through examination and empirical testing of the patient's beliefs, not through

54   Aaron T. Beck

philosophic debate or persuasion by the therapist. Patients learn to become their own therapists, employing the skills learned in Cognitive Therapy: examining the evidence for and against their interpretations, looking for alternative explanations or courses of action, and behaving in ways which are congruent with more adaptive ways of thinking. Clients derive new meanings and interpretations of events. They are not given substitute beliefs by the therapist.

Until Cognitive Therapy began to address personality disorders, it was assumed that all cognitions and behavior patterns could be changed through empirical analysis, logical discourse, behavioral experiments, gradual steps and practice (Young, 1990). The affective arousal necessary for new learning, however, seems to be even more important in treating personality disorders. Thus, Cognitive Therapy uses more experiential techniques to create structural change in treating more difficult disorders (Beck, Freeman and Associates, 1990).

Therapy Relationship

Like Kelly and others, Beck endorses the collaborative role of the client. This position assumes that clients can be active in their therapy and gives impetus to the notion of self-help. It is consistent with the theoretical premises that (1) one's internal communication is accessible to introspection, (2) these beliefs have highly personal meanings unrelated to classic psychoanalytic theory, and (3) these meanings can be deduced by the clients rather than interpreted by the therapist.

Beck took this collaboration and directed it towards the examination and testing of the patient's beliefs, as if they were hypotheses to be supported or nullified. Unlike anyone else, Beck 'turned the client into a colleague who researches verifiable reality' (Wessler, 1986: 5).

Contributions to the Theory of Depression

Beck's Model of Depression

Beck's cognitive model of depression posits that in nonendogenous unipolar depression, individuals have a cognitive vulnerability to depression which is triggered by stressful life events (Kovacs and Beck, 1978). This cognitive vulnerability consists of negative, maladaptive schemas: cognitive structures containing dysfunctional beliefs and presumed to be established by early learning experiences. These schemas are latent and out of the individual's awareness until triggered by a personally meaningful and schema-congruent life event. In the case of depression, schemas often reflect loss, deprivation, worthlessness or defeat. They also appear related to personality.

The triggering of depressogenic schemas generates negative expectations, sadness, self-recriminations, and apathy stemming from biased and distorted information processing. As a consequence of pessimism, hopelessness or apathy, the individual becomes less active, takes fewer risks and avoids social contact. Reduced performance is then interpreted as a sign of failure or worthlessness, reinforcing the negative schema about the self.

In 1987, Beck reformulated his theory of depression to yield six different, but overlapping, models which describe or explain its etiology, its evolutionary significance, and other concepts not fully explicated in its initial design (Beck, 1987a). This refinement clearly identified this initial, descriptive model with non-endogenous, unipolar depression, not all types of depressions nor their etiologies. Thus, cognitive theory uses personality modes, dysfunctional beliefs, and stressful life events to explain non-endogenous depression (Haaga, Dyck and Ernst, 1991).

Primacy of Cognition The primacy of cognition in depression reformulates the model of depression from being a mood state to being a cognitive one as well. According to Beck's theory, in depression there is a malfunctioning of normal information processing and there are specific beliefs and attitudes which are triggered by particular life events, leading to other symptoms. In depression there is a negative cognitive shift in information processing so that much relevant positive information is screened out and negative self-relevant information is selected, attended to and incorporated (Beck, 1967).

Beck's theory does not argue that cognitions cause depression or any other disorder, although the notion of cognitive vulnerability has been investigated in relationship to relapse. Beck considers the activation of schemas to be a mechanism by which depression develops, not its cause. The cause may be due to any interaction among genetic, biological, developmental, personality, environmental, and cognitive factors (Beck, 1967).

Nevertheless, once depressed, all individuals show common cognitive features regardless of the causes of various types of depression. These features include cognitive distortions, cognitive deficits, and a negative view of the self, the world, and the future, known as the cognitive triad.

Cognitive Vulnerability in Depression Just as there is a biological vulnerability to depression there is a cognitive one: specifically, schemas incorporating negative views of the self, one's personal world, and the future. These beliefs are absolute, learned from life experiences, and connected to strong affect. Examples of depressogenic beliefs are 'I am worthless,' 'I am unlovable,' and 'I am helpless.'

In his reformulation of his theory of depression, Beck (1983, 1987a) hypothesized that certain types of individuals would be more sensitive to specific types of stressful life events than others. A study of outpatients at Beck's clinic identified two broad types or modes of personality, sociotropy and autonomy, which are presumed to respond to different types of environmental contingencies in the etiology of depression (Beck, Epstein and Harrison, 1983). Sociotropy is characterized by a reliance on positive social interaction for gratification. Depressions occurring in patients of this type were found to have been precipitated by a disruption of social bonding (Beck, 1983), a finding consistent with Bowlby's (1977, 1979) thesis that such disruption is essential to depression. Another group of patients, however, was found to represent a second personality mode, autonomy. Autonomy is characterized by needs for achievement, mobility or freedom from control by others, and a preference for solitude. Autonomous individuals were found to become depressed when thwarted from attaining goals (Beck, 1983). These personality types or modes are meant to represent extreme ends of a dimension and not dichotomous and exclusive categories.

Beck elaborated his cognitive theory of depression in this way to respond to Bowlby's (1977, 1979) work on attachment and the disruption of social bonds as a precursor to depression. Beck (1987a) also cites the influence of criticisms (for instance Coyne and Gotlib, 1983) that Cognitive Therapy paid insufficient attention to people's social environments in the etiology of depression as impetus to include this clinical formulation of the personality modes in a theory of depression.

Cognitive Deficits in Depression   In depression, normal cognitive processing is altered by the activation of schemas, and several functions become impaired such as perception, recall, inference, and long-term memory. Problem-solving difficulties, perhaps resulting from cognitive rigidity, limit one's abilities to generate solutions to problems (Nezu, Nezu and Perri, 1989; Weishaar and Beck, 1990).

Cognitive Distortions   Beck's theory of depression describes the thinking of depressed persons as being full of errors in logic, called cognitive distortions (Beck, 1976). In terms of his information-processing model, cognitive distortions are the mechanisms which bias the deciphering of information in a negative way. One might define the role of cognitive distortions as 'schema maintenance,' for they influence information processing in a way to uphold the patient's core beliefs, however maladaptive they may be (Young, 1990). Cognitive distortions include over-generalization, dichotomous thinking, selective abstraction, minimization or magnification, arbitrary inference, and personalization.

There is debate, as will be discussed in Chapter 4, as to whether the cognitions of depressed persons are any more distorted than those of nondepressed persons. It may be that they are biased in a negative way, whereas the cognitions of nondepressed people are biased in a positive way. Alternatively, the cognitions of depressed individuals may reflect more pessimism than those of nondepressed individuals, but are not necessarily distortions of reality.

Cognitive Triad Beck coined the term the *cognitive triad* to describe the depressogenic program that becomes activated in depression. The cognitive triad reflects a view of the self as a failure, a view of the world that is thwarting and hostile, and a view of the future as hopeless. Bandura's (1977a, 1986) work is somewhat related, for his concepts of self-efficacy and outcome efficacy deal with the expectancies people have about their abilities and the likelihood of reinforcement.

Haaga, Dyck and Ernst (1991) suggest that the negative view of the world is actually a negative view of one's personal world, not the state of the world in general. Thus, the cognitive triad actually consists of a view of the self and two of its components: the self in relationship to the world, and the self in relationship to the future. Two aspects of the cognitive triad, a negative view of the self and a negative view of the future have been found to be associated with suicide risk (Weishaar and Beck, 1992).

Theoretical Contributions to the Study of Suicide
As a logical outgrowth of his depression research, Beck investigated cognitive factors in suicide. He found that hopelessness, or the extreme negative view of the future, is the key psychological variable in suicidality. Dr Maria Kovacs, who intially came to work with him on his suicide research, believes Beck's conceptualization of hopelessness as a cognitive construct is among his most important theoretical contributions.

Hopelessness is defined as a stable schema incorporating negative expectancies. This conceptual shift allows clinical intervention to identify the source of the hopelessness, clarify the problems by reducing the cognitive distortions which make problems seem irresolvable, and begin problem-solving. Conceptualizing hopelessness as a cognitive construct is also a useful explanatory device for clients: hopelessness is an attitude, not a reflection of reality. It remits when depression remits and, therefore, is not to be acted upon.

Beck's ability to demonstrate a relationship between high levels of hopelessness and suicide intent is an important contribution to the field of suicide research and is an important clinical observation for suicide risk assessment and prediction. Beck has substantiated the association between hopelessness and suicide risk through longitudinal research on both inpatients (Beck et al., 1985) and outpatients (Beck et al., 1990a). Scores of nine or above on the Beck Hopelessness Scale (Beck et al., 1974) were predictive of eventual suicide over a period of five to ten years. Use of the Hopelessness Scale yields a high percentage of false positives, but its clinical utility is substantial. Additional findings support the relationship between low self-concept, or negative view of the self, and suicide risk (Beck and Stewart, 1989).

Cognitive Profiles
In explicating the cognitive bias present in various syndromes, Beck and his colleagues have described cognitive profiles for psychological disorders, including personality disorders (Beck, 1976; Beck et al., 1979; Beck, Freeman and Associates, 1990; Beck and Weishaar, 1989a, 1989b). While individuals have idiosyncratic cognitions, there are pervasive themes within each diagnostic category which reflect how information is biased. Such profiles are clinically useful in conceptualizing cases and intervening in a way which targets core cognitive processes.

Cognitive Specificity
Beck attributes the application of Cognitive Therapy across diverse disorders to this notion of cognitive specificity: 'each disorder has its own specific cognitive conceptualization and relevant strategies that are embraced under the general principles of Cognitive Therapy' (Beck, 1991a: 368).

The hypothesis of cognitive specificity, that each disorder has its own typical cognitive content, has been mainly investigated by comparing the cognitions of depressed and anxious patients. Using the Cognitions Checklist, depressed patients scored higher on Loss–Defeat subscales and anxious patients scored higher on the

Danger subscale (Beck et al., 1987). Another study (Beck et al., 1986) found that, compared to anxious patients, depressed patients were more likely to predict high probabilities of negative outcomes to their problems and low probabilities of positive outcomes. Further, M.S. Greenberg and Beck (1989) found, on self-endorsement and recall, that depressed patients endorsed cognitions of depressive content (such as loss) while anxious patients endorsed cognitions with anxiety content (such as danger). Moreover, a factor analytic study of all the cognitive scales designed to measure the cognitive content of depression and anxiety yielded appropriate loadings on the depression and anxiety factors (D.A. Clark, Beck and Brown, 1989).

Clinical Significance of Beck's Theory of Depression
The structural organization of cognition has implications for a theory of psychotherapy. Beck's theory describes core and more derivative cognitions. Core cognitions, embedded in schemas, need to be reached and modified for fundamental and lasting change to occur.

Part of the art of Cognitive Therapy is choosing the most fruitful cognition to examine. This means, theoretically, that all thoughts are not of equal importance, for their importance reflects their place in one's cognitive organization (Beck et al., 1979). David M. Clark says, 'I suppose one of the biggest problems in Cognitive Therapy is that anyone you see who's at all emotionally distressed will have an enormous number of negative thoughts, most of which are totally irrelevant. The art of Cognitive Therapy is to know which thoughts are driving the system and just go for those. When you watch Tim actually working, it's very noticeable that he doesn't seem to be doing very much therapy at all to start up with the patient. What he's doing, I think, he often is maneuvering around and around until he gets into some sort of thoughts which have plenty of affect attached to them. He looks for affect and then mines that particular area.'

Beck's theory assumes that thoughts associated with affect tend to be more representative of deeper beliefs and assumptions than are less emotionally-connected statements. The emergence of themes across situations and over time is also presumed to reflect underlying assumptions.

Other clinically relevant statements have to do with self-schema (Markus, 1977), or self-referential information; expectations or predictions about the future; and causal attributions or inferences about the cause of events, including behavior (Hollon and Kriss, 1984; Shaw and Segal, 1988). Expectations and causal attributions have received more attention than other types of cognitions in marital therapy research (Baucom, 1989).

An alternative cognitive model of depression, Seligman's reformulated learned helplessness model (Abramson, Seligman and Teasdale, 1978; Peterson and Seligman, 1985) is based on causal attributions. The learned helplessness model of depression posits that, in the face of negative, uncontrollable events, internal (vs. external), stable (vs. unstable) and global (vs. specific) attributions of causality are associated with depression. A further reformulation of a specific subtype of depression, 'hopelessness depression,' also posits inferential style as contributing to stable and global attributions of negative events, negative inferences about the self, and negative inferences about the consequences of negative events (Abramson, Metalsky and Alloy, 1989). Thus, a person's attributional or explanatory style may be a cognitive vulnerability for depressive episodes (Peterson and Seligman, 1985).

Safran et al. (1986) offer a conceptual framework of core cognitive processes to indicate which automatic thoughts disclosed in a therapy session are most likely to reflect core or, in their terms, higher order cognitions. They argue that the thoughts and assumptions which affect self-perception are more central than other types of cognitions. They also identify Beck's (1983) classification of sociotropic and autonomous personalities and their corresponding emphasis on lovability and competence as prevailing themes to watch for. They reiterate Beck's (Beck et al., 1979) guidelines of observing consistency of themes across situations and attending to the cognitions accompanying affective shifts. In addition, they point out that although Ellis may work on modifying core constructs by challenging irrational beliefs, RET does not deal with central constructs that are idiosyncratic for each patient. Beck's Cognitive Therapy does explore the highly personal meanings of these organizing principles.

Empirical Tests of the Cognitive Model of Depression

Tests of Treatment Efficacy

Tests of Beck's model of depression fall into two areas: (1) its clinical efficacy and (2) its theoretical soundness. The therapeutic effectiveness of Cognitive Therapy in the treatment of unipolar, nonpsychotic depressive disorders is well-supported. A meta-analysis of 28 outcome studies (Dobson, 1989) demonstrates its superiority or equivalence to other treatments, including antidepressant medication. In their review of empirical studies of

Cognitive Therapy, Hollon and Najavits (1988) state that Cognitve Therapy alone is comparable to tricyclic antidepressant medication in terms of acute symptom reduction and that the combination of the two may be superior to either one alone.

The strength of Cognitive Therapy may be most apparent in preventing relapse. Six studies indicate that Cognitive Therapy is superior to pharmacotherapy in preventing relapse or recurrence of depression (Evans et al., 1992; Hollon and Najavits, 1988; Shea et al., 1992). Even in the NIMH collaborative study, in which Cognitive Therapy was found equivalent in direct comparisons to other modalities, there is evidence of its superiority at the one-year follow-up stage (Shea et al., 1992). Hollon and Najavits (1988: 651) conclude, 'Clearly, something very powerful is provided by Cognitive Therapy that survives the termination of treatment.'

Tests of Theoretical Principles
While Cognitive Therapy has been demonstrated to be effective in the treatment of unipolar depression, the mechanisms of change are not clear. Cognitive Therapy works, but no one knows how. Cognitive Therapy is believed to produce changes in existing beliefs and in the way information is processed by the individual. These changes, theoretically, lead to decreases in overt symptomatology. It is presumably the training in identifying and modifying one's beliefs (Beck et al., 1979; Hollon and Najavits, 1988) and engaging in more deliberate information processing (Hollon and Garber, 1990) that is responsible for the change. Beck and others (Hollon and Beck, 1979; Hollon and Garber, 1990) argue that the process of empirical hypothesis testing is the most powerful tool used to change beliefs and the way information is processed by the individual. Thus, data gathered by the client through verbal examination and behavioral experiments are used to create change.

Support for Descritpive Features of the Model
An extensive review of the empirical support for Beck's theory of depression is provided by Haaga, Dyck and Ernst (1991). They summarize research findings particularly relevant to Beck's stressor–vulnerability model, which describes sufficient conditions for depression. The model has both descriptive components and suggestions of causality, with which some researchers have taken issue.

Haaga, Dyck and Ernst (1991) concluded that all subtypes of depression are associated with increased negative thinking, but not all thinking is negative. The concept of the cognitive triad is supported, but it is not clear whether the triad is conceptually a single dimension with overlapping components and whether all components are necessary for depression. It may be that elevated levels in only one component of the triad may be sufficient for depression. It is also not clear whether depressive thinking is automatic, in a rigorous sense: that is, initiated without awareness and difficult to inhibit. Studies of subclinical dysphoria suggest that the process is indeed automatic, but studies with depressed subjects are needed. Haaga, Dyck and Ernst (1991) report that the severity of negative cognitions correlates positively with the severity of noncognitive symptoms, and that this relationship cannot be attributed to statistical artifacts. Lastly, the authors conclude that there is evidence of a cognitive bias in depression, which is defined as a tendency to make judgments in a systematic and consistently negative manner. There is less evidence for cognitive distortion or seeing the world unrealistically. The greatest evidence for distortion among depressed individuals has to do with underestimations of highly positive feedback.

Several cognitive changes in depression have been substantiated in clinical samples. They are: (1) an increase of negative automatic thoughts, (2) negative expectancies for success, (3) negatively biased recall of self-referent information, (4) a notably high level of dysfunctional attitudes, and (5) a bias toward internal, stable and global attributions to failure experiences (Shaw and Segal, 1988).

Support for Causal Features of the Model
Although Beck does not claim that his model of depression is causal, the notion of cognitive vulnerability as a predisposition to depression, and the description of how personality modes may interact with specific types of stressors are suggestive of causal features. Haaga, Dyck and Ernst (1991) conclude that measures of cognitive vulnerability, as operationalized by dysfunctional beliefs, have usually found beliefs to be at normal levels after depression remits. They therefore conclude that dysfunctional beliefs are state-dependent features in individuals. Nevertheless, they maintain that it is premature to abandon hypotheses of cognitive vulnerability.

Similarly, initial studies of the proposed interactions between personality modes and stressful life events in predicting depression recurrence are inconclusive. No direct tests of the interactions of sociotropy and autonomy with life events have been made because of methodological issues. What studies exist, however indirect, offer mixed suppport for the association between 'personality type' and the type of event leading to depression. Hammen and her colleagues (1989) reported a relationship between life events and type of personality in depression. A subsequent, more refined study

(Hammen, Ellicott and Gitlin, 1989) found this relationship true only for those scoring high in autonomy on the Sociotropy–Autonomy Scale (Beck, Epstein and Harrison, 1983). Segal, Shaw and Vella (1989) found congruence of life events only among sociotropic subjects who relapsed. The utility of such investigations is the test of congruence between type of life event and depressive subtype. More generally speaking, it begins to address the relationship between cognitive vulnerability, broadly defined by a personality dimension, and life stress leading to depression.

Finally, Haaga, Dyck and Ernst (1991) conclude that no study has incorporated all the variables of Beck's model in a longitudinal design that could test his onset hypothesis. These variables would be personality modes, a measure of dysfunctional beliefs under appropriately challenging conditions, stressors, and the identification of depression status during follow-up – all among a sample of never-before-depressed subjects. Thus, there is more evidence, at this point, for the descriptive features of Beck's model of depression than for the causal features.

Support for Primacy of Cognition
Although it has been argued recently that Beck's endorsement of cognitive primacy in psychopathology is of conceptual primacy and not causal or temporal primacy (Alford and Carr, 1992), there is some research evidence in support of cognitive mediation in depression. Rush and his associates (Rush et al., 1981) found that patients treated with Cognitive Therapy, but not pharmacotherapy, experienced changes in beliefs about themselves and their futures prior to changes in vegetative symptoms. A further study (Rush et al., 1982) found greater changes in measures of hopelessness midway through a course of treatment with Cognitive Therapy than with drug treatment. Rush, Weissenberger and Eaves (1986) found that changes in cognition preceded changes in affect. Teasdale and Fennell (1982) found that reduction of active negative thought content led to the greatest reduction in negative affect in depressed persons. Blackburn and Bishop (1983) found evidence of greater change in cognitive content and process following Cognitive Therapy, with or without medication, than drug treatment alone. In contrast to these findings, Simons, Garfield and Murphy (1984) found no differential changes in automatic thoughts or underlying beliefs between subjects treated with Cognitive Therapy and those receiving pharmacotherapy.

Contributions to Research and Accountability in Psychotherapy

Beck's work is clearly built on the interplay between clinical observations and testable research hypotheses. His theoretical formulations have direct clinical applications and his clinical observations lead to further theoretical refinements.

Beck's use of research to create and develop a system of psychotherapy is a contribution which has had many ramifications. Dr Michael Mahoney says, 'I think Beck individually and then collectively with his collaborators and students introduced a level of respectability to research and psychotherapy research dealing with cognitive processes that had not been there before.' Dr Albert Ellis similarly cites Beck's solid research as a major contribution to the field of cognitive psychotherapies. Dr Donald Meichenbaum credits Beck's use of clinical populations as lending credibility and legitimacy to the cognitive conceptualization of depression and to psychotherapy research in general. Dr Jesse Wright, originator of the first inpatient Cognitive Therapy treatment program at the University of Louisville, believes the intellectual rigor of Cognitve Therapy has been an important contribution to psychotherapy. 'Cognitive Therapy was revolutionary,' he says, 'to somebody, at least from my perspective, who came out of more of a hard science background – physiology, biochemistry and pharmacology – and was looking for something in the aspect of psychiatry that had something close to that.'

Many say that Beck's treatment manual for depression set a standard of accountability in reporting what actually goes on in psychotherapy which has since been emulated by other researchers and clinicians. While some have argued that Beck's treatment manual for depression, for example, does not capture the heart of his own psychotherapeutic style, such a manual is teachable, testable and accessible to many therapists.

Assessment Scales

In the development of his theory, Beck operationalized a number of concepts for the assessment and treatment of depression and other disorders. The Beck Depression Inventory (BDI) (Beck et al., 1961; Beck and Steer, 1987) includes psychological symptoms of depression such as pessimism, sense of failure and guilt along with vegetative signs. Studies of the BDI found that suicidal wishes correlated more closely with negative attitude than with vegetative symptoms (Beck, Lester and Albert, 1973). This suggested that psychotherapy might be more helpful in reducing suicidal risk than would pharmacotherapy. The BDI has been used in hundreds of studies and its validity and reliability are well documented (Beck and Steer, 1987).

The BDI has beeen found to correlate with suicide intent when a broad heterogeneous population is studied, such as in general medical practice. When a more homogeneous population is studied, such as a sample of depressed, inpatient suicide ideators or depressed outpatients, the Beck Hopelessness Scale (BHS) (Beck et al., 1974) and the Beck Self-Concept Test (BST) (Beck et al., 1990b) are better correlates of suicidal intent. Scales specifically devised for suicide research are the Suicide Intent Scale (SIS) (Beck, Schuyler and Herman, 1974) which assesses the severity of someone's intent to die at the time of a recent suicide attempt, and the Scale for Suicide Ideation (SSI) (Beck, Kovacs and Weissman, 1979) which assesses the degree to which someone is currently thinking about suicide. Beck's Self-Concept Test (Beck et al., 1990b) has also been found related to suicide risk (Beck and Stewart, 1989).

In addition to the BDI and the Beck Self-Concept Test are two assessment scales used in the study of depression: the Dysfunctional Attitude Scale (DAS) (Weissman, 1979; Weissman and Beck, 1978) and the Sociotropy–Autonomy Scale (Beck, Epstein and Harrison, 1983). The Dysfunctional Attitude Scale has been used in many studies as a measure of cognitive vulnerability to depression (Segal, 1988; Shaw and Segal, 1988). Difficulties operationalizing the concept of latent schemas and the meaning of stability or change in dysfunctional beliefs have precluded a clear consensus on the utility of this scale. The Sociotropy–Autonomy Scale is designed to measure personality dimensions, specifically to study their relationships to life stress events in the development of symptomatology.

Contributions to a Theory of Anxiety

Beck's cognitive theory gained prominence in the area of depression. Yet applications of the cognitive model have grown. Beck has developed the cognitive model of anxiety from his initial conceptualization of psychopathology resulting from faulty information processing. The cognitive themes apparent in depression are deprivation, defeat, and loss; the prevailing theme in anxiety is threat. Anxiety reactions are on a continuum with normal physiological responses, but are exaggerated reactions to perceived danger. Beck takes an evolutionary perspective by proposing that anxiety, originating as the fight, flight or freeze response observable in animal behavior, became less adaptive over millenia as danger became less physical and more psychosocial in nature. Anxiety disorders are viewed as extreme threat reactions (Beck, Emery and Greenberg, 1985). The central cognitions in anxiety consist of unrealistic perceptions of danger, catastrophic interpretations about loss of control, or perceived negative changes in a relationship (D.M. Clark and Beck, 1988). As in depression, there may be dysfunctional beliefs or schemas that pose vulnerabilities to anxiety. In addition, the cognitive distortions supporting such underlying beliefs involve overestimating the probability of the feared event, overestimating the severity of the feared event, underestimating one's ability to cope with the feared event, and underestimating rescue factors or the presence of people or environmental factors that could help (Beck, 1976). Beck follows Richard Lazarus' (1966) stress model to articulate how cognitive distortions contribute to the anxiety response, for, at each point of appraisal and reappraisal of a situation, distorted or biased thinking can misrepresent the degree of danger or ability to cope.

Beck's anxiety model offers a theoretical contribution in its emphasis on the role of the individual's beliefs and interpretations of events, including his or her own physiological reactions. It is the patient's catastrophic misinterpretation of bodily responses as signs of impending doom that escalates anxiety and is conceptualized as precipitating panic (Beck, Emery and Greenberg, 1985; Clark, 1986, 1988). The cognitive theory of recurrent panic suggests the following sequence: a variety of factors (such as mild anxiety, exercise, excitement, caffeine) produce mild sensations which are interpreted in a catastrophic way. This produces a marked increase in anxiety, which leads to a further increase in bodily sensations, creating a vicious cycle which culminates in a panic attack. Stress-induced hyperventilation may also be a part of this cycle if the somatic sensations are interpreted as a sign of immediate danger (Salkovskis and Clark, 1991).

Ideational Content in Anxiety
Beck demonstrated that anxiety states have ideational content (Beck, Laude and Bohnert, 1974) and that people often make very specific interpretations of their symptoms. In panic, for example, a rapid heart rate may be interpreted as the onset of a heart attack, derealization as a precursor of insanity, and breathlessness as a sign of inevitable suffocation. Different anxiety disorders are characterized by different ideational content; for example, social phobia revolves around the fear of negative evaluation by others (D.M. Clark and Beck, 1988), and simple phobias involve an exaggerated perception of danger in a specific object or situation.

Evolutionary Significance of Anxiety

Beck's theories on anxiety disorders and phobias owe a good deal to evolutionary theory. He uses an evolutionary model to explain the adaptive value of physiological arousal in the anxiety reaction: it prepares the animal for flight or fight. Human beings, possessing primate physiology but responsive to psychosocial cues, may over-respond to environmental threats, either signs of physical danger or social threats. Cognition plays various roles in the anxiety response process, for we perceive cues, interpret them as signs of danger, estimate our resources with which to cope with the threat, and assess the risk involved. Beck's model of anxiety, particularly the anxiety associated with panic, focuses on how the interpretation of one's own physical reactions can escalate anxiety, leading persons to interpret their own physiological responses as signs of internal disaster.

Influence of Richard Lazarus

Beck also acknowledges his debt to Richard Lazarus (1966) in the formulation of his theories, not only for Lazarus' emphasis on the role of cognition in human behavior, but for his conceptualizations of 'primary' and 'secondary' appraisals. In describing an individual's response to stressful situations, Lazarus states that a person initially makes a 'primary appraisal' of the degree of threat involved, and then makes a 'secondary appraisal' of the available resources to counter the stressor. Finally, the individual makes a reappraisal of the stressor in the context of these resources. Beck says, 'Lazarus did influence me a lot with the whole idea of appraisal. It was consistent with what I thought.' Beck's use of primary and secondary appraisal in his anxiety model pertains to how a person assesses the risk of a situation and his or her ability to cope with danger, complete with how the person might over-estimate threat and underestimate coping resourses (Beck, 1976; Beck, Emery and Greenberg, 1985).

Efficacy of Cognitive Therapy of Anxiety

Studies of the efficacy of Cognitive Therapy in the treatment of Generalized Anxiety Disorder (Butler et al., 1991) and particularly of panic demonstrate its effectiveness. Treatment based on the cognitive model of panic (Beck, 1987b, 1988a; D.M. Clark, 1986) yielded almost complete reduction of panic attacks after 12–16 weeks of treatment (Sokol, Beck and Clark, 1989; Sokol et al., 1989). A further study, using purely cognitive procedures without exposure found reductions in panic as well (Salkovskis, Clark and Hackmann, 1990). Although there are relatively few outcome studies on Cognitive Therapy for anxiety disorders as compared to those on depression, initial results are positive.

Tests of the Cognitive Theory of Anxiety

The theory behind the cognitive treatment of anxiety is also undergoing examination. Clark and Beck (1988: 145) have articulated four postulates to test the cognitive model. They are: (1) the thinking of anxious persons will be characterized by thoughts concerned with the perception of danger; (2) within individuals, anxiety ratings will correlate with the believability and frequency of thoughts concerned with danger; (3) the temporal occurrence of thoughts concerned with danger will be such that they could logically contribute to the initiation or maintained activation of the anxiety program; and (4) the experimental manipulation of the frequency and believability of thoughts concerned with the perception of danger will have systematic effects on patients' levels of anxiety.

In their review of the literature, Clark and Beck (1988) found that six studies had investigated the nature of the thoughts of anxious patients and all six had found the thoughts related to danger. The second prediction was also upheld, with correlations found between anxiety levels and the believability of anxious thoughts. There is some support for Clark and Beck's third prediction. Beck, Laude and Bohnert (1974) and Last and Blanchard (1982) found that phobics and other anxious patients reported danger-related thoughts before their anxiety peaked, suggesting that such thoughts contributed to arousal. Finally, Clark and Beck report that although experimental manipulations of the frequency and/or believability of negative thoughts among depressed patients had been conducted, no comparable experiments had been conducted with anxious patients.

Since Clark and Beck's review, there has accumulated more evidence, from research on panic, to support the role of cognitions in anxiety disorders. A study of patients diagnosed as having panic disorder with agoraphobia found that all subjects identified catastrophic cognitions pertaining to physical illness, death, mental illness, loss of self-control and social embarrassment (Robinson and Birchwood, 1991). Consistent with the cognitive model which postulates that panic attacks result from the catastrophic misinterpretations of somatic symptoms, specific links between certain cognitions (for example, 'I am having a heart attack') and physical symptoms (such as tightness in the chest) were found.

Additional evidence suggesting the mediational role of cognitions in escalating anxiety is a study by Ehlers and her colleagues (1988) which used false heart rate feedback to induce panic. A further study (Ehlers, 1991) found that fear of body sensations associated with anxiety is characteristic of patients with panic disorder and is also found to a lesser degree among infrequent panickers and patients with other anxiety disorders. High symptom sensitivity and self-reported low coping ability were specific to anxious patients as compared to nonpatient controls.

Theoretical Contributions to Couples' Therapy

Beck wrote a self-help book for couples, *Love Is Never Enough* (1988b), which describes the role of cognitions in distressed relationships. This contribution added to growing evidence that relationship difficulties stem from dysfunctional beliefs as well as communication deficits and other problematic behavioral patterns. Partners may have unrealistic or unreasonable expectations and standards about relationships in general and about their own relationship and partner in particular (Beck, 1988b). Causal attributions, or blame, for problems is also a common type of cognition in distressed partnerships (Epstein and Baucom, 1989).

The same cognitive mechanisms operating in depression and anxiety operate in relationship problems. Specifically, schemas are triggered by life events, biasing information processing and contributing to emotional distress. Cognitive distortions, such as overgeneralization about a partner's characteristics, or arbitrary inference and mind-reading, are common among couples.

While *Love is Never Enough* is based on clinical experience rather than on clinical laboratory research, a number of other cognitive–behavioral researchers have focused on marital distress, both in terms of assessing the types of cognitions which contribute to conflict and the types of interventions which can reduce interpersonal strife (see Epstein and Baucom, 1989 for a review). 'A cognitive–behavioral approach,' write Epstein and Baucom (1989: 492) 'focuses on how spouses often process information about their relationships inappropriately, either deriving invalid conclusions about events, or evaluating those events according to unreasonable standards.'

Beck's book is meant for the public, not specifically for clinicians. However, Drs Frank Dattilio and Christine Padesky have published a manual for therapists, *Cognitive Therapy with Couples* (1990). Dattilio and Padesky write that there are three main goals in Cognitive Therapy with couples. They are: (1) modification of unrealistic expectations in the relationship, (2) correction of faulty attributions in relationship interactions, and (3) the use of self-instructional procedures to decrease destructive interaction.

To date, outcome studies comparing cognitive and behavioral techniques, alone and in combination, have found few differences in the effectiveness of these approaches (Baucom, 1989; Baucom and Lester, 1986; Baucom, Sayers and Sher, 1990; Emmelkamp et al., 1988; Huber and Milstein, 1985; Margolin and Weiss, 1978). Both cognitive restructuring alone and Behavior Marital Therapy alone have been successful in promoting cognitive change (Emmelkamp et al., 1988; Epstein, Pretzer and Fleming, 1982). Cognitive restructuring has also been found to be effective in creating behavior change in couples (Emmelkamp et al., 1988; Baucom, 1985).

Contributions to a Theory of Personality Disorders

Evolutionary Strategies
In *Cognitive Therapy of Personality Disorders* (Beck, Freeman and Associates, 1990), Beck again uses evolutionary theory and an information-processing model to develop his theory. Beck's model of personality disorders posits that prototypes of our personality patterns could be considered 'strategies' which influenced survival and reproductive success during hominid evolution. Present-day personality disorders may be exaggerated expressions of those primitive strategies. Information processing, which relies on underlying beliefs embedded in schemas, determines how an individual evaluates a situation. 'The psychological sequence,' write Beck, Freeman and Associates (1990: 22), 'progresses then from evaluation to affective and motivational arousal, and finally to selection, and implementation of a relevant strategy. We regard the basic structures (schemas) upon which these cognitive, affective, and motivational processes are dependent as the fundamental units of personality.'

Elaboration of Schema Concept
In his theory of personality disorders, Beck further elaborates his schema concept. Schemas, as presented by such theorists as Bartlett (1932) and Piaget (1926, 1936/1952), are structures which integrate and assign meanings to events. Beck's schema concept is similar to Kelly's (1955) notion of personal constructs. Beck describes schemas as having structural qualities such as breadth (whether they are narrow, discrete or broad), flexibility or rigidity (reflecting their capacity for modification) and density (their relative prominence in the cognitive organization). Beck also discusses schema valence or level of activation. When schemas are

latent they are not involved in information processing; when they are activated, they direct all cognitive processing.

In psychopathology, highly personalized idiosyncratic schemas are activated and probably inhibit more adaptive or appropriate schemas from operating (Beck, 1964, 1967; Beck, Emery and Greenberg, 1985). In the case of personality disorders, these idiosyncratic schemas are operative on an even more continuous basis than during an episode of depression or anxiety.

'Individuals with personality disorders show the same repetitive behaviors in many more situations than do other people. The typical maladaptive schemas in personality disorders are evoked across many or even most situations, have a compulsive quality, and are less easy to control or modify than are their counterparts in other people . . . In sum, relative to other people, their dysfunctional attitudes and behaviors are overgeneralized, inflexible, imperative, and resistant to change' (Beck, Freeman and Associates, 1990: 29).

Cognitive Profiles

Following the *continuity hypothesis*, the types of beliefs and attitudes apparent in personality disorders are exaggerated forms of beliefs held by individuals not having personality disorders.

As in normal individuals, there are relationships between beliefs and attitudes and overt behaviors. Each personality disorder is characterized by a set of beliefs, attitudes, affects and strategies, forming a *cognitive profile* for that diagnosis. For example, a basic belief of the dependent personality is 'I am helpless' and the corresponding strategy is one of attachment. The dysfunctional beliefs anchoring the personality disorder originated as a result of the interaction between the individual's genetic predisposition and exposure to undesirable influences from other people and specific traumatic events.

In an evolutionary sense, behavioral strategies are designed to ensure survival and reproduction. In a developmental sense, they arise either out of compensation or fear, or as a result of reinforcement in an individual's learning history.

Individualized case conceptualization is essential to the Cognitive Therapy of personality disorders. The therapist needs to know the client's view of himself or herself, the view of others, the client's basic beliefs, overt strategies or behaviors, and the consequences or effects of those beliefs and strategies (Beck, Freeman and Associates, 1990).

Differences from Cognitive Therapy of Depression and Anxiety

Cognitive Therapy with personality disorders differs from Beck's original model of psychotherapy in several ways. First, there are challenges posed to the establishment of a collaborative relationship. In fact, Beck, Freeman and Associates list 19 such obstacles which could inhibit collaborative empiricism. Thus, greater attention to such things as the activation of schemas within the therapy relationship is required. Second, the origin of schemas is explored to a greater extent in working with personality disorders, particularly in the case of early trauma. This often entails a greater attention to early childhood experience in order to conceptualize the establishment and maintenance of a schema. Third, because the personality disordered patient's beliefs are so rigidly held, logical discourse and behavioral experimentation may not be sufficient for change. Cognitive Therapy of personality disorders makes greater use of role play, with role reversal, imagery, and reliving of childhood experiences to elicit schemas and respond to them.

Differences from Traditional Approaches to Personality Disorders

James Pretzer has spoken and written extensively on Cognitive Therapy of personality disorders (Pretzer, 1983, 1985, 1989, 1990; Pretzer and Fleming, 1989). He contrasts Cognitive Therapy with more psychodynamic approaches. 'One of the complaints I had,' he says, 'with the object relations people was however wonderful their insights are, the terminology being used is so obscure that it's really hard to figure out exactly what they're saying and what one would do about it in real life. Whereas the cognitive approaches are easier to grasp and provide a really good framework for then using a wide range of interventions systematically. With a cognitive perspective, it's possible to come up with a reasonably concise model of what's going on with some pretty clear suggestions about what to do in terms of intervention and what sequence of interventions is going to be most promising. You still have all the interpersonal complexities of working with borderlines to contend with, but it's much easier to navigate those waters if you have an idea as to where you're headed and what you want to accomplish.'

Cognitive Therapy of Personality Disorders (Beck, Freeman and Associates, 1990) is based on theoretical and clinical material, for there are few well-controlled outcome studies on the efficacy of cognitive–behavioral interventions for personality disorders.

Yet, preliminary case studies appear promising. One of the strengths of the approach, say several practicing Cognitive Therapists, is the individualized conceptualization of clients' problems. In addition, the clinical flexibility apparent in the use of diverse techniques nevertheless serves a unified and cohesive theory of psychopathology.

Theoretical Directions

As Beck's theories have evolved, he has come to rely more on writings in cognitive psychology, social psychology, and evolutionary biology (Beck, 1991b). Current Cognitive Therapy integrates theoretical dimensions from both psychology and biology, and Beck predicts that Cognitive Therapy will draw upon these areas further for its development of theory. In the future, interdisciplinary endeavors might investigate, for example, how schemas are established, how cognitive change occurs, and how cognitions, affect, and behavior can promote change in each other.

Beck has drawn on a rich history of psychotherapy as well from these related fields to develop a view of psychological functioning which is based on notions of adaptation to our physical and social environments. In order to adapt successfully, individuals must perceive, integrate and respond to environmental information. Beck's Cognitive Therapy helps individuals to examine their perceptions, to test and deliberate beliefs and assumptions, and to arrive at adaptive conclusions and solutions. This is achieved within a collaborative therapeutic relationship which gives considerable control to the patient as he or she examines his or her views of self, world, and relationship to others. Beck's contributions to this process and the practice of psychotherapy are discussed in the next chapter.

3

Practical Contributions

Overview

Beck's Cognitive Therapy changed the way psychotherapy is conducted in a number of ways, some of which are likely to have lasting effects on the nature and process of psychotherapy. Already the influence of cognitive therapies is apparent in the increased attention being paid by several psychotherapeutic modalities to current experience and the products of consciousness.

Beck's break from traditional psychoanalysis changed the role of the therapist, the nature of the therapeutic relationship, the way in which therapy is conducted, and the goals of therapy. Along with behavior therapists, Beck demonstrated that structured, short-term therapy can be helpful. Yet, he differed from behaviorists in his manner of case conceptualization and general therapeutic goals. Beck states,

> I believe that the 'common factors' among various psychotherapies rely primarily on *cognitive change* whether this is brought about through the therapeutic relationship, abreactive techniques, or explanation or interpretation. We certainly consider the therapeutic alliance as a 'common factor' shared with other therapies. But we also believe that the sharp and explicit focus on changing belief systems, reinforcing and refining reality testing, and developing coping strategies makes for a more robust therapy. (Beck, 1991b: 12)

Beck has devised a structured, short-term therapy which is present-centered and problem-oriented for depression and anxiety disorders. In working with personality disorders, therapy is longer and childhood experience tends to be more important since maladaptive schemas, established early in life, play a dominant role in many areas of functioning.

In order to review Beck's practical contributions to psychotherapy, his innovations in approach, techniques and strategies, I have divided them into (1) innovations in psychotherapy process and (2) innovations in clinical procedures and format.

Innovations in Psychotherapy Process

Cognitive Therapy is an active, structured form of therapy. Therapeutic strategies are derived from a cognitive conceptualization of each case and specific therapeutic principles guide the course of therapy. The format of therapy sessions is designed to enhance a working relationship with the client and to focus on specific tasks to be accomplished in the therapy hour as well as those to be conducted between therapy sessions. Cognitive case conceptualization, the underlying principles of collaborative empiricism, Socratic dialogue and guided discovery (Beck, 1976; Beck et al., 1979), and the format of therapy are all innovations in psychotherapy process, as is the short-term focus of Cognitive Therapy.

Case Conceptualization
Case conceptualization is based on the cognitive model of emotional disorders (Beck, 1976). This is an inductive approach, for the therapist must first understand the cognitive processing and content accompanying the client's distress as opposed to making a priori generalizations about the client on the basis of either diagnosis or problems on a problem list. Beck says, 'Instead of using pinpoint interventions for each problem, I have a series of methods that apply the theory on the basis of conceptualization. For instance, when we use assertiveness training, we don't use it simply to take care of the patient's lack of assertiveness, but we would be dealing with a more global problem that the person has a great evaluative fear. We're working at many levels with any technique.'

The cognitive model posits that behaviors and emotions are driven by underlying schemas, and any observable behavior can be derived from a number of schemas. So, for example, someone preoccupied with somatic complaints might have a schema related to vulnerability to harm and illness, defectiveness, or something else entirely. One man, who believed he had a tumor somewhere in his body, had a schema related to unrelenting standards. He felt he had not performed up to the standards inculcated by a critical father and, therefore, deserved to be punished by having a tumor. Thus, the therapist must understand both the cognitive profile of a disorder and the beliefs unique to that client.

Knowing someone's cognitive profile helps to guide therapeutic style. For example, it might help the therapist decide whether to give the person choices, as is helpful with a client who doesn't want to feel controlled, or to be more directive, as might convey connection to someone who feels uncared for and lacking in guidance. Case conceptualization is so important in Cognitive Therapy that Dr Jacqueline Persons has devoted a book to it, *Cognitive Therapy in Practice: A Case Formulation Approach* (1989).

The cognitive model is presented to the client as a rationale for the treatment approach and for the selection of each specific treatment strategy (D.M. Clark and Beck, 1988). Treatment procedures and strategies serve the conceptual model, and the application of the same procedure for two different individuals might yield very different outcomes, largely because of the relevance of the procedure to the client's cognitive makeup. For example, use of the Daily Record of Dysfunctional Thoughts (see Figure 3.1) is helpful for someone who has difficulty remembering events which triggered affect and for someone who needs to be more specific about what's going through his or her mind. However, Persons (1990) describes a case in which a young woman wrote reams of automatic thoughts about social and school situations instead of participating in them. Thus, she used the technique as an avoidance maneuver.

An example of a cognitive conceptualization of borderline personality disorder is provided by Pretzer (1989, 1990). The cognitive profile of the borderline personality explains the mood swings and erratic behavior characteristic of the disorder in terms of underlying beliefs. According to the cognitive conceptualization, the borderline patient has three basic assumptions which pose understandable and constant conflicts. (Each individual patient also has additional beliefs based on his or her history.) These beliefs are: the world is dangerous and malevolent; I am powerless and vulnerable; and I am inherently unacceptable. The cognitions of patients with borderline personality disorder are also characterized by dichotomous or all-or-nothing thinking. The combination of these assumptions and that type of cognitive distortion leads to extreme interpretations of events and emotional instability. For example, if one is powerless and vulnerable, then one might need to depend on someone else. However, the borderlines' belief that they are inherently unacceptable makes dependence risky, for it could lead to rejection, abandonment, or attack when the unacceptability is discovered. Moreover, others may prove themselves suddenly and absolutely unreliable and untrustworthy. This can lead to unstable interpersonal relationships.

DATE	SITUATION	EMOTION(S)	AUTOMATIC THOUGHT(S)	RATIONAL RESPONSE	OUTCOME
	Describe: 1. Actual event leading to unpleasant emotion, or 2. Stream of thoughts, daydream, or recollection, leading to unpleasant emotion.	1. Specify sad/ anxious/angry, etc. 2. Rate degree of emotion, 1–100.	1. Write automatic thought(s) that preceded emotion(s). 2. Rate belief in automatic thought(s), 0–100%.	1. Write rational response to automatic thought(s). 2. Rate belief in rational response, 0–100%.	1. Re-rate belief in automatic thought(s), 0–100%. 2. Specify and rate subsequent emotions 0–100.

Explanation: When you experience an unpleasant emotion, note the situation that seemed to stimulate the emotion (if the emotion occurred while you were thinking, daydreaming, etc., please note this.) Then note the automatic thought associated with the emotion. Record the degree to which you believe this thought: 0% = not at all; 100% = completely. In rating degree of emotion: 1 = a trace; 100 = the most intense possible.

Figure 3.1 *Daily Record of Dysfunctional Thoughts* (Beck et al., 1979)

Collaborative Empiricism

Collaborative empiricism means that the patient is viewed as a personal scientist (cf. Kelly, 1955) who is capable of working with the therapist in conceptualizing the problem, identifying salient cognitions, and investigating and testing the validity of those cognitions, which are posed as hypotheses. In Cognitive Therapy, both the therapist and the client are active. The therapist does not wait for the client to raise material, and both contribute to the agenda. Questions, as opposed to interpretations, are the principal therapeutic tools. The patient is active as well, assuming more responsibility as therapy progresses for such things as the design of behavioral experiments and problem-solving.

Bernard Shulman contrasts the stance of the psychoanalyst with the stance of the cognitive therapist.

> In general, classical psychoanalytic technique requires relative passivity in the therapist, who waits for the patient to bring in products of unconscious wishes and defenses against them and then interprets them.
>
> Cognitive therapists do not work this way. Adler and his followers, Perls and the Gestalt movement, Albert Ellis, Aaron Beck and Viktor Frankl would never work that way. They would be *active* therapists, eagerly seeking to change referential frame or perceptual Gestalt of the client. (Shulman, 1988: 98)

Jeffrey Young identifies the active stance of the Cognitive Therapist as a distinctive trait of the therapy. 'The therapist is extremely active; planning strategies and implementing techniques. The active stance of the therapist, the strategic attitude of the therapist, is still a significant difference from traditional psychotherapy. In fact, when I teach the approach to people who are trained in another orientation, the thing they have the most difficulty getting used to is the very high demand on the therapist to be constantly formulating, reformulating, planning, and then doing something.'

Collaboration operationalizes Beck's phenomenological approach, for the client is treated as a co-investigator. The client's perceptions of the problem are seen as valid, not as a smokescreen for hidden drives or unconscious motivations. Conceptualization and investigation begin on the basis of the client's experience, not on the therapist's reformulation or preconceived ideas. This approach provides a lot of data, since, with guidance and training, cognitions are accessible to the client. The model itself is also accessible to the client, for it is straightforward and easy to understand, and enlists the client as an active agent, thereby giving the client some sense of control over the process. As the client learns the model and the requisite skills, he or she develops competencies in self-help. Such competencies are presumed to guard against relapse. The collaborative nature of Cognitive Therapy also demystifies the process, for clients are involved in setting goals, making abstract concepts concrete through homework between sessions, and providing feedback on therapy difficulties and progress. 'Beck was really introducing a form of therapy that wasn't mysterious in the psychoanalytic sense. He used language that was very understandable by clients and other therapists alike, and was going about it with the kind of common sense, pragmatic strategy that scientists use, but that the everyday person, if they're trained in it, could also use,' says Michael Mahoney.

David M. Clark states, 'The idea is that the data are always the person's thoughts, and once you stick with that it's very difficult to go dramatically wrong, to do very inappropriate things. With other therapies, particularly psychodynamic ones, in the hands of very skilled people, they can do some very good things. But also, they're easy to abuse because there's no easy feedback from the patient when you're going wrong. And of course, there's lots of ways in which the therapist can interpret what's happening negatively with the patient, which actually helps to maintain the therapist's distorted view that they're doing something useful when they're not. Whereas you really can't do that as a Cognitive Therapist. I think that's very powerful. It's very difficult to do any harm with Cognitive Therapy.'

Empirical Tests of Beliefs   The idea of empirically testing beliefs is an innovation in psychotherapy, including the cognitive therapies. Hollon and Najavits (1988) point out that while empirical hypothesis testing is the primary vehicle of change in Cognitive Therapy, Rational-Emotive Therapy (A. Ellis, 1973, 1980) and its offshoots (such as Systematic Rational Restructuring: Goldfried, DeCanteceo and Weinberg, 1974) rely on appeals to rationality. Meichenbaum's Self-Instructional Training (Meichenbaum 1974, 1975a, 1977) uses repetition to produce cognitive change. The patient practices first aloud, then covertly, cognitions the therapist believes to be more adaptive. Meichenbaum's other cognitive therapy, Stress Inoculation Training (Meichenbaum, 1975b, 1985) involves a skills training application phase which uses a combination of rationality and repetition-based efforts to change beliefs. It also includes the opportunity for later application practice.

While collaboration and the use of conscious material did not originate with Beck, he initiated the experimental component into therapy. Mahoney says, 'He was willing to say to a client, "Well, let's test that. Let's see what happens if . . ." The experimental component was there, to some extent, with the behaviorists, but much less in an exploratory way, much more in a prescriptive way. The behaviorists tended to have their techniques already developed and it was just a matter of applying them, getting the right technology connected with the right person. Beck's was much more of an open-ended therapy. Yes, there was a format for it and some assumptions, but it really cast the individual as a collaborator and an active agent in the therapeutic process in a way I don't think had been done before.'

An example of collaborative empiricism appears in *Cognitive Therapy of Depression* (Beck et al., 1979: 79). In this case, the patient has reported continuous automatic thoughts concerning whether people like him or dislike him. Based on the client's report, the therapist develops hypotheses which could identify logical inconsistencies as well as basic assumptions. The therapist then checks these hypotheses with the patient: 'You spend a lot of time guessing how each person you meet feels about you. Most of your attention to environmental events appears to be concentrated on whether or not you are a likeable person. Even events that have little or no relation to that question – such as the way the checker acts at the supermarket – are interpreted by you to be relevant to the question of whether you are likeable or not. Does this observation seem to fit the facts?'

The therapist's comments serve several purposes. One is to have the patient consider the hypotheses presented by the therapist. Sometimes patients disagree with such formulations and new ones are developed jointly. This builds collaboration. In addition, as the therapist formulates the client's perceptions and interpretations as hypotheses, the therapist helps the patient to view his or her thoughts as a personal view of reality and not necessarily as the only true perspective. However, the therapist has not debated the validity of the patient's view outright.

From this collaborative stance, several hypotheses might be generated to test the patient's interpretations. For example, Hypothesis 1 might be: Your automatic response to any encounter with another person is 'he likes me, he likes me not.' The test would be to observe and self-monitor how frequently you question people's reactions to you. Hypothesis 2 would be: Since you are depressed, most of your expectations and interpretations will be negative. The test would be to count positive and negative interpretations. Hypothesis 3 would be: You are inclined to read negative responses into other people's reactions to you when there is no reason for them to have any reaction to you at all. The test would be to ask yourself after each encounter, '(1) Did I feel hurt or rejected by the encounter?, (2) Is there any evidence the other person even noticed me?, and (3) If s/he did notice me, is there any evidence that the reaction was anything but neutral?' (Beck et al., 1979: 80). These hypotheses are treated as conjectures, not as facts. If they are confirmed, then there is a basis from which to discover the patient's underlying assumptions.

Socratic Dialogue
Socratic dialogue is the term used by Beck to describe the manner in which Cognitive Therapists use questions to promote cognitive change. Instead of providing answers to client's dilemmas or debating their perceptions and interpretations, a Cognitive Therapist helps the patient to arrive at his or her own answers by carefully crafting a series of questions to first understand the client's conclusions and then open those conclusions to include other possible alternatives. The purpose is to help clients to evaluate and provide answers to their own thoughts. Through such questioning the client is less likely to feel defensive or required to agree with the therapist's interpretation. If the client is not made to feel defensive, additional material such as the meanings of events, fantasies, fears, predictions, and the like are more likely to be forthcoming. Socratic dialogue is fueled by curiosity and is an attempt to fully understand the patient's point of view. It is not a manipulation to 'trap' the patient in contradictions or to blatantly expose his or her beliefs as fallacious. It is a nonjudgmental way of modeling how to examine one's assumptions.

Socratic dialogue helps the client arrive at logical conclusions based on the questions posed by the therapist. Questions are used to (1) clarify or define problems, (2) assist in the identification of thoughts, pictorial images or assumptions, (3) examine the meanings of events for the client, and (4) assess the consequences of specific thoughts and behaviors (Beck and Young, 1985).

Socratic dialogue, says Gary Emery, focuses the attention on the thinking process itself. Ruth Greenberg adds, 'Cognitive Therapy sharpens the focus on the moment and I think the technique of questioning is going to remain a part of the interviewing tradition of psychotherapists of whatever persuasion. You can ask people what their experience right now is, what their feelings are, what's going through their minds. In the answers to those simple questions, you're going to get information that's absolutely pregnant with meaning.'

John Rush describes watching Beck in therapy: 'He's a very good listener. He'll be quiet for quite a while in spite of the fact that

Cognitive Therapy involves talking a lot. He'll listen for quite a while, and then he'll summarize things and quickly put a bit of a twist on the way it's summarized, and then ask the patient if that's how they feel or think or does that represent what they're doing. So, he has this give and take style in an interview which I think appears informal and nonthreatening. It has a certain kind of flow and flexibility to it. It is very patient-driven.

'My impression is that he's looking for openings. The patient's talking about something, then talking about something else, and he's looking for openings to kind of raise some questions for the patient. He uses a lot of questions, which I think is not very threatening, and he avoids nasty personal questions. He operates from a genuine curiosity, really trying to understand the patient's point of view. He raises these questions so he can get a better view of how the patient sees things. The patient himself or herself is beginning to stand back from their point of view and ask themselves the same questions. Was it really that way? Was your boss really angry at you? Is that level of feeling out of proportion to what you described as happening? Would you always feel this way or is it only in this circumstance? So, as he's trying to understand the world from the patient's point of view, the patient's beginning to move to a more objective questioning stance himself.'

The following example of Socratic dialogue illustrates how the therapist assists a depressed patient in examining the utility of staying in bed all day (Beck et al., 1979: 70):

Therapist: What is the probability that you will go back to bed when you leave the office?
Patient: About 100 per cent.
Therapist: Why are you going back to bed?
Patient: Because I want to.
Therapist: What is the reason you want to?
Patient: Because I'll feel better.
Therapist: For how long?
Patient: A few minutes.
Therapist: And what will happen after that?
Patient: I suppose I'll feel worse again.
Therapist: How do you know?
Patient: Because this happens every time.
Therapist: Are you sure of that? . . . Have there been any times when lying in bed made you feel better for a period of time?
Patient: I don't think so.
Therapist: Have you found that not giving in to the urge to return to bed has helped you at all?
Patient: I guess when I get active, I feel better.
Therapist: Now to return to your wish to go to bed. What are the reasons for going to bed?

Patient: So I'll feel better.
Therapist: What other reasons do you have for going to bed?
Patient: Well, I know theoretically that I will feel worse later.
Therapist: So, are there reasons for not going to bed and doing something constructive?
Patient: I know that when I get involved in things I feel better.
Therapist: Why is that?
Patient: Because it takes my mind off how bad I feel and I am able to concentrate on other things.

This transcript indicates how clients can reach conclusions strictly through the use of careful questions rather than by giving advice or instructions. Notice how the therapist had the client express both sides of the argument and even challenge the validity of the reasons for pursuing constructive activity. This allowed a full examination of cognitions in making a decision.

Guided Discovery

The third principle of the cognitive therapy process is guided discovery, which refers generally to the investigative process by which patients 'discover' their own illogic or misperceptions as opposed to the therapist persuading them to adopt a point of view (Beck and Young, 1985). Guided discovery has also come to mean the identification of themes which run through the patient's present perceptions and beliefs and their connection to experiences in the past (Beck and Weishaar, 1989a). Guided discovery is a verbal enterprise in which the therapist might ask the patient to delineate themes apparent in his or her automatic thoughts, use imagery to evoke salient cognitions, or conduct an historical review of a schema to elicit the reasons for the steadfast maintenance of such a belief.

The following scenario illustrates the use of guided discovery to identify themes in automatic thoughts as well as to draw connections between thought and affect. The case is of a young man troubled by anxiety as a consequence of trying to live up to parental expectations of perfection (Beck and Weishaar, 1989a:313):

Therapist: What types of situations are most upsetting to you?
Patient: When I do poorly in sports, particularly swimming. I'm on the swim team. Also, if I make a mistake, even when I play cards with my roommates. I feel really upset if I get rejected by a girl.
Therapist: What thoughts go through your mind, let's say, when you don't do so well at swimming?
Patient: I think people think much less of me, that I'm not a winner.
Therapist: And how about if you make a mistake playing cards?
Patient: I doubt my own intelligence.
Therapist: And if a girl rejects you?

Patient: It means I'm not special. I lose value as a person.
Therapist: Do you see any connections here, among these thoughts?
Patient: Well, I guess my mood depends on what other people think of me. But that's important. I don't want to be lonely.
Therapist: What would that mean to you, to be lonely?
Patient: It would mean there's something wrong with me, that I'm a loser.

The therapist might hypothesize that this patient had the following beliefs: that his worth is determined by others, that if he is not special he is a loser, or that there is something inherently wrong with him that would cause people to reject him.

Guided discovery could proceed by looking for historical evidence, such as early messages from significant others, and current evidence, such as how his own behavior might reinforce these beliefs, to substantiate any of these hypotheses.

Format of the Interview

Beck has written that an important discriminating feature of Cognitive Therapy is the format of the interview (Beck, 1991b). It is a structured interview with an agenda, feedback and homework assignments. Setting an agenda is to decide, at the beginning of the session, which problems, topics and tasks will be discussed. Both the therapist and the client contribute to the agenda and decide together how to prioritize the items. Practitioners of less structured approaches often see an agenda as the therapist exerting too much control over the session. Yet, by making the agenda explicit and collaborative, the therapist is less likely to assert his or her own biases in terms of topics to be discussed or length of time devoted to topics. In addition, clients quickly learn to bring in lists of topics to put on the agenda and are less likely to forget or minimize items they had wished to discuss.

Feedback is an integral part of the therapeutic interview, giving the therapist the opportunity to check his or her understandings and perceptions. It allows the therapist to correct any misconceptions. It also allows the client to clarify statements, to express difficulties with the therapist or with therapy, or to verify that therapy is on target. Feedback is routinely solicited throughout the session and especially at the end of the session. At this time, also, the therapist may ask the client to summarize what was covered in the session. Feedback helps to build and maintain collaboration and promotes an openness of disclosure. The therapist's acceptance of feedback and his or her efforts to respond constructively to it can model self-acceptance and may also afford the opportunity to use the therapeutic relationship to explore beliefs and assumptions about relationships, causal attributions, and other core constructs.

Homework assignments are tasks to be completed between therapy sessions and give the patient the opportunity to apply what is learned in therapy sessions. Homework is not unique to Cognitive Therapy, but its purpose is different from that in behavior therapy. It is not intended solely to afford practice in skills acquisition, but to test beliefs in real life situations as opposed to discussing them abstractly. Tasks are mutually determined by the therapist and patient, usually with the therapist taking a more directive role in early sessions. Homework assignments are the most effective ways for clients to gather data, test hypotheses and begin to modify maladaptive assumptions (Beck and Young, 1985). They are believed both to shift the focus of therapy from the subjective and abstract to more concrete and objective concerns (Beck and Young, 1985) and to promote cross-situational learning or generalization (Shaw, 1988). The patient's reactions to homework assignments are always discussed to identify any distortions in the patient's conclusions, to discover the meanings of the outcomes for the patient, and to reinforce the formation of new, more adaptive thinking.

Short-term Model of Therapy
Another innovation in the psychotherapeutic process is that Cognitive Therapy is relatively brief. Behavior therapy is also short-term, but is not focused on the patient's internal world. In the original treatment outcome studies on depression, the length of treatment with Cognitive Therapy was 20 sessions over a 12-week period. Positive results have similarly been found in the clinic within 12 to 20 sessions for the treatment of unipolar depression. D.M. Clark and Beck (1988) report that the treatment of anxiety generally lasts between 5 and 20 sessions, and remarkable decreases in panic attacks have been achieved in 12 sessions (Salkovskis and Clark, 1991).

In *Cognitive Therapy and the Emotional Disorders*, Beck explains that Cognitive Therapy does not require as much time as psychoanalysis because 'discussions center around concepts that are essentially within the patient's awareness' (Beck, 1976: 317). Thus, data are accessible to the patient. Moreover, formulations are comprehensible to the patient and can be operationalized and tested between sessions through homework experiences. The rate of progress in Cognitive Therapy is enhanced by activity outside the therapy session. In contrast to the therapeutic relationship being the sole mechanism of change as in psychoanalysis, very specific techniques such as homework are presumed to promote change (Shaw, 1988; Goldfried, 1988).

Arthur Freeman describes Beck's contribution as creating a dynamically oriented (but not psychodynamic in the analytic sense) therapy that works quickly. Beck, says Freeman, 'effectively draws on a number of theories and models and puts them together in a very effective way. Beck references his debt to Horney and Adler, and also the idea of using the here and now of an ego-oriented approach, of helping the patient to use logical analytic skills. Cognitive Therapy will be remembered most for the fact that we can help people quickly.'

One of the early advantages of Cognitive Therapy was that it was highly successful in treating depression and anxiety in a very short time. As its applications widened to include personality disorders and more chronic depressions such as dysthymic disorder, the length of treatment increased. Jeffrey Young identifies a number of features which keep Cognitive Therapy unique, even when it is longer-term: the active and strategic stance of the therapist, the focus on the patient's self-perception even though it may be a deeper view of the self, the effort to link treatment around the patient's conscious perceptions as well as unconscious themes, and the length of treatment in Cognitive Therapy relative to psychoanalysis. Says Young, 'It's still much shorter-term than traditional therapy. Even with it being longer, even as long as a year and one-half or two years, it's still significantly shorter than a typical analytic treatment of a comparable case. So, if you could cut a treatment that's typically five years to a year and one-half or two years, that's still a significantly shorter treatment. I would say another major difference is in analytic therapy very often the patients can be in treatment for a long time and not get any change. Whereas, I think because Cognitive Therapy maintained its change orientation, not just insight orientation, it is more likely to lead to observable changes that the patient can actually see. We don't consider insight to be the final proof of the treatment. The proof of treatment is still there's actual change in the person's life functioning, happiness, and whatever you want to use. If there isn't that change, we still consider ourselves as failing.'

Innovations in Clinical Procedures

The basic procedural sequence of Cognitive Therapy is: (1) preparing the client and providing a cognitive rationale, (2) training in self-monitoring of thoughts, (3) application of behavioral techniques, (4) identifying and responding to cognitions, (5) examining beliefs and assumptions, and (6) termination and relapse prevention (Beck et al., 1979). These steps provide a format for a discussion of innovations in how Cognitive Therapy is conducted.

Rationale
Providing a cognitive rationale entails explaining the model to the client utilizing examples from the client's life to illustrate the role of beliefs, images, perceptions, and other cognitions in the presenting problems. The therapist asks the client for his or her own explanation of the problems and, as the client's attributions, perceptions, and other cognitions are explored, the therapist may inquire about the strength of these beliefs, the possibility of alternative points of view, and the meanings of events for the client. The therapist does not rush to challenge the client's perspective, but attempts to identify core cognitions.

The cognitive model is presented in terms of the role that thoughts and images play in our reactions to events. Hollon and Garber (1990) use an 'A–B–C' model to demonstrate how affective responses at point C to events at point A are seen as determined, in part, by interpretations at point B. Although this is a simple model, it is not meant to be simplistic; the cognitive mediation that goes on at point B is often complex and out of the individual's awareness. While the cognitive model is presented in the initial sessions, a great deal of attention is paid to case conceptualization before interventions are attempted. Nevertheless, reframing a problem or initiating another hypothesis is often possible in early sessions and may provide insight into the operation of biases in the client's information processing. The identification of another possible interpretation or 'rival hypothesis' begins to create disequilibrium in the client's belief system.

One of the effects of providing a rationale to the client is that it demystifies therapy and makes it accessible to the client, thus encouraging a collaborative relationship. The client then joins in the process of identifying goals for therapy and formulating a plan to address presenting problems. A rationale for the approach to therapy is provided initially and a rationale for each strategy or homework assignment is presented throughout the course of treatment. This contrasts with a more distant therapeutic stance and allows for continuous feedback between client and therapist.

Beck et al. (1979: 73) describe the way the therapist might explain the cognitive approach to the client: 'When depressed persons consider their experiences, they are generally drawn to the most negative meanings that can conceivably be attributed to those events. When this occurs, the negative thinking feels realistic to the patient. The more believable this negative thinking is, the more upset the patient will feel.'

Cognitive Therapy is a teachable method of therapy, an approach that patients can understand and utilize. The model also leads to specific treatment interventions, so patients see it as practical. Thus, Cognitive Therapy utilizes an educational framework, encourages self-help, and generates personally relevant interventions and experiments for patients. By demystifying the therapy process, Cognitive Therapy allows for therapists to be judged on how well or competently they are providing the therapy, says Brian Shaw. This has implications for outcome research, for it makes it possible to examine whether subjects received the therapy that was intended. It also has clinical implications because it assumes that the therapy itself, albeit difficult to separate from the therapist doing it, contains active ingredients for change. Moreover, it may be possible to delineate mechanisms of change apart from the therapeutic relationship. The Cognitive Therapy Rating Scale (Young and Beck, 1980) is used in the training and evaluation of Cognitive Therapists.

Beck and Young (1985: 20) have identified therapist characteristics which are assumed to contribute to treatment efficacy.

Cognitive Therapists should ideally (1) demonstrate the 'non-specific' therapy skills of warmth, genuineness, sincerity, and openness; (2) be skilled at seeing events through the patient's perspective; be able to suspend their own personal assumptions and biases while listening to patients describe their reactions and interpretations; (3) reason logically and elicit a more convincing interpretation of the same events; plan strategies several steps ahead, anticipating the desired outcome; and (4) be active, providing structure and direction to the therapy process. Thus Cognitive Therapy appears to work best with therapists who can provide the empathy of a nondirective therapist, take a phenomenological perspective and collaborate with the client, be active and creative in destabilizing maladaptive beliefs while helping to generate new learning experiences, and direct therapy without simply imposing a set of techniques.

Self-Monitoring

Training in self-monitoring occurs in initial sessions. Clients are taught to attend to the thoughts accompanying their distress. Beck says, 'Having done a lot of free association myself and having worked with patients, what I discovered was that the salient type of thoughts are not the kinds of things that the individual reports in "streaming" or even becomes very much aware of until their attention is focused on it. People are simply not accustomed to state their self evaluative types of thoughts, and yet they're monitoring their coercive types of thinking. There's a particular sequence that we discovered that was very important, and that was to first notice the affect, or in some cases the particular form of behavior, and then to focus on what went on before. Unless you utilize this particular method or ask the questions such as, "What is going through your mind right now?" these thoughts are simply not identified or recognized.'

Michael Mahoney says one of Beck's therapeutic innovations was having people pay more attention to what they were thinking. 'He really began the trend toward people thought listing and keeping track of thoughts, particularly using their emotional reactions as a cue to examine what they were just thinking about.'

Once patients could see the associations among their thoughts, feelings and behaviors and could learn ways to modify their thinking, they could then apply those skills at times of distress. Patients can be encouraged to monitor their thoughts in therapy sessions and check perceptions with the therapist, as is demonstrated in the example of a therapist having to postpone a future appointment (Beck et al., 1979: 152):

> *Patient*: That's okay, I know you have to go to a meeting. You know, I think I should tell you, I got the thought that you were rejecting me. I don't know why. Because if I think about it, it's obvious you have to cancel the appointment.
> *Therapist*: Was there any evidence which supported your idea?
> *Patient*: Well, frankly, I wondered whether you could make an extra effort and see me. And I don't even know whether you'll be in the area.

In this case, the patient and therapist were able to clarify and test the patient's cognitions as they occurred. This provided a successful experience for the patient in the use of these skills. It also could allow the therapist to respond to the patient's concerns, correct any misconceptions, and support the patient in further identification of thoughts about the relationship.

Behavioral Strategies

Behavioral activation strategies are often used early in Cognitive Therapy, particularly in treating depression and some anxiety states (such as panic, phobias). The general purpose of these strategies in the treatment of depression is to increase goal-directed and problem-solving behaviors (Beck et al., 1979; Hollon and Garber, 1990). In the treatment of phobias, exposure to a feared stimulus generates salient or 'hot' cognitions which are not available otherwise (Beck, Emery and Greenberg, 1985). In the case of panic, a behavioral intervention such as respiratory control for hyperventilation (Clark, Salkovskis and Chalkley, 1985) may work quickly to bring symptoms under control. In Cognitive Therapy, various behavioral techniques are used to promote cognitive change. Increasing the daily activity of a depressed patient may directly contradict beliefs of ineffectiveness or predictions that he or she is more contented in bed. Reducing avoidance in an anxious patient at least reveals cognitions that are stimulated only in the feared situation and are the necessary targets of intervention. Exposure to the feared situation can also challenge catastrophic predictions. Later in therapy, behavioral experiments designed to meet the explicit needs of each patient are used to provide data which contradict existing maladaptive beliefs.

Bandura (1977a) maintained that one of the most effective ways to change cognitions is to change performance, but this finding does not contradict the cognitive model, for in order for behavioral change to be maintained and generalized to new settings, the experience must also change the patient's notion of self-efficacy. In Cognitive Therapy, the therapist always checks what the client has learned from a behavioral experiment, for the client's conclusions are the targets of change, not just observable behavior. For example, an agoraphobic client may attribute her successful journey outside her home to luck or the behaviors of others. Self-efficacy is enhanced by the correct attributions of success.

Identifying Cognitions
The first type of cognitions which patients are typically taught to identify are those most easily available to introspection, automatic thoughts. In many cases, clients must place themselves in problematic situations in order to evoke these thoughts. This can be done through *in vivo* exposure, imagery or role play. Clients are taught to ask themselves particular questions which reveal the meanings of events and the underlying beliefs operating in distressing situations. This process of identifying cognitions is a contribution to psychotherapy because of the types of thoughts considered important; the training in self-inquiry accomplished by the client; and the use of exposure, role-playing and imagery to gain access to salient cognitions.

D.M. Clark and Beck (1988) describe two parallel streams of thought which operate simultaneously. The first, which patients can readily report, consists of descriptions of how the person is thinking or feeling; they are more superficial, voluntary thoughts. The second stream consists of the person's appraisal of self or the situation and are linked to affect. An example of the first type is 'I was worried about my speech.' An example of the second is, 'Everyone is laughing at me.' This second stream of thought is comprised of thoughts which seem to have a life of their own, which come 'automatically' and spontaneously, and which go unexamined. The difference between the two streams of thought is reflected in statements made by patients like, 'I know *objectively* there is no danger, but I still *feel* like something terrible is about to happen.' The 'feeling' statement is the more important one.

Automatic thoughts reflect deeper beliefs and assumptions and, although they are generally more accessible and easily identified than beliefs, they are often difficult to pin down. One reason is state-dependent memory: patients are more likely to retrieve memories when they are experiencing the emotions congruent with those memories: for example, negative memories when depressed (D.M. Clark and Teasdale, 1982). Cognitive avoidance, or the suppression of distressing thoughts and images, also makes it difficult for patients to identify the exact nature of their cognitions and any association between cognition and affect. For example, a patient might say, 'I feel anxious and have no idea why' or might speak in general terms rather than vivid detail, repeatedly open their eyes during imagery, or minimize the impact of a traumatic event. A Cognitive Therapist would gently persist in questioning to elicit the avoided cognitions and, with the patient's agreement, decrease avoidance by returning the patient to a distressing image or topic and gradually increasing their time exposed to it. A third reason that patients have difficulty identifying cognitions is that sometimes, even when cognitive avoidance is not operating, images, particularly those associated with anxiety, are very brief. In addition, D.M. Clark and Beck (1988) report that images accompanying very high anxiety may be bizarre, and patients are therefore reluctant to volunteer them until the therapist explains that they are a normal component of high anxiety.

Numerous techniques to elicit cognitions have been designed by Beck and his colleagues (Beck et al., 1979; Beck, Emery and Greenberg, 1985; D.M. Clark and Beck, 1988). Beck states that since the mid 1970s he cannot take credit for the innovative techniques and strategies used in Cognitive Therapy, for his students have developed many of them. What is highly innovative on his part, however, is the creation of a conceptual model which can generate countless techniques to elicit cognitions, deactivate specific cognitive distortions, and test maladaptive assumptions. *Cognitive Therapy of Depression* was written originally as a handbook explicating techniques and strategies used in the treatment of depression. It was a collaborative effort, with John Rush, Brian Shaw, Gary Emery, Maria Kovacs, and Steven Hollon all contributing to how therapy was conducted. The second half of *Anxiety Disorders and Phobias: A Cognitive Perspective* is devoted to techniques and was written by Gary Emery. The most popular self-help book on Cognitive Therapy, *Feeling Good* (1980) by Dr David Burns, is a compendium of techniques created by the therapists at Beck's Center for Cognitive Therapy.

D.M. Clark and Beck (1988) review some of the ways Cognitive Therapists help clients to identify cognitions. One way is to have the client recall a recent emotional experience and then recall the cognitions associated with the onset and maintenance of the emotional reaction. Typical questions from a Cognitive Therapist are, 'What went through your mind just then?,' 'Did you have any pictures in your mind just then?' In treating anxiety, the therapist might ask 'When you were at your most anxious, what was the worst thing you thought might happen?' In other cases, such as depression, the therapist might ask in reference to an event 'What does that mean to you?,' 'What would be so bad if that happened?' or 'What does that say about you?' in order to explore dire predictions, attributions, meanings, and self-evaluations.

One of the hallmarks of the Cognitive Therapy process is writing down elicited cognitions. This serves several purposes: (1) it makes cognitions more concrete and less elusive; (2) it can be useful in promoting the recall of additional, more frightening thoughts (D.M. Clark and Beck, 1988); (3) it accurately stores predictions and expectations prior to behavioral experiments, thus preventing misrecall (Hollon and Garber, 1990); and (4) it aids self-monitoring and the identification of the associations among thoughts, affect, and behavior. Recording thoughts occurs in session by the therapist and as homework by the client using a Daily Record of Dysfunctional Thoughts (Beck et al., 1979; see Figure 3.1).

Mood shifts during a therapy session can initially be used to demonstrate the association between thoughts and feelings and can be used to assess cognitions as they occur. *In vivo* or imaginal exposure to anxiety-provoking situations is also used to elicit cognitions which the patient learns to monitor and rate in terms of believability. Reliving an emotional experience through imagery or an interpersonal interaction through role play are also ways in which deeper, affect-laden, core cognitions are reached. Even when automatic thoughts are difficult to elicit, the therapist can use imagery to return the patient to the stressful scene in order to distinguish the meanings of events. One patient, who had waited frantically to be picked up from work by her daughter, appeared immobilized as she described the incident. Although she was unable to articulate the specific thoughts going through her mind at the time, she suddenly said after a period of silence, 'I just knew I'd be all alone forever.'

The technique of identifying cognitions in Cognitive Therapy contrasts with the nondirective techniques of free association and 'consciousness streaming.' The Cognitive Therapist gently proceeds to explore meanings, alternatives, and misconceptions when the client is reviewing distressing material. The Cognitive Therapist needs to have the client experience affect in order to identify the important cognitions, and will attempt to keep the client 'in the moment' to report salient cognitions. In consciousness streaming, a technique intended to reduce resistance (Mahoney, 1983, 1990), the client is requested to 'spontaneously share the flow of thoughts, feelings, images, memories, fantasies, and so on' (Szykula et al., 1989: 301). In contrast to free association, in consciousness streaming the therapist invites the client to withhold any thoughts they find too uncomfortable to share with the therapist, and makes no theoretical interpretations of the client's verbalizations. Consciousness streaming is recommended as a way to elicit cognitions pertaining to the 'therapeutically relevant verbalizations' of identity, personal power, values, and reality or problem-orientation (Mahoney, 1985a). It is not viewed yet as a tool in the client change process.

Once the more accessible cognitions are identified, beliefs and assumptions can be determined. Beliefs may be expressed spontaneously as rules or values, or as more absolute statements which are firmly held. They are often identified by their emotional valence as well. In the absence of the spontaneous expression of beliefs, identification of dysfunctional assumptions occurs in a three-stage process (Beck et al., 1979). First, the patient recognizes and reports automatic thoughts. Second, the patient, with the therapist's guidance, identifies general themes present in the automatic thoughts. Third, the therapist and patient formulate the patient's central rules about his or her life. Clues to underlying assumptions are apparent in the types of cognitive distortions present (for instance the patient who overgeneralizes may have assumptions characterized by overgeneralizations), the frequent use of particular kinds of words (such as harshly self-critical words), the types of events to which the patient overly responds, either in a positive or negative way (such as job, relationship), or the patient's reactions to the behaviors of others (such as causal attributions).

As mentioned in Chapter 2, Cognitive Therapists are most interested in beliefs about the self, including self-efficacy; beliefs about one's personal world, including attributions of causality; and beliefs about the future, including predictions and attitudes reflecting hopelessness. Some cognitive theorists emphasize the importance of self-perceptions or self-schema (Markus, 1977; Safran et al., 1986; Segal, 1988). Others also emphasize causal attributions and expectations about the future (Hollon and Kriss, 1984; Shaw and Segal, 1988). What differentiates Cognitive Therapy from other cognitive therapies is the attention paid to idiosyncratic beliefs which have highly personal meanings.

The idiosyncratic meaning of an event is conveyed in the following passage in which the therapist asks a depressed patient about the meaning of failing a test (Beck et al., 1979: 145–6):

> *Therapist*: How can failing a test make you depressed?
> *Patient*: Well, if I fail, I'll never get into law school.
> *Therapist*: So, failing the test means a lot to you. But if failing a test could drive people into clinical depression, wouldn't you expect everyone who failed the test to have a depression? . . . Did everyone who failed get depressed enough to require treatment?
> *Patient*: No, but it depends on how important the test was to the person.
> *Therapist*: Right, and who decides the importance?
> *Patient*: I do.

Examining Beliefs

Cognitive Therapy is often misunderstood as a collection of techniques, perhaps because it does lend itself to the generation of intervention strategies and is a pragmatic approach to psychotherapy. Some researchers have encouraged dismantling studies of Cognitive Therapy in order to discover its active ingredients and to determine whether the behavioral techniques create the change or whether cognitive strategies alone are efficacious (Dobson, 1989). What's cognitive about Cognitive Therapy is the conceptual model of human behavior and the target of therapy: cognitive change. Beck says, 'What I have is a series of methods that are going to apply the theory to a particular case, not necessarily on the basis of the [specific] problem "out there," but on the basis of the conceptualization. We're working at many levels and any technique not only has the immediate practical level but has a metalevel which you have to take into account.'

Many innovative techniques have been developed in Cognitive Therapy to examine a patient's beliefs. Indeed, specialized techniques have been developed for various disorders (see Emery,

Hollon and Bedrosian, 1981; Freeman, 1983; Freeman et al., 1989; Young, 1982). In addition, many strategies and techniques have been borrowed from other modalities such as behavior therapy and Gestalt therapy. In reference to the use of techniques, Beck (1991b: 12) states,

> I have consistently maintained that cognitive therapists can choose from a variety of therapeutic methods as long as they adhere to a number of principles: (1) the methods are consistent with the cognitive model of psychotherapy and can be logically related to the theory of therapeutic change; (2) the therapists base their choice of techniques on a comprehensive conceptualization of the case and an understanding of the patient's introspective capacity, style of problem-solving, sensitivity, etc.; (3) the basic principles of collaborative empiricism and guided discovery are utilized; and (4) the standard structure of the interview is followed unless there are compelling reasons for deviating from it. In most Axis I cases the standard cognitive and behavioral techniques suffice to produce lasting effects.

Beck acknowledges his debt to behavior therapy for providing features of the therapeutic interview: setting goals for therapy, breaking problems into component parts, operationalizing procedures, monitoring progress, and making behavioral assignments. Specific behavioral techniques such as *in vivo* exposure and respiratory control are evident in Cognitive Therapy's treatment of anxiety disorders. Similarly, behavioral techniques such as activity scheduling and graded task assignment are used in the treatment of depression.

Beck's emphasis on questioning was derived from Rogerian Client-Centered Therapy and Ellis' Socratic questioning (Beck, 1991b). RET also influenced Beck's use of testing beliefs, but not disputing them philosophically. Psychodrama and Gestalt therapy have been influential in Cognitive Therapy's use of emotive techniques, especially in the treatment of personality disorders. In working with personality disorders, it appears especially helpful to produce an affective experience by inducing imagery of childhood experiences which played a critical role in the establishment of maladaptive schemas (Beck, 1991b; Beck, Freeman and Associates, 1990; Edwards, 1989, 1990; Young, 1990).

In the process of examining their beliefs, clients are asked a number of questions which promote disequilibrium in existing beliefs and allow the possibility of alternative conclusions. First, the client is asked to review the evidence for a given belief or, in the case of a testable prediction, to collect more data. The second step is to ask the client to generate alternative explanations in addition to the ones he or she held initially. The third question is whether the initial belief, if true or accurate, actually means what the client believes (Hollon and Garber, 1990). Additional questions may pertain to how a belief functions for the client, including the affective and behavioral sequelae of maintaining the belief; the implications or predictions if the belief is true; the advantages or disadvantages of maintaining the belief; and the positive steps the patient may take to effect change. During the process of clarifying a belief, gathering data, examining the evidence, and problem-solving the therapist helps the patient to identify and counteract the operation of cognitive distortions (Beck, 1976) which bias the processing of new information. Behavioral experiments are designed to test what would happen if the client behaved in a novel way, such as acting contrary to a 'should'. The experimental nature of such a task involves the patient predicting a result, carrying out the experiment, and discussing the results with the therapist.

This same process of examination can be conducted with cognitions at various levels, from automatic thoughts to more basic beliefs. When working at the level of more basic beliefs or schemas, evidence in support of the schema is obtained through historical review: which life events were interpreted by the client as being supportive of the schema? Were there events which contradicted the schema? Often, in such a review, it becomes apparent that the client started to behave in ways that were congruent with a schema. For example, an adult with the belief that she is an outsider, is 'different,' may have been shy as a child. When she wasn't chosen for games or invited to participate in group activities, she would conclude, 'No one likes me because there's something wrong with me.' This belief prevented her from joining in and learning the social skills which are usually practiced and developed in childhood and adolescence. Her awkwardness and anxiety were interpreted as signs of being defective, not signs that her isolation had prevented the acquisition of skills. By adulthood, she had reinforced the schema through her own avoidance behavior.

In the process of examining the patient's beliefs, it is the patient who must recognize underlying beliefs and test their validity. The therapist guides or helps the patient to infer assumptions, but does not jump to conclusions about the patient's assumptions or provide solutions or substitute beliefs for the patient.

> Once therapy moves beyond the concrete data of automatic thoughts and observable behaviors, there is a danger that therapeutic intervention will miss the mark. At this point, therapists are particularly vulnerable to the risk of presenting their own biases – what they speculate the patient's beliefs are. If the therapist, however, will listen to and work

with the patient, therapy is more likely to stay on target. (Beck et al., 1979: 247)

Beck's interviewing style reflects this focus on the patient's interpretation of events, with the therapist stepping back from the role of expert. His style has often been compared to that of the television detective 'Columbo,' someone who is generally intelligent, but situationally ignorant, whose inquisitiveness belies his shrewdness. Jeffrey Young says that Beck projects an image 'of being grandfatherly, kind, caring, completely nonthreatening. That's the image. At the same time being extremely shrewd and intelligent about what's really going on. I used to call it "the Columbo approach": the combination of looking as if you don't know what you're doing, while knowing everything you're doing. That's what he does as a therapist; saying things like, "What do you mean by that?" or "What do you think about this idea?", never pushing anything at anyone, soft pedaling it, but knowing exactly what the strategy is. It's extremely effective. I think he's a great therapist.'

The Cognitive Therapist proceeds by questioning, framing hypotheses for further testing, and checking with the patient as to whether the therapist accurately understands the patient's point of view. A direct challenge of the patient's belief system may be construed as an attack or lack of empathy, as a confusing move which the client may agree with out of compliance or reject outright, or as a cause for termination. Beck's contribution to the process of psychotherapy is that it is a client-driven therapy which is still structured and directed. It uses questioning as a central therapeutic tool and homework between sessions, as well as work within sessions, as a mechanism of change.

Termination and Relapse Prevention

Termination is discussed early in Cognitive Therapy as part of the rationale for using the cognitive model, for one goal of therapy is to teach clients how to do Cognitive Therapy themselves. This is compatible with Goldfried's (1980a) perspective that psychotherapy trains people in skills for coping with their lives. It is also presumed to guard against relapse, for clients can implement the methods they learned in therapy on future occasions. In closing sessions, clients may review new perspectives and are encouraged to anticipate and practice dealing with future difficulties, either through role play or cognitive rehearsal. This practice is similar to the preparedness intrinsic in Meichenbaum's (1975b, 1977, 1985) Stress Inoculation Training.

Over the course of therapy, the client has assumed more respon-sibility for identifying problems, generating solutions, and applying newly learned behaviors and attitudes outside of therapy sessions. The therapist moves from being a guide to being a consultant, and the frequency of sessions is reduced. Therapy is discontinued gradually, usually with a couple of booster sessions scheduled over several months.

This approach to termination contrasts with longer-term therapies in which criteria for and expectations of termination are not discussed at the outset. Independence and self-reliance are explicit therapeutic goals in Cognitive Therapy, even though the therapeutic relationship may be quite strong. This approach reflects an underlying assumption in Cognitive Therapy, and in behavior therapy as well, that real change occurs as a function of what goes on between sessions, not solely within the session (Goldfried, 1988). Thus, termination has been planned for by discussing it early in treatment so that it is an expectation; by teaching the patient therapeutic, self-help skills; and by gradually shifting the control of therapy to the patient within the supportive context of a collaborative relationship.

Conclusion

Beck has been very specific in providing therapeutic guidelines. Cognitive Therapy is readily operationalized, teachable, and testable. Tests of its efficacy have been quite supportive, while tests of cognitive theory have yielded mixed results. In other words, Cognitive Therapy works, but no one is sure how.

By creating a therapy that is direct and specific, Beck has opened Cognitive Therapy to much scrutiny. It has been scientifically examined perhaps more than any other form of psychotherapy. The criticisms of Cognitive Therapy range from philosophic differences with other schools of therapy to details of research design. The criticisms of Cognitive Therapy and the rebuttals by cognitivists have generated further research endeavors and provided lively debate on the nature and measurement of cognition itself, mechanisms of change, goals of psychotherapy, the role of the therapeutic relationship, and the search for common principles among various psychotherapies. These issues will be presented in the next chapter.

4

Criticisms and Rebuttals

Overview

Despite its demonstrated efficacy, Cognitive Therapy has been criticized by a number of schools – biological psychiatry, behavioral psychology, and psychoanalysis most notably – on practical and theoretical grounds. The extensive research on the cognitive theory of depression is perhaps unrivaled in psychotherapy. It has raised questions concerning not only the design of studies supporting or challenging the effectiveness of Cognitive Therapy, but the validity of cognitive theory and its ability to describe, explain, and predict all types of depression. Extensive analyses have been made of various constructs comprising cognitive theory, yielding mixed results (Barnett and Gotlib, 1988; Coyne and Gotlib, 1986; Haaga, Dyck and Ernst, 1991). Some of the questions and criticisms voiced have led to the refinement and development of the theory (Beck, 1987a, 1991a).

On philosophical grounds, Cognitive Therapy has been called too mentalist (Rachlin, 1988; Skinner, 1977; Wolpe, 1978), too rationalist (Mahoney, 1984; Mahoney and Gabriel, 1987), too distant from basic science (Hawkins, 1989; Rachlin, 1988; Skinner, 1977; Wolpe, 1989), and too separate from the data of cognitive psychology (Power, 1987).

On a practical level, Cognitive Therapy has been criticized as being too superficial and simplistic, as avoidant of affect, as neglectful of the therapeutic relationship, and as adding little or 'nothing' (Wolpe, 1985: 113) to strategies and methods employed by behavior therapy (Beidel and Turner, 1986; Krantz, 1985; Wolpe, 1985).

Perhaps because of the amount of research done on Beck's Cognitive Therapy, it has stood to represent all cognitive therapies and, sometimes, all short-term therapies when criticism is leveled by opposing schools of thought. At the same time, there are strong differences of opinion within the domain of cognitive therapies and theories.

As is often the case in philosophical debates, false dichotomies have been created between Cognitive Therapy and other modalities: for example, Cognitive Therapy vs. behavior therapy, Cognitive Therapy vs. experiential therapies, or Cognitive Therapy vs. pharmacotherapy. In actuality, Cognitive Therapy does not contradict any of these models and, indeed, employs them when appropriate. As psychotherapy integration proceeds (see Goldfried 1980b, 1992; Beck, 1991b) questions may arise about the continued uniqueness of Cognitive Therapy, but current inquiries deal mostly with its theoretical base and the demonstration of cognitive change in psychopathology and recovery.

While it is often difficult to separate practical issues from theoretical ones, this chapter will deal separately with criticisms of the way in which Cognitive Therapy is done and criticisms of cognitive theory. In other words, some critics doubt that Cognitive Therapy will work because of 'active ingredients' it lacks. Others believe it does work, but not for the reasons purported by Beck's cognitive theory.

History of Criticisms of Cognitive Therapy

Cognitive Therapy rose to prominence at a time of upheaval in psychotherapy and of rapid growth in the fields of cognitive science and information processing. It developed in an era of social action, self-awareness, and self-help. Behavior therapy, which was a radical departure from the dominant psychoanalytic and psycho-dynamic models, had grown rapidly. A great appeal of behavior therapy was that it rested on scientific principles of learning: classical and operant conditioning. Behaviors could be observed, quantified, and changed by following certain procedures. Therapists didn't need to deal with mental constructs and infer what was going on with the patient; they could see it.

Behavior therapy grew out of experimental psychology and has always been tied to laboratory findings. That is one of its strengths. The initial and persistent objections to Cogniitve Therapy by behaviorists have much to do with its perceived break with basic science, as exemplified by a reliance on self-report, paper-and-pencil measures, and a lack of adequate demonstration that cognitions operate by principles other than conditioning.

For many behaviorists, most notably Wolpe and Skinner, cognitive therapies represented a return to mentalism and were, therefore, linked to psychoanalysis. Skinner opposed the use of hypothetical constructs to explain behavior and believed that speculations about mental processes would impede the search for practical ways of predicting and controlling behavior (Bry, 1991).

Wolpe became the ardent defender of behaviorism, castigated cognitivists Bandura, Beck, Ellis, Arnold Lazarus, Mahoney, Meichenbaum, and Goldfried as 'malcontents,' and argued that cognitions are a form of behavior, for they follow the same laws of reinforcement and extinction as motor and autonomic responses (Wolpe, 1976b, 1978). Thus, argued Wolpe, there should be no separate field of cognitive therapies.

The distinctions between behavior therapy and Cognitive Therapy, the degree to which they are integrated or should be integrated, and the philosophic principles on which they are based are argued today. Resurgence in such debate surfaces as new treatments (such as Cognitive Therapy for panic disorder) are developed (Alford and Carr, 1992) or as there are calls to dismantle Cognitive Therapy for depression to see whether recovery is due to changes in cognitive processing or to improving behavioral deficits (Dobson, 1989; Krantz, 1985).

Another early area of criticism had to do with Cognitive Therapy's efficacy. It appeared too superficial or simple to effect lasting change. Although it is widely recognized now as an efficacious treatment for unipolar depression, each new application is met with some reserve. Cognitive Therapy is accumulating evidence as an effective treatment for anxiety disorders, including panic disorder, but critics are skeptical about its utility with personality disorders, which have traditionally been treated with long-term therapies.

As Cognitive Therapy began to look promising in treatment outcome research, attention shifted to cognitive theory. The therapy worked, but was it based on sound principles? Was Cognitive Therapy really positing that negative thoughts cause depression? Although this idea has been disclaimed by Beck, it persists as a misunderstanding. What has remained of importance, however, is the notion of a cognitive vulnerability to depression and how it might operate.

The concept of a cognitive vulnerability to depression continues to be key to the theory and elusive to demonstration at this point. Criticisms have focused on how difficult it is to identify the nature of such a vulnerability, to measure it, and to prove its influential (if not causal) role. Again, this echoes Skinner's warning that cognitions are inferred constructs. As such, they are subject to many types of experimenter's error.

Other criticisms dealing with cognitive theory have to do with the purportedly limited view of depression proposed by the cognitive model of depression. Specifically, cognitive theory ignores environmental factors, particularly interpersonal ones, in the ontogeny of depression. Additionally, the extent to which depressive cognitions are distorted has been questioned, as has the goal of 'rationality' in psychotherapy.

Cognitive Therapy has grown along with several trends in cognitive–behavior therapy, specifically constructivism and psychotherapy integration. These movements within the field have also challenged Cognitive Therapy. In recent years, there has been less emphasis on Cognitive Therapy as an information-processing model and more emphasis on its phenomenological nature. The shift may reflect the basic premise of Cognitive Therapy that how the patient constructs his or her reality is critical, as opposed to relying on a more mechanistic computer analogy of human experience that was more popular in the 1970s. Constructivism puts the emphasis on the patient's reality without disputing whether it is accurate or rational. In this way, it is assumed, the therapist is less likely to impose a reality on the patient's experience. It is a popular view and very influential on how the various cognitive therapies currently define themselves (see A. Ellis, 1990).

Psychotherapy integration, a movement initiated primarily by Marvin Goldfried and Paul Wachtel in the 1980s, calls on various modalities to find common principles and complementary methods of therapeutic change. Beck believes that Cognitive Therapy is *the* integrative therapy (Beck, 1991b) while others criticize its apparent inattention to the psychotherapeutic relationship, early childhood experience, and emotion. Offshoots of the cognitive model have been developed which pay explicit attention to affect (Safran and Greenberg, 1988), the therapeutic relationship (Liotti, 1991; Safran and Segal, 1990), and early childhood experiences (Young, 1990).

Cognitive Therapy grew as experimental psychology became primarily cognitive in nature and benefited from concepts used in experimental cognitive and social psychology (Hollon and Garber, 1990). Yet, Cognitive Therapy has been criticized for being out of touch with contemporary cognitive psychology (Power, 1987; Power and Champion, 1986) and not addressing the issue of conscious versus nonconscious cognitive processes (Brewin, 1989; Power, 1989). Cognitive Therapy has been described as based on empiricism and 'light on theory' (Alford and Norcross, 1991: 185). Some critics encourage Cognitive Therapy to rest its theory increasingly on mental models (Power and Champion, 1986).

Criticisms by Behavior Therapy

A review of the criticisms of Cognitive Therapy begins with those leveled at all cognitive therapies by behavior therapy. Cognitive Therapy and behavior therapy have an historical relationship, for Cognitive Therapy was developed coincidentally with the cognitive revolution in psychology. Beck's Cognitive Therapy was embraced by cognitivists within behavior therapy, but was also strongly reacted against by radical behaviorists. Thus, criticisms of anything cognitive were forceful. In addition, some of the original criticisms by behaviorists, both legitimate arguments and misunderstandings of Cognitive Therapy, persist today. Thus, the criticisms by behaviorists have theoretical and historical importance.

The criticisms by behaviorists are not directed solely at Beck's Cognitive Therapy, but at all cognitive therapies. They stem from theoretical differences concerning the role of cognition in behavior change, and originated in the context of the 'cognitive revolution' in psychology. Much of the fervor behind behaviorism's criticisms deals with the fact that cognitivists changed the face of behavior therapy (leading to cognitive–behavior therapy) rather than separating from it entirely. In response, one camp of behaviorists did secede from the Association for Advancement of Behavior Therapy rather than be part of an organization which also represented a cognitive membership. Others remained perplexed as to why cognitive approaches were being validated as distinct from behavioral ones (Thyer, 1992), for as Wolpe originally put it, 'cognition is a subclass of behavior' (Wolpe, 1976b: 114).

Far from being moribund, the debate about the place of cognitive therapies within psychology, particularly its uneasy alliance with behavior therapy, remains lively. A special miniseries in the journal *Behavior Therapy*, edited by Houts and Follette (1992), considers the philosophical and theoretical bases of behavior therapy after two decades of mix with cognitivists.

Wolpe's Criticisms and Rebuttals by Cognitive Therapists
Joseph Wolpe's landmark criticisms of cognitive therapies appeared in a series of articles remembered for their tone as well as their content (Wolpe, 1976a, 1976b, 1978). In their rejoinder to Wolpe, Beck and Mahoney (1979) identify four assumptions which underlie Wolpe's criticisms. They are:

(1) Determinism precludes both free will and personal causation; (2) cognitive theorists violate the assumptions of physicalism by invoking a nonbiological entity called mind; (3) human learning is adequately explained by the principles of conditioning; and (4) cognitions are

scientifically legitimate variables only if they are considered behaviors in which case they are governed by the principles of behavioral theory. (1979: 94)

In response to Wolpe's first assumption, Beck and Mahoney (1979) argue that behaviors and cognitions influence one another reciprocally, that causation cannot be reduced to a primary or initial force. Free will or free choice operates within a context of determinism, predictability, or cause and effect relationships; they are not mutually exclusive.

To address Wolpe's second assumption, Beck and Mahoney (1979) deny that cognitive theorists believe in the existence of the 'mind' separate from human biology. This Cartesian dichotomy of mind versus body has been foisted onto cognitivists and has contributed to such misconceptions as cognitive therapies giving causal roles to cognitions in the etiology of depression and anxiety. Beck (1984, Beck et al., 1979) has repeatedly denied such a reductionistic stance. In Cognitive Therapy, cognition is assigned a central role in the development of psychopathology, but not necessarily one that is causal or temporally primal.

The separation of mind and body also allows for the cognitive therapies to be viewed in opposition to behavior therapy when they share commonalities, and has fostered competition between the two approaches. A recent example is the argument that Beck's cognitive treatment of panic disorder is inconsistent with conditioning theory (Seligman, 1988; Wolpe and Rowan, 1988). Alford and Carr (1992) explain how Beck's model is an integrative perspective which is compatible with contemporary classical conditioning theory and also incorporates a phenomenological perspective. It includes the meaning of perceived relationships among events, not just the observer's view of those relationships.

The third assumption, that all learning is explained by conditioning, has been challenged since Bandura's (1969, 1974) work. Current criticisms of behavior therapy point out the limitations of simple conditioning models (Davey, 1987; Erwin, 1992; Siddle and Remington, 1987), and some critics advocate the use of mental models from cognitive science in behavior therapy (Power, 1991), although this view is not unanimous.

Beck and Mahoney (1979) disagree also with Wolpe's fourth assumption, that thoughts are legitimate variables only if they are viewed as a subclass of behavior. They say that behavior therapy had yet to define itself and had yet to distinguish behavior from nonbehavior. Thus, cognitions could not be subsumed under an amorphous category.

In the same issue of the *American Psychologist*, Arnold Lazarus

(1979: 100) states that a major difference between behaviorists and cognitive–behaviorists is that cognitive–behavior therapists do not view cognitions, or what were then called 'private events,' as background factors, but as 'preeminently significant'. Cognitive and affective [including autonomic] processes are interactive, argues Lazarus. Moreover, 'Wolpe misses the essential fact that the cognitive orientation places a different emphasis (not a different construction) on the importance of "thinking behaviors".'

Beck and Mahoney further identify three criticisms made by Wolpe which they dispute on empirical grounds: (1) that cognitive therapists are not familiar with behavior therapy practice; (2) that cognitive distortions are rare in behavior disorders; and (3) that cognitive strategies do not add to the power of behavior therapy. These criticisms, too, continue today.

The assertion that cognitive therapists are unfamiliar with the practice of behavior therapy was contradicted in 1977 by an historical review of the training of cognitive therapists (Mahoney, 1977). Most had been trained as behavior modifiers. It is further contradicted today by the percentage of cognitive therapists who hold membership in the Association for Advancement of Behavior Therapy (Craighead, 1990). Nevertheless, as recently as 1988, Skinner (1988) argued that skepticism about the adequacy of behaviorism is an inverse function of one's understanding of it.

Wolpe's contention that cognitivists knew little of the practice of behavior therapy was directed at Beck's (1976) statement that, in theoretical formulations, behaviorists bypass cognitions. Beck was not referring to the practice of behavior therapy, which claimed to use cognitive techniques. Behavior therapy labeled the supportive strategies of reassurance, guidance, persuasion, and re-education as cognitive techniques. Actually, these so-called 'cognitive techniques' are not the strategies used in Cognitive Therapy. At the time of this debate, the strategies used in Cognitive Therapy were identifying automatic thoughts, testing their validity through behavioral experiments and examining evidence, applying rules of logic to evidence, and considering alternatives (Beck, 1976). Thus, cognitivists were largely trained in behavior therapy, but developed intervention strategies to address an expanded view of the role of cognitions.

Moreover, the way cognitive therapists considered cognitions was very different from the way behaviorists such as Wolpe acknowledged but downplayed cognitions. As Davison (1980) points out, Wolpe himself was always mediational and not radically behavioristic, but explained such things as perception in conditioning terms. For cognitive theorists, wrote Davison, reinforcement schedules are, at best, of peripheral interest. What truly defines a cognitive viewpoint is the structuring of experience (or what is popularly referred to nowadays as information processing). Humankind imposes a structure on life, and it is this that behavior therapists are being urged to attend to. This is what the cognitive revolution in behavior therapy is all about, and it is not what Wolpe asserts to us has existed over the past twenty years. (1980: 207)

The statement that cognitive distortions are rare in behavior disorders is challenged empirically by Beck and Mahoney (1979), who discuss a number of studies, including the noteworthy Beck, Laude and Bohnert (1974) study which found that those diagnosed with 'free floating anxiety' actually had danger-related thoughts and images.

In the years intervening since the publication of this debate, cognitions have been demonstrated to exist in abundance in a variety of disorders. Yet the role of distortion of thought processes remains unknown. Two questions remain: (1) Are the cognitions of depressed and anxious people distorted while the cognitions of normal people are not? and (2) Is a goal of therapy to make thinking more 'rational' or a more accurate reflection or consensual version of reality? These questions touch on several theoretical issues, including the multi-causality of depression, 'depressive realism,' the relationship between cognitive vulnerability and cognitive distortions, and the nature of Cognitive Therapy, whether rationalist or constructivist.

Finally, Wolpe's criticism that cognitive strategies add nothing to the efficacy of behavior therapy remains unresolved but hotly debated. The behavioral position has been most recently articulated by Beidel and Turner (1986) based on a review of cognitive therapy and outcome studies. They conclude that there is no empirical support for the superiority of cognitive–behavior therapy over traditional behavior therapy and that cognitive–behavior therapy does not address aspects of a disorder beyond those addressed by classic behavioral techniques.

Beck's Cognitive Therapy utilizes both cognitive and behavioral techniques and they have rarely been compared to each other. Nevertheless, Shaw's (1977) study of depressed students found 'pure' Cognitive Therapy to be more efficacious than behavior therapy and nondirective therapy. F.G. Taylor and Marshall (1977) found that while behavior therapy and Cognitive Therapy both were effective in treating depressed college students, Beck's Cognitive Therapy was superior. Recently, a meta-analysis of Cognitive Therapy for depression (Dobson, 1989) found nine studies which compared Beck's Cognitive Therapy and behavior therapies. 'On the basis of these data,' concludes the author, 'the average cognitive therapy client had an outcome superior to that of 67% of the behavior therapy clients' (Dobson, 1989: 415).

Cognitive therapy has also been applied to anxiety disorders, long the bastion of behavior therapy. The highly successful cognitive treatment package for panic disorder (D.M. Clark, Salkovskis and Chalkley, 1985; Salkovskis, Jones and Clark, 1986; Sokol et al., 1989; Beck, 1988a) employs the cognitive techniques of challenging misinterpretations of bodily sensations as they occur during panic attacks and modifying beliefs which lead to catastrophic conclusions. These are accompanied by the behavioral technique of exposure to physical sensations as well as a technique to quiet hyperventilation called 'respiratory control'.

In order to test the effectiveness of cognitive techniques alone, a series of studies were conducted to rule out nonspecific treatment effects (Beck, 1988a) and the effects of behavioral techniques (D.M. Clark, Salkovskis and Chalkley, 1985; Salkovskis, Clark and Hackmann, 1991). Clark, Salkovskis and Chalkley (1985) achieved significant reductions in panic during a treatment phase when patients received anti-exposure instructions. Salkovskis, Clark and Hackmann (1991) excluded exposure and respiratory control and used only verbal techniques for challenging misinterpretations of bodily sensations. This 'pure' cognitive treatment of two sessions within ten days reduced misinterpretations and frequency of panic attacks in four out of five patients. The patient whose beliefs did not change had no change in panic frequency. An additional test of nonspecific effects was conducted by initially giving some patients a nonfocal treatment directed at negative thinking about life problems, followed by focal treatment on misinterpretations. Others received anxiety-specific treatment focusing on misinterpretations. Reductions in misinterpretations and panic frequency occurred during the focal cognitive treatment, but not during the nonfocal treatment.

Despite its demonstrated efficacy, it is still not known how Cognitive Therapy effects change. Understanding this process is a fundamental theoretical challenge and one that is of great and active interest.

Criticisms of the Practical Aspects of Cognitive Therapy

Criticisms of Cognitive Therapy practice are most closely associated with psychodynamic perspectives. Criticisms include the view that Cognitive Therapy is too technique-oriented due to its research derivation, too present-centered, overly focused on symptoms without appreciation for complex problem areas or hidden conflicts, inattentive to emotion, and unappreciative of the therapeutic relationship. As part of this last point, some have argued that Cognitive Therapy pays no attention to transference, countertransference, and termination issues, all important in the attachment which occurs between a depressed client and a therapist.

Critics from both the psychodynamic and cognitive science camps also accuse Cognitive Therapy of ignoring the role of unconscious processes (Karasu, 1990; Power and Champion, 1986; Raimy, 1980). And some question whether the therapist can distinguish between dysfunctional thoughts and more realistic or adaptive ones (Raimy, 1980). This leads to theoretical debates concerning the role of rationality in therapy and to philosophical differences over the use of a phenomenological approach which utilizes the patient's self-report as basic data.

The following are criticisms directed at Cognitive Therapy:

Cognitive Therapy is a Simplistic Set of Techniques
Many of the criticisms of how Cognitive Therapy is conducted are based on *Cognitive Therapy of Depression* (Beck et al., 1979), which was developed from the treatment manual used in the early depression studies (Kovacs et al., 1981; Rush et al., 1977). *Cognitive Therapy of Depression* was commended for making explicit what goes on in therapy, and the efficacy of the approach is well-documented (Dobson, 1989). Nevertheless, the view of Cognitive Therapy presented in the book is of a technique-oriented therapy which focuses initially on symptom reduction. This perception lends itself to criticisms that Cognitive Therapy is simplistic, that the emphasis on techniques underestimates the skill required to be a Cognitive Therapist, and that Cognitive Therapy offers a formulaic approach to complex problems (Karasu, 1990).

Cognitive Therapists generally agree that these criticisms are reactions to *Cognitive Therapy of Depression*, but also point out that since Cognitive Therapy actually provided therapeutic guidelines, strategies, and techniques, readers may have focused on them exclusively.

It is not the techniques that make it Cognitive Therapy, argues Judy Beck, but the conceptualization: 'It's interesting that many people label themselves Cognitive Therapists who use cognitive techniques, but don't have a cognitive conceptualization. And I think that's backwards. If you use a cognitive conceptualization, then probably whatever you're doing is Cognitive Therapy.'

Ruth Greenberg, co-author of *Anxiety Disorders and Phobias: A*

Cognitive Perspective (Beck, Emery and Greenberg, 1985), states that as cognitive therapies develop, Cognitive Therapy is less distinctive than it was and people may return to the technical aspects as its distinction. 'The easiest way to tell where it starts and where it stops is to focus on the most basic technical aspects, the kinds of things that were written up in *Feeling Good* [David Burns' 1980 popular self-help book on Cognitive Therapy]: the Thought Record and the Pleasure Prediction Sheets, the simple behavioral techniques and so forth. I think it's easy to imagine that that really is Cognitive Therapy, that it really consists of setting down random thoughts that have some negativity in them without a consideration of the whole psychological system. I think that kind of superficial technical Cognitive Therapy is really an easy whipping boy. It's a straw man people set up and then knock down.'

Beck's reaction to statements that Cognitive Therapy is simplistic is directed at psychiatry. 'Many psychiatrists are biologically oriented so they consider themselves pragmatic, but if they were pushed to state their theoretical orientation, it would be psychodynamic. One of the things I've noticed is that there's a kind of resistance in the field to a new paradigm. It leads people to minimize the efficacy of Cognitive Therapy and discount it.'

Beck believes that Cognitive Therapy was more readily accepted by psychology because it was undergoing its own cognitive revolution and because academic psychologists are more persuaded by empirical findings than are psychiatrists in general.

Jeffrey Young, director of the Cognitive Therapy Center of New York, states that many of the criticisms of Cognitive Therapy are aimed at the early version of the theory. The hostile reaction to Cognitive Therapy is a separate issue. Says Young, 'I think a lot of that comes from the fact that a lot of people who were trained analytically were being told by cognitive therapists, "Everything you're doing is really almost a waste of time; all the things you believe are important in the therapy – the therapy relationship, the early origins, the insight – these things are really a waste of time. And all you really have to do is look at the symptom, take it at face value, use certain techniques, and the person feels better and they're out the door!" So, the original formulation undercuts traditional views so drastically that it's experienced as an enormous threat to people who are, for example, analytically oriented. I think a lot of hostility was really hitting them at the core of their beliefs.'

Cognitive Therapy was considered superficial because it provided clinical instructions on the use of various cognitive and behavioral techniques. Other reasons include its short-term and present-centered nature, and its apparent neglect of the therapeutic relationship.

Cognitive Therapy is Short-Term

The short-term nature of Cognitive Therapy is inextricably tied to criticisms that it is a 'cookbook' therapy or collection of techniques. Criticisms of its relative brevity are shared with other problem-oriented therapies, particularly behavior therapy. Both are criticized for having symptom reduction as the goal and are predicted to have limited utility, probably restricted to the treatment of phobias and uncomplicated, unipolar depression.

Outcome studies of Cognitive Therapy, however, do not show its effects to be short-lived (Hollon and Garber, 1990). Short-term Cognitive Therapy has long-term effects and lower relapse rates than pharmacotherapy (Evans et al., 1992) and other forms of psychotherapy (Shea et al., 1992) in the treatment of depression.

As Cognitive Therapy seeks wider applications in areas such as personality disorders, length of treatment increases. In addition, it is expanding into new clinical areas without benefit of empirical data to back the theory. Arthur Freeman, co-author of *Cognitive Therapy of Personality Disorders* (Beck, Freeman and Associates, 1990), finds this to be a valid criticism. 'We've written a book on personality disorders,' he says, 'but have not extensively tested the model as was done on depression and anxiety. The book preceded the extensive studies. What we explain in the book is that this is a preliminary book to get people thinking about doing more research, but we can't ignore the population because they exist in the clinical caseload.'

Some cognitive–behavior therapists, including Donald Meichenbaum, think that Beck has overextended the cognitive model to the treatment of couples, for Beck has less personal experience treating couples than he has treating individuals with personality disorders. Beck's book for couples *Love Is Never Enough* (Beck, 1988b) was written as a self-help book for the general public and lacks a research base.

The fact that Cognitive Therapy was derived from research and lends itself to being operationalized for further research applications is thus an advantage and a source of criticism. The advantage, as Brian Shaw puts it, is that it is testable. 'I think that probably Cognitive Therapy will go down as one of the approaches that really, sincerely, from the beginning was oriented toward tests and evaluations. The disadvantage is that the overt simplicity of the model misleads some to see it as simplistic and to underestimate the therapeutic skill required to practice sound Cognitive Therapy.'

Cognitive Therapy is Mechanical and too Easy to Learn
As was evident in the National Institute of Mental Health Treatment of Depression Collaborative Research Program, it is not easy to train novice Cognitive Therapists quickly to become good Cognitive Therapists. The main reason Beck resigned from the project was that NIMH insisted on the continued use of barely adequate Cognitive Therapists. Jeffrey Young describes the situation thusly: 'What happened when we tried to teach people Cognitive Therapy who aren't really imbued with the whole model and tried to do it in a short time was people absorbed it in a rote way. I call it "technical cognitive therapy," when you end up having people not attuned to the interpersonal component of the therapy, being trained in thought records, but without much sensitivity to the feelings and to the therapy process and to what the patient's really saying. The technique overrides what should be commonsense in the relationship. So, I feel that was a mistake – the emphasis on technique rather than on blending the technique with good interpersonal rapport and sensitivity.'

Analysis of the NIMH Collaborative Study found site differences (Elkin et al., 1989) which can be due to patient characteristics or therapist characteristics. Brian Shaw, who took over training Cognitive Therapists from Beck and Young, believes the site differences are due to therapist differences.

Power writes,

> good therapists from different persuasions are probably more similar to each other than they are to bad therapists of their own persuasion. These therapist effects, for example, seem to have led to the lack of differentiation between different types of therapy in the recent NIMH Collaborative Depression Study in which therapist differences overwhelmed treatment effects. (Elkin et al., 1989). (1991: 2)

Cognitive Therapy is too Present-Centered and Focused on Symptom Relief
The criticism that Cognitive Therapy is too focused on present symptoms reflects three separate complaints: (1) the ultimate goal of Cognitive Therapy is symptom relief; (2) Cognitive Therapy focuses on superficial levels of cognition; and (3) Cognitive Therapy pays scant attention to childhood experiences. All these criticisms contribute to a perspective that Cognitive Therapy lacks depth of understanding of psychopathology and is probably inadequate to deal with personality issues, complex problem areas, and hidden conflicts (Karasu, 1990).

The misunderstanding that the only goal of Cognitive Therapy is symptom relief may stem from the expedient way in which

Cognitive Therapy often works. Indeed, some patients may leave therapy when they feel better but before schemas have been modified.

Beck et al. (1979: 23) argue for a full understanding of the depressive syndrome and not a superficial view: 'We believe that the tendency of many psychotherapists to ignore traditional nosological categories and to concentrate simply on the patient's problems is restrictive and may lead to unfortunate consequences.' Although the focus of initial sessions is on symptom relief as well as on establishing and building a collaborative relationship and conceptualizing the patient's underlying beliefs and assumptions, the focus of later sessions moves to deeper-level cognitions.

'As therapy progresses and the patient's symptoms lessen, the focus of therapy shifts to changing faulty assumptions – those basic beliefs that predispose the person to depression. Changing his erroneous or dysfunctional assumptions has a direct effect upon the patient's ability to avoid future depressions' (Beck et al., 1979: 244). The exploration of more stable cognitions requires an understanding of the interpersonal factors and personal history of the patient which established these beliefs.

Critics of Cognitive Therapy have argued that symptom reduction without attention to personality factors can lead to relapse (Karasu, 1990). It is interesting to note that one of the strengths of Cognitive Therapy appears to be a prophylactic effect and lower relapse rates (Evans et al., 1992; Hollon and Garber, 1990; Shea et al., 1992).

Cognitive Therapy has also been misunderstood as a method of altering negative thinking using a formulaic approach to modifying clients' thoughts. The initial appeal of working at the level of automatic thoughts is that they are available and accessible. However, not all of them are useful. As David Clark says, 'Anyone who is at all distressed will have an enormous number of negative thoughts, most of which are totally irrelevant. They're sort of rubbish, really. They're not driving the system.'

Cognitive Therapists need to be aware of the meanings of events and experiences to the client, some of which are conveyed by affect and by a general theme or tone in the patient's discourse. 'By relying exclusively on the immediate raw data of the automatic thoughts, the therapist misses the crucial – but unexpressed – meaning' (Beck et al., 1979: 30). The therapist needs to enter into the patient's phenomenological world and check the accuracy of his or her perceptions.

In response to the criticism that Cognitive Therapy is formulaic, Beck et al. (1979: 29) write, 'There is no standard format that can be applied systematically to all patients to obtain the crucial data and change the idiosyncratic patterns.' A cognitive conceptualization of each case is necessary.

Two examples using the same technique, recording and responding to negative automatic thoughts, illustrate how conceptualization is more important than technique. Caire (1992) describes a case in which a patient did not improve despite her challenge of negative thoughts because she was responding to superficial thoughts. It was only when the patient stopped avoiding negative affect that the more central beliefs or core constructs emerged. Caire's work supports Beck's formulation that it is necessary to follow automatic thoughts to the beliefs from which they are derived (Beck et al., 1979). These beliefs are tied to emotions that are often avoided. Caire also reiterates the importance of recording thoughts as a way of representing problems concretely and as a way to track cognitions and emotions over time. Caire argues that using a standard technique, recording and responding to automatic thoughts, reduces cognitive and emotional avoidance by forcing clients to focus on the most powerful cognitions.

In contrast to Caire's case findings, Persons (1990) describes how a client used the Daily Record of Dysfunctional Thoughts as a means of avoiding situations in which irrational beliefs about herself were triggered. By conceptualizing the client's behavior as avoidance, Persons prescribed behavioral experiments to test her beliefs: the client was to make a commitment to school and socializing, and was to increase her activities accordingly. Her depression and anxiety improved quickly. Underscoring the importance of conceptualization over technique, Persons concludes, 'whether or not the patient benefits from treatment depends less on the particular intervention strategies used than on whether the strategies allow the patient to obtain evidence that disconfirms his or her central irrational beliefs about the self' (1990: 133).

Finally, Cognitive Therapy has been criticized as being too present-centered and symptom-oriented because it pays little attention to childhood experiences. In Beck's 1979 volume, he does state that patients who believe they are depressed solely because of childhood experiences need to be oriented to the rationale of Cognitive Therapy. 'It may be more useful for the therapist to discuss the fact that one can change a pattern of thinking or behavior without identifying the cause and course of previous learning' (Beck et al., 1979: 145).

Initially, Cognitive Therapy was interested in early experiences as a way to understand the origins of beliefs and schemas.

However, these early experiences were not to be 'relived' or worked on directly. More recently, there has been increased interest in early experiences, particularly as Cognitive Therapy has taken on more complex cases involving personality problems and chronic depressions.

In these cases, early, formative experiences and historical material are explored to identify beliefs, to review the evidence used over time to maintain these beliefs, and to modify the beliefs through emotive techniques and role play. As historical evidence in support of a negative view of self, for example, is reviewed, it is examined for bias, missing data, or interpretive errors. Core beliefs can be restructured through such a review. Examples of such attention to childhood experiences are found in *Cognitive Therapy of Personality Disorders* (Beck, Freeman and Associates, 1990) and in a newer form of Cognitve Therapy, Schema-Focused Cognitive Therapy (Young, 1990).

Emotive techniques such as spontaneous and guided imagery are often used to identify the source and etiology of core beliefs and schemas. By having a patient trace an emotion back to an earlier experience, memory can be retrieved. In addition, the patient's perceptions and interpretations of that experience *as it happened* may be critical to their subsequent beliefs. Spontaneous imagery may also identify a schema or core cognition without actual historical connections being made, for the imagery provides meaningful cognitive content associated with affect.

While Beck's Cognitive Therapy has always used imagery (Beck, 1970b, 1976), the applications just discussed are very new. In addition, Cognitive Therapy does not stay mired in the past. Rather it uses historical material to understand and reframe existing beliefs. Historical material provides yet another way to challenge cognitive constructs.

Judy Beck says, 'People who still believe Cognitive Therapy is really only Cognitive Therapy of depression can't really get a handle on this, and it does seem too mystical to them. To me it's just an outgrowth because basically you're still getting out these underlying beliefs, and you're helping the patient restructure them in a different format. Then when the imagery exercise is over, we process what went on and have the patient write out the old belief and the new belief and how much they believe each one, and maybe put it on a flash card and read it every day for a few weeks.'

Cognitive Therapy does not Give Sufficient Attention to Emotion

Cognitive Therapy has been criticized for the role it ascribes to emotion in cognitive theory and its apparent lack of utilization of emotion in therapy. Cognitive theory has been criticized for conceptualizing emotion as 'a post cognitive phenomenon' (Greenberg and Safran, 1987: 40). The notions that cognition precedes emotion and that people's emotional reactions to events are determined by the private meanings attached to those events are implicit in Cognitive Therapy. Critics of this perspective characterize it thusly: 'Deviant meanings are held to constitute the cognitive distortions that form the core of emotional disorders; these personal meanings are the primary targets of change in cognitive therapy' (Greenberg and Safran, 1987: 40). Further, Mahoney (1980: 159) argues that cognitive therapies 'tend to view feelings narrowly, as phenomenal artifacts that are to be controlled rather than experienced.'

Thus, critics of Cognitive Therapy would view emotion, not as a consequence, but as an equal source of information to cognition. Criticisms of Beck's view and use of emotion are examined at both the theoretical and practical levels.

Emotion in Cognitive Theory   According to Beck's theory of depression (Beck, 1967: 287) 'the affective response (as well as the behavioral and physiological responses) is determined by the way the individual structures experience.' However, this relationship between cognition and emotion is not linear. Beck posits that a feedback loop occurs in depression: the depressed person's negative cognitions precipitate sad affect which, in turn, is interpreted negatively, leading to further bad feeling. In addition to this reciprocal interaction between thought and feeling is the influence of a person's developmental and learning histories, for early losses or other traumas may predispose someone to depression (Beck, 1967).

In the 1980s a debate between R. Lazarus (1982, 1984) and Zajonc (1980, 1984) pitted cognition and emotion against each other in a chicken-and-egg race for temporal primacy. Cognitive Therapy was placed in the 'cognitive primacy' camp, although Beck has never argued in favor of a linear causality of depression or any other syndrome. Beck, in fact, distinguishes between primacy and causality. He says that once depression is established, cognitions shape the affective, behavioral and motivational responses. Cognitions are an integral part of depression, on par with these other responses (Beck, 1991a: 371). The causes of depression can be any combination of biological, genetic, stress or personality factors (Beck, 1967).

Beck's cognitive model of depression is not a theory of emotion *per se* (Shaw, 1979), but in recent years he has written about the evolutionary significance of depression (Beck, 1987a) and anxiety (Beck, Emery and Greenberg, 1985). Although depression and anxiety are maladaptive states for contemporary humans, Beck postulates that in early human evolution they were adaptive. According to his scheme, depression is a biologically wired-in response to disappointment which inhibits the organism from expending energy fruitlessly; it is a conserving mechanism (Beck, 1987a). Anxiety is a built-in system of responses to threat and danger in which physiological arousal leads to flight, fight, or freeze reactions. In premodern times, danger was largely from physical threats. In modern societies, threat is psychosocial, yet we overrespond as if to physical danger (Beck, Emery and Greenberg, 1985).

In Beck's theory, 'emotion is viewed as an important part of depression but not as a major feature of the disorder' (Wright, 1988: 555). Other researchers, however, have more thoroughly described the influence of emotion on cognitive processing (Bower, 1981; Breslow, Kocsis and Belkin, 1981; L.S. Greenberg and Safran, 1984; Mayer and Bower, 1985). Depressed mood has been found to stimulate cognitive distortions, such as selective recall of negative versus positive memories. Modifying affect, by cognitive, behavioral or other means, is thus presumed to alter cognitive distortions and thereby affect treatment outcome (Wright, 1988).

In addition to research on the impact of emotion on cognitive activity, theories of emotion are being developed in conjunction with findings in cognitive psychology. The work of Safran and others (L.S. Greenberg and Safran, 1987; Mahoney, 1990; Safran and Greenberg, 1988) extends beyond the scope of Beck's work not only to validate emotion as an untapped realm within the cognitive therapies, but to establish it as 'tacit knowing' (L.S. Greenberg and Safran, 1987: 166), thus linking it to experiential therapies (L.S. Greenberg, Safran and Rice, 1989), constructivist/existential views of self-knowledge (Mahoney, 1990), ecological adaptation (Safran and Greenberg, 1988), and the view that emotions are action tendencies that link the human organism to the world (L.S. Greenberg and Safran, 1987; Mahoney, 1990; Safran and Greenberg, 1988).

Emotion in the Practice of Cognitive Therapy   Beck devotes a chapter of *Cognitive Therapy of Depression* to the role of emotions in Cognitive Therapy. He states (Beck et al., 1979: 36), 'Cognitive therapy draws heavily on "emotional techniques" as part of the therapeutic repetoire' and goes on to list 'sensory awareness' and flooding as important tools as long as they are used for the purpose of cognitive change. In this same volume, however, he criticizes the use of 'abreactive' therapies which encourage emotional ventilation, but ignore the role of ideation in excessive emotion and the value of cognitive techniques in the alleviation of emotional distress.

As early as 1970, Beck (1970a, 1970b) wrote of the importance of imagery as a source of cognitive data. Imagery work emerged again in Freeman's (1981) writings on dream restructuring and importantly in Beck, Emery and Greenberg's (1985) book on anxiety disorders. Imagery features prominently in anxiety disorders as clients often report horrific and vivid imagery instead of automatic thoughts. With Beck's anxiety book, the use of imagery in Cognitive Therapy gained new recognition and emphasis. Currently, imagery techniques have undergone a renaissance and are used for changing basic beliefs and schemas (Edwards, 1989, 1990; Young, 1990).

In terms of Cognitive Therapy practice, emotional arousal is necessary for cognitive change (Beck and Weishaar, 1989a, 1989b). Often such arousal needs to be stimulated in the therapy session to gain access to salient or 'hot' cognitions (Safran and Greenberg, 1982b). For example, the use of *in vivo* exposure generates affect-laden cognitions which are then open to testing and modification. For example, in the treatment of panic disorder, inducing a panic state within a therapy session achieves several goals: (1) it reveals catastrophic cognitions which contribute to the escalation of symptoms; (2) it provides exposure to feared physiological sensations; and (3) it serves as a behavioral experiment which can disprove faulty conclusions about the consequences of panic.

The use of emotive techniques is especially valuable in cases of emotional and/or cognitive avoidance. Imagery is extensively used to bypass defenses of rationalization and intellectualization, to link vague somatic complaints or affective states with schemas (Young, 1990), to identify the source of core beliefs, and to restructure intrusive and disruptive images as in trauma cases (Padesky, 1990).

Newman (1991) describes several methods of affect enhancement in Cognitive Therapy, including imagery, role-playing, and *in vivo* experimentation. He recommends the use of standard relaxation techniques as a prelude to imagery exercises. He also states that imaginal situations in the exercise could be any which the client would find too uncomfortable to experience in real life. This includes actual memories, hypothetical encounters in the present, or anticipated events.

In summary, Cognitive Therapy has not incorporated emotion into a comprehensive theory, but sees it in a reciprocal relationship with cognition. In terms of clinical practice, Cognitive Therapy maintains that emotional arousal is necessary to gain access to core cognitive constructs and to make changes in them. Thus, emotive techniques are used not for ventilation of affect, but for fundamental cognitive change.

Cognitive Therapy has Rationality as a Goal

A criticism related to the alleged unemotionality of Cognitive Therapy is that it champions rationality as a goal of psychotherapy. This particular criticism is directed at many cognitive–behavior therapies, not just Beck's Cognitive Therapy. It has been articulated most extensively by Mahoney (Mahoney, 1980, 1988; Mahoney and Gabriel, 1987), who contrasts what he calls 'rationalist' cognitive therapies with constructivism.

In 1980, Mahoney wrote that, among other problems, cognitive therapies 'place an excessive emphasis on the role of rationality in adaptation' (Mahoney, 1980: 159). Moreover,

> in the cognitive therapies, the term 'rationality' has come to imply a naively simplistic form of 'good reasoning'. It is presumed that there is a 'right' way to think – i.e., one which is rational and therefore 'good'. Wrong ('irrational') thinking patterns are said to lead to distress. Remedial training in rational thinking is the strategy of choice. (Mahoney, 1980: 169)

In contrast to this rationalist view is constructivism, which challenges 'the idea that reality is fundamentally external and stable and argues that human thought is not meaningfully separable from human feeling and action' (Mahoney and Gabriel, 1987: 46). Constructivist approaches to psychotherapy such as cognitive developmental therapy (Mahoney, 1990) and structural cognitive therapy (Guidano, 1987; Guidano and Liotti, 1983) view problems as manifestations of former adaptive strategies rather than as perceptual or conceptual errors. The therapy which follows from this view is more exploratory than remedial, the therapist is less directive and more passive, and there is greater emphasis on attachment theory (Bowlby, 1977, 1979) in regard to the therapeutic relationship in order to provide a 'safe context' for exploration of self and world.

Beck's Cognitive Therapy does fit a few, but not all, of the many specific criticisms leveled at rationalist cognitive therapies

(Mahoney and Gabriel, 1987). For example, Cognitive Therapy is problem-focused and does attempt to minimize relapse. It does not, however, propose that insight is sufficient for change, or that all problems are due to irrational thinking. Beck eschews the word 'irrational' in reference to maladaptive thoughts, for at one time in the person's life these beliefs made sense. Dysfunctional beliefs contribute to psychological disorders because they interfere with normal cognitive processing, not because they are irrational (Beck and Weishaar, 1989a).

Both Beck and Albert Ellis have taken issue with being labeled 'rationalists'. Ellis responded with an article, 'Is rational–emotive therapy (RET) "rationalist" or "constructivist"'? (1990).

Of Beck's Cognitive Therapy, Mahoney now says, 'I made the mistake of calling it rationalist in something, I think it was in the foreword to my 1984 volume with Mario Reda [Reda and Mahoney, 1984]. True to his form, Tim related he was surprised that I considered him a rationalist. He felt that George Kelly had been a significant influence on his early writing and thinking; that he viewed himself more as a constructivist. It's probably an individual difference in how people read him and where they see the emphasis. I certainly know colleagues who would be inclined to place Beck and Cognitive Therapy at the rationalist end of the continuum. But I would really respect both his request and his assertion that the heart of the system is really not preoccupied with rationality as much as with adaptation. Certainly, his interest in Darwin and evolutionary issues is more constructivist than rationalist. So, at this point, I classify him as constructivist.'

Beck believes his view of constructivism is close to Kelly's view. In contrast to his own approach is that of Mahoney and others to whom he refers as 'idealists'. He says, 'I think my own theory is much more in line with George Kelly who proposes that the external reality is extracted, synthesized, and integrated according to certain structures, which he calls constructs and which other people call schemas. However, there are other constructivists who I would call idealists philosophically in that external reality seems to be much less important, if it has importance at all, as compared with internal reality.

'I would personally think that the internal reality is in some ways a replica of external reality, although it may not be perfect, but it's shaped probably by evolutionary factors so that we will utilize what goes on outside us, that exists outside us, in such a way as to fulfill our evolutionary objectives. So there is some correspondence between the two: our internal reality is continuously being subjected to correction by external reality. Otherwise we would go about like zombies and could not continue to exist, let alone pass on our genes to the next generation.

'Now where we construct our own reality has to do with particularly those areas that have specific significance in terms of critical meaning. In this particular case, important meanings have to do with survival and reproduction. In those areas, the blurring of reality is strongest, and the domination of internal schemas is the greatest. We are much more likely to construct our reality according to internal as opposed to external factors. For objects and distance we can be very much [external] reality-oriented.

'One group of constructivists, which I would call idealists, seem to discard, totally, the significance of the outside world and believe the only thing that's important is the inside world. A number of methods are used to open up windows to the internal world, such as free association, which has an analogue technique known as "streaming," and a technique of looking at one's image in the mirror. These are methods that are intended to bring the person in touch with his internal reality.

'The problem with this is it discards the notion of the importance of the outside world and puts the entire emphasis on internal phenomenology. Since the only thing that counts is what goes on inside the person's head, then anything goes, which means any method is acceptable as long as it opens up some kind of channels to the individual's phenomenology. There are no restraints, constraints, or direction to the methods that are used. There is no constraint on the therapist himself. Such things as outcome data become irrelevant because what's important is what the person actually experiences. It seems to be taken for granted that if the individual gets greater contact with his internal world, he would then achieve his purpose. There are no criteria for whether the person has been helped or not other than the individual's satisfaction with the process. So the process, then, becomes more important than the outcome.

'This seems to me to be a total reversal of what's been happening in the behavior therapy movement. In the cognitive therapy movement such things as operationalizing procedures, evaluating the efficacy of procedures, working to have results and outcomes are all very important. This has now been jettisoned in favor of the process itself.'

A recent article on the use of consciousness 'streaming' in a case study acknowledges that the utility of the technique is in the exploratory stages of therapy. Its utility in change processes is unknown (Szykula et al, 1989).

On the other side of the rationalist–constructivist debate are those who think Cognitive Therapy has not gone far enough in prescribing rational thinking as a goal of therapy (Baron et al., 1990; Moshman and Hoover, 1989). Baron et al. (1990) present criteria and guidelines for rational ('actively open minded') thinking which are reminiscent of D'Zurilla and Goldfried's (1971) problem-solving model. Moshman and Hoover (1989) see a natural devlopmental trend in humans toward increasing rationality. They describe a way to foster rationality which is not anathema to an organismic/contructivist perspective.

Richard Lazarus has been critical of the notion of rationality being key to adaptation. In response to a paper written by Goldfried (1980b), Lazarus places himself at odds with 'Goldfried, Ellis and, in fact, the behaviorist tradition' by writing,

> Although people can be helped by getting them to see the hard realities and illusory and irrational nature of their assumptions about living, we often also need the luxury of some illusions and therapy in some instances might better revolve around helping the person think more positively about his or her plight rather than fixating on the painful truth. So much of life is ambiguous that there is much room for variation in appraisal. (Lazarus, 1980: 124)

The therapeutic goal of rational thinking is tied to the theoretical debate about the extent to which distorted thinking contributes to psychological distress. This debate will be discussed in the section on criticsms of cognitive theory.

Cognitive Therapy Does Not Acknowledge Unconscious Processes

Raimy (1980) identified two primary objections to the assumptions made by cognitive therapies: (1) that the therapist can readily distinguish between dysfunctional thoughts and more realistic thoughts that produce adaptive behavior; and (2) that the patient's interpretation of events must be accepted as 'basic "rock bottom" data' (Raimy, 1980: 155).

Implicit in this second objection is the criticism that Cognitive Therapy does not appreciate how unconscious processes could affect the presentation of 'data' by the client. Beck rejects the Freudian notion of the unconscious, a portion of the mind containing information whose escape must be defended against. Because of his reaction to Freud's concept of unconscious motivation, Beck said, 'the concept of unconscious processes is largely irrelevant to Cognitive Therapy' (Sacco and Beck, 1985: 5).

Beck views consciousness on a continuum and focuses on conscious or preconscious meaning. This view ignores unconscious goals, conflicts, and intentions, for the Cognitive Therapist does not interpret such speculations to the client. Although the concepts of unconscious goals and motivations are not congruent with the practice of Cognitive Therapy, they are congruent with current concepts in cognitive science (Power, 1989), an area to which many cognitive therapists have turned in the last decade.

Power (1987) distinguishes between conscious or controlled and unconscious or automatic processes. Automatic processes are modular, parallel and fast; controlled processes are sequential and slow. Clearly, Beck's concept of 'automatic thoughts' (Beck, 1976) touches on this view of unconscious processes. More important, however, is the relationship of conscious and unconscious processes to a cognitive theory of emotion. According to Power, 'faciliatory and inhibitory effects are necessary within any theory of emotion to account for different types of interactions between emotions. Similarly . . . between episodes of depression the depressive may be able to inhibit the entry into awareness of the automatic processing of negative material, whereas during depression conscious processes appear to facilitate this negative processing' (Power, 1987: 247).

Within the field of cognitive behavior therapies, some theorists are examining the role of unconscious processes in experience as well as the similarities and differences between psychoanalytic and cognitive–behavioral conceptualizations of the unconscious (Meichenbaum and Gilmore, 1984; Safran and Greenberg, 1987). Interestingly, the push for a rapprochement between such theoretically disparate modalities comes from developments in cognitive science (Power, 1989).

Cognitive Therapy Does Not Use The Therapy
Relationship For Therapeutic Change
The major criticism of Cognitive Therapy from psychoanalytic and psychodynamic schools is that Cognitive Therapy neglects the therapeutic relationship as a context for or agent of change. Indeed, this has been a growing criticism within the cognitive school (Mahoney, 1980; Safran and Segal, 1990). Newer brands of cognitive therapies have attempted to address this perceived deficit (Guidano and Liotti, 1983; Safran and Segal, 1990; Young, 1990).

The growing attention to the therapeutic relationship may be part of a movement in the cognitive therapies noted years ago by Richard Lazarus (1980) toward psychodynamic concepts. More recently, Power (1991) has observed that just as there was a 'cognitive drift' in the practice of behavior therapy, there is now a 'psychoanalytic drift' in the practice of Cognitive Therapy.

Beck describes the role of the Cognitive Therapist as that of a 'guide who helps the client understand how beliefs and attitudes influence affect and behavior' (Beck et al., 1979: 301). In early writings, Beck does not elaborate on what it takes to be a good Cognitive Therapist besides the warmth, genuineness, and unconditional positive regard that are highlighted in Rogers' (1951) Client-Centered Therapy. Later writing (Beck et al., 1979; Beck and Young, 1985) states that a Cognitive Therapist must also have a full understanding of the cognitive conceptualization, be creative and active, and be knowledgeable of behavioral and cognitive strategies.

In psychoanalytic and psychodynamic therapies, the therapeutic relationship is used extensively as a reflection of how the client interacts with key figures in his or her life. It is also considered the context of therapeutic change. The development and resolution of the transference relationship is the cornerstone of psychoanalytic therapies.

The therapeutic relationship is important in Cognitive Therapy as the basis of collaborative empiricism. Thus, the relationship serves as a motivating and energizing force for a strategy of change, rather than being the locus of change itself. In Beck's Cognitive Therapy, the therapist rarely reveals his or her own feelings, experiences or opinions, and then does so 'judiciously' (Beck et al., 1979: 52).

Transference issues are treated as are other automatic thoughts (Beck and Young, 1985; Wright, 1988), to be 'confronted head on' by trying to correct the cognitive distortions which contribute to passivity, lack of intiative, or oppositionalism (Beck et al., 1979: 58). Safran and Segal (1990) note, however, that it is not asssumed in Cognitive Therapy that changes in the patient's perceptions as a result of addressing these distortions will necessarily generalize to perceptions and behaviors outside of the therapy.

Countertransference issues are regarded as signals for therapists to work on their own automatic thoughts and assumptions. Further, in treating depression, the therapist must often work hard not to get caught up in the patient's negative view.

The use of collaborative agendas and regular feedback are integral parts of the structure of Cognitive Therapy sessions and are designed to minimize difficulties in the therapy relationship. One may thus view Cognitive Therapy as encouraging positive, but not idealized, transference in the sessions by actively soliciting the client's wishes for the direction of the session and by demystifying therapy or the image of the omnipotent therapist.

In an article on therapeutic change, Strupp rejects 'the notion of psychotherapy as a "treatment" and as a set of "techniques" aimed at the amelioration of "disorders" or "symptoms" unless one uses these terms in a highly metaphoric sense' (Strupp, 1988: 78). Rather, he writes, 'the therapist must be capable of understanding the often disguised and symbolic meanings of the patient's behavior in relation to the therapist and provide meaningful feedback to the patient' (Strupp, 1988: 79).

Similarly, Power (1989) encourages Cognitive Therapists to use the therapeutic relationship as a psychoanalyst would.

> In more general conditions such as depression in which it is likely that early attachment problems form a significant factor, then the individual's current significant relationships and the transference relationship will reflect these earlier distortions. In such cases, a focus on the transference issues, whether positive or negative, provides one of the most powerful tools potentially at the disposal of the cognitive therapist. (Power, 1989: 552)

Termination issues may also be critical for depressed patients. These may be crucial in short-term therapies since the termination phase may have to become the focus of therapy almost as soon as a therapeutic alliance is founded (Power, 1989). Cognitive Therapy does not address termination in an interpersonal sense, but rather as an expectation introduced in early sessions to prepare clients for their increasing responsibility over the course of therapy.

In contrast to the psychoanalytic view, Cognitive Therapy maintains that a good therapeutic relationship is not sufficient for change to occur. In response to Strupp, for example, Shaw argues, 'At issue here is not the friendly interpersonal environment, but what the therapist's skill or competence does in applying the treatment' (Shaw, 1988: 84). Treatment, according to Shaw, is a way of behaving toward the client in order to manage his or her problems or symptoms. It is based on a conceptualization which is congruent with a theory. One might say that, in Cognitive Therapy, there is at least as much emphasis on the conceptualization as on the relationship.

Nevertheless, says, Jeffrey Young, 'you have to acknowledge that no matter what therapy you do, the relationship is going to be at least 50 per cent. If you lose that 50 per cent, no matter what techniques you're using, you're losing half of the potency of therapy as a whole.'

The area traditionally emphasizing the importance of the therapeutic relationship is work with personality disorders. In *Cognitive Therapy of Personality Disorders* (Beck, Freeman and Associates, 1990), Beck describes personality disorders as interpersonal 'strategies' which are the result of interactions between genetic factors and rigidly held schemas. They pose particular challenges to building a therapeutic alliance. Beck and Freeman describe 19 problems in collaboration which are likely to arise in working with characterological disorders. Examples include: the patient may lack the skill to be collaborative, the patient's fears of change and becoming a 'new' self may contribute to noncompliance, and the goals of therapy may be vague and amorphous. The authors emphasize the ability to conceptualize these problems as being schema-driven as the key to maintaining collaboration.

Concentration on the therapeutic relationship has increased within the cognitive school in the past decade. There has been a flourishing of interest in John Bowlby's (1969, 1973, 1980) attachment theory as a foundation for the relationship between therapist and client. Drawing on Bowlby's work, constructivist therapists view the therapeutic relationship as providing a safe context in which the client can explore and examine interactions with the world (Bowlby, 1979; Guidano, 1987, 1991; Mahoney and Gabriel, 1987).

More explicitly, Liotti (1991) describes how abnormal patterns of attachment within the therapy relationship represent earlier attachments. Such abnormal patterns are categorized as anxious resistant, avoidant, and disorganized/disoriented attachments. Knowledge of these attachment patterns can guide assessment and schema change.

As part of the central role of attachment theory, there is currently an emphasis on interpersonal schemas (Liotti, 1991; Safran, 1990; Safran and Segal, 1990). An interpersonal schema is a knowledge structure that contains information relevant to the maintenance of interpersonal relatedness (Safran, 1986, 1987). The basic goal of maintaining relatedness is biologically wired-in, whereas the specific strategies to accomplish this are learned.

There is current debate, as will be discussed in the following sections, whether clinical deficits are cognitive or interpersonal in nature (Coyne and Gotlib, 1983, 1986; Krantz, 1985; Segal and Shaw, 1986a,b). There are likely to be complex interactions between cognitive and interpersonal deficits, for cognitive processes operate in interpersonal contexts. The current focus on the therapeutic relationship highlights this.

Criticisms of Cognitive Theory

Beck's Cognitive Therapy for depression has been researched and scrutinized perhaps to a greater degree than any other theory and therapy. While outcome studies are supportive of its efficacy (Dobson, 1989; Elkin et al., 1989; Hollon et al., 1992), several questions remain concerning cognitive theory. Aspects of Beck's theory of depression have been substantiated empirically, such as (1) increased negativity of cognitions about the self, (2) increased hopelessness, (3) specificity of themes of loss to depressive syndromes rather than to psychopathology in general, and (4) mood congruent recall (Haaga, Dyck and Ernst, 1991). However, major features of the theory are not well-supported, including the assumption that depressive thinking is illogical or inaccurate, and the notion of a cognitive vulnerability to depression. Furthermore, critics have argued that Beck's theory does not adequately consider environmental factors such as life events (Krantz, 1985) and interpersonal interactions (Coyne and Gotlib, 1983) in the etiology of depression.

Beck has responded to these criticisms by reformulating his theory to include six separable but overlapping models of depression: cross-sectional, structural, stressor-vulnerability, reciprocal-interaction, psychobiological, and evolutionary. These models are descriptive, explanatory or etiological (Beck, 1987a). They can be tested separately or in combination with one another. Dyck and Stewart (1991) discuss how to operationalize the stressor-vulnerability model, but as yet it remains unsubstantiated (Haaga, Dyck and Ernst, 1991). In addition, Beck has responded to the growing interest in Bowlby's attachment theory as it relates to depression by adding the personality dimensions of sociotropy and autonomy to his theory (Beck, 1983; Beck, Epstein and Harrison, 1983). Specifically, this elaboration addresses the association between loss of a relationship and the onset of depression by identifying interpersonal loss as a stressor most likely to affect a broad category of personality, sociotropy.

Additional criticism of Beck's model has to do with its lack of congruence with contemporary cognitive psychology. In cognitive science, there is particular focus on the roles of conscious and nonconscious cognitive processing (Brewin, 1989; Power, 1987). There is also curent debate on the structure of internal representations, whether or not they are verbally accessible, and, practically speaking, how to access them.

Whereas Beck writes of schemas, Bower (1981) conceptualizes cognitive structures of associative networks. More complex structures such as mental models (Power and Champion, 1986) or headed records (Morton, Hammersly and Bikerian, 1985) have also been proposed. Whether internal representations are hierarchical or heterarchical is also debated. Finally, it is unclear whether verbally and situationally accessible representations are stored in the same memory system, but encoded differently, or whether they are stored in separate memory systems (as in, for example, Moscovitch, 1985; see Brewin, 1989).

While much of these debates is beyond the scope of Beck's research, findings have implications for how to measure schemas and for the explanatory power of Beck's model. For example, Brewin (1989) suggests that Cognitive Therapy for depression works by gaining access to nonconscious situational memories. Other cognitive–behavior therapies work by altering verbally accessible knowledge (providing plausible new information to alter misconceptions) or by promoting self-regulatory strategies (such as reattribution training, problem-solving training, or coping statements).

Criticisms of Beck's Cognitive Model of Depression

Cognitive theory posits that nonendogenous, unipolar depression results from an interaction of biological, genetic, stress or personality factors which activate depressogenic schemas. 'Activation of the schemas [is] the mechanism by which depression develops, not a cause' (Beck, 1991a: 371).

Activation of these latent schemas leads to biased cognitive processing and errors in perception and inference which are manifested in pervasively negative views of one's self, one's future, and one's personal world. This last aspect of the triad, a negative view of the world, has been modified slightly in recent years. It does not mean a negative view of the world in general, but rather 'one's fitness for meeting life's demands' (Haaga, Dyck and Ernst, 1991: 218).

The keystones of the cognitive model are the concepts of the cognitive triad, distorted cognitive processing, and maladaptive schemas (Beck, 1987a; Beck et al., 1979). While there is empirical support for the cognitive triad, the notions of distorted thinking and latent schemas are problematic.

Distorted Thinking

In their review of empirical studies of Cognitive Therapy, Haaga, Dyck and Ernst, (1991) state that there is evidence of a negative bias in the judgments of depressed persons. However, depressed individuals may be pessimistic without necessarily distorting reality. These authors advocate conceptualizing the thinking of dysphoric people as biased rather than distorted.

It had been reported earlier that depressed individuals viewed negative feedback realistically (Alloy and Abramson, 1979) and that nondepressed subjects were too optimistic in their reactions to feedback (Coyne and Gotlib, 1983). This came to be known as 'depressive realism'. However, the design of the Alloy and Abramson study did not really allow demonstration of this conclusion (Haaga, Dyck and Ernst, 1991; Segal and Shaw, 1986a). Subsequent research found that the relative realism of dysphoric and nondysphoric groups varies as a function of the match between the feedback to be perceived and the subjects' prior beliefs (Dykman et al., 1989).

In contrast to the notion of depressive realism, depressed patients have been found to recall feedback as significantly more negative than it had been while psychiatric and normal controls were more accurate (Gotlib, 1983). Depressed patients also overestimated self-punishments and underestimated self-reinforcements in a learning task; the control subjects were accurate (Gotlib, 1981). Highly symptomatic nonclinical subjects have also been found to underestimate high rates of positive feedback (DeMonbreun and Craighead, 1977).

It has been argued that Beck's model erroneously assumes that nondepressive thinking is logical, rational, and free of distortions when it actually may be positively skewed (Power and Champion, 1986). Beliefs of nondepressed persons may rest on their usefulness and viability, not on logic (Power, 1989). Indeed, illusory bias has been demonstrated to be an adaptive mechanism in the face of life-threatening events in adults (Taylor, 1983) as has unrealistic optimism in the face of demonstrated failure in children (Bjorklund and Green, 1992).

Beck actually argues that nondepressed individuals have a greater capacity to self-correct their initial appraisals, not that their thinking is free from bias or distortions (Beck and Weishaar, 1989a). A negative bias in thinking is most likely to occur when data are not immediately present, are not concrete, are ambiguous, and are relevant to self-evaluation (Riskind, 1983).

Beck now proposes the following: (1) the nondepressed cognitive organization has a positive bias; (2) as it shifts towards depression, the positive cognitive bias is neutralized; (3) as depression develops, a negative bias occurs; (4) in bipolar cases there is a swing into an exaggerated positive bias as the manic phase develops (Beck, 1991a: 372).

Cognitive Vulnerability to Depression
Central to the cognitive model of depression is the notion of cognitive vulnerability: depressogenic schemas which are established by a person's learning history and which contain negative beliefs, usually reflecting themes of deprivation, defeat, abandonment,

worthlessness or loss. These schemas are latent until triggered by an event related to the schema content. Several problems exist in demonstrating this construct: (1) the schema concept is vaguely defined and lacks consensus and uniformity in its use; (2) it is difficult to measure a latent cognitive structure; and (3) it has not yet been demonstrated how personality variables interact with stressful life events to contribute to the onset and maintenance of depression.

Schema Concept
The meaning of schema in Beck's cognitive theory of depression has not been clear in its application. One definition of a schema is a dysfunctional belief which can be operationalized in paper-and-pencil questionnaires, such as the Dysfunctional Attitude Scale (DAS) (Weissman, 1979; Weissman and Beck, 1978). 'Basic beliefs' and 'schemas' have been used interchangeably (Haaga, Dyck and Ernst, 1991).

A second definition is that a schema is a cognitive structure comprised of many elements. The self-schema, for example, is defined as 'an organized unit or cluster of self-descriptions . . . Activation of one of these elements, due to its nesting within such a structure, will spread to other related negative elements, culminating in the phenomenological experience of a negative view of self' (Segal et al., 1988: 473). Although Beck refers to schemas as cognitive *structures* (Beck, 1987a), it is the *content* of these structures which is assessed in research and addressed in therapy. Structural change is inferred when belief change is evident.

Segal (1988) presents an extensive review of research on the schema construct and the difficulties in demonstrating its predictive capacity in depression. Measurement difficulties include (1) demonstrating the existence of dysfunctional beliefs before an initial depressive episode, and (2) demonstrating schematic processing independent of the effects of depressed mood on the dependent variables used.

Segal (1988) advocates the definition of schema in cognitive-structural terms, which is consistent with its usage in cognitive psychology and social cognition. Methods used to assess general knowledge structures such as semantic networks (Bower, 1981) could be applied to the self-schema construct to verify whether information about the self is similarly organized.

Segal's proposal helps Cognitive Therapy research resolve issues of how to measure schemas when they are latent, for it bypasses the use of paper-and-pencil measures which only reflect the depressed person's negative verbalizations and focuses on measures of cognitive structure and organization. Measures used in cognitive psychology such as semantic priming, intrusions on nonpresented material in free recall, and release from proactive inhibition 'allow for constructs used in information processing to be assessed without directly asking subjects about them, and in this sense reflect processes that are thought to be more automatic' (Segal, 1988: 151).

Measuring Cognitive Vulnerability
The move toward models from cognitive psychology and social cognition comes after years of research which attempted to measure schemas by questionnaire, usually the DAS (Weissman and Beck, 1978). These studies are reviewed in the famous Coyne and Gotlib (1983, 1986) articles along with rejoinders by Segal and Shaw (1986a, 1986b). An additional review is presented by Barnett and Gotlib (1988). Basically, the research has been hindered by a lack of procedures suitable for priming latent beliefs (Haaga, Dyck and Ernst, 1991; Riskind and Rholes, 1984) and by the use of a measure (the DAS) which has been criticized as too general a measure to be specific to depression. However, in two studies, it appears that elevated DAS scores in a nondepressed phase indicated a vulnerability to future depressive symptoms (Rush, Weissenberger and Eaves, 1986; Simons et al., 1986). Thus, the hypothesis that dysfunctional beliefs pose a cognitive vulnerability to depression remains viable, but has not been demonstrated conclusively.

As discussed above, measuring schemas as cognitive *structures* (clustered or interconnected mental operations) rather than their expression in verbalized self-report may resolve existing dilemmas.

Environmental Factors in Depression
Several researchers (including Barnett and Gotlib, 1988; Coyne and Gotlib, 1983, 1986; Krantz, 1985) have criticized Beck's cognitive model of depression for minimizing the importance of environmental and social factors in the onset and maintenance of depression. These critics cite evidence that depressed individuals often face serious and numerous negative life events and also may confront unsupportive reactions to their depressions from spouses and other family members. These factors are often cited to challenge the notion that depressed individuals have distorted perceptions of their life situations, for their lives may indeed be as bad as they seem.

These criticisms led to two reformulations of Beck's model. One was the inclusion of personality types, autonomous and sociotropic (Beck, 1983; Beck, Epstein and Harrison, 1983), and the type of stressors likely to activate the dysfunctional beliefs of these types. Autonomous individuals are most sensitive to being thwarted or to failure. Sociotropic individuals are sensitive to personal rejection or loss of a relationship. Thus, Beck introduced the idea of a personality type interacting with a specifically meaningful life event which, in turn, can lead to depression.

The second refinement of Beck's theory of depression was the expansion of his initial model to include six separate models: cross-sectional, structural, stressor-vulnerability, reciprocal-interaction, psychobiological, and evolutionary (Beck, 1987a). The reciprocal-interaction model addresses the interpersonal dynamics contributing to depression. Beck argues that problematic interactions between patient and spouse, for example, reflect mutually reinforcing interactions of beliefs of the individuals. Moreover, the reciprocal-interaction model is most applicable to the maintenance of depression rather than its onset.

The areas of personality dimensions and social and environmental factors remain of great interest in the etiology of depression. The interactions of personality and cognitive variables with life events as risk factors for depression have not yet been adequately determined, but are the focus of much current research.

Conclusion

Beck developed a theory of psychopathology and a form of psychotherapy which stood in contrast to the dominant approaches of the 1960s: psychoanalysis and behaviorism. He was explicit about how to conduct Cognitive Therapy and devised tests of its efficacy. These innovations exposed Cognitive Therapy to much scrutiny and criticism for its theoretical differences with other modalities and, more recently, lack of support for causal features of the depression model. Over the years, several criticisms, such as the lack of attention to interpersonal and environmental factors in the onset of depression, have led to refinements of Beck's model (Beck, 1987a). Currently, there is support for many of the descriptive features of his model of depression.

The demonstrated efficacy of Cognitive Therapy in the treatment of unipolar depression and anxiety has led to further clinical applications which may test the limits of the therapy. As Cognitive Therapy is used to treat personality disorders and more chronic depressions, it becomes longer-term and employs the therapeutic relationship and emotive techniques to a greater extent. It will be interesting to see whether Cognitive Therapy maintains its distinctiveness in the future and whether it emerges, as Beck (1991b) predicts, as *the* integrative psychotherapy.

5

The Overall Influence of Aaron T. Beck

Overview

Aaron T. Beck has significantly and substantially influenced the practice and direction of psychotherapy in the last 30 years. His influence is so integrated with the cognitive movement in psychology that he both created innovations and responded to those of his colleagues. Thus, he shares with other cognitivists the credit for attention paid to clients' phenomenological views and for the elucidation of the role of cognition in behavior change and emotional well-being.

Beck has also made unique contributions to the field. At the theoretical level, he revised the way we think about psychopathology by shifting from a motivational model to an information-processing one. By emphasizing information processing instead of drives and hidden motivations, he directed attention to *how* psychological functioning operates during distress, not *why* people behave the way they do. Products of this information processing, thoughts and images, were accessible and available to clients as well as to therapists. This shifted the therapeutic relationship to a more collaborative balance, with therapist and client co-investigating both the content of cognitions and how they became activated. Thus, the therapeutic relationship changed to a partnership, and the nature of the data investigated changed from unconscious to conscious or preconscious with greater emphasis on present experience. Beck also introduced the therapeutic principle of empirically testing the patient's cognitions rather than providing alternative perspectives and coping self-statements, or philosophically debating the validity of the patient's beliefs.

Beck drew on a long history of psychotherapy, owing debts to Adler, Horney and Kelly as well as to Freud. The schema concept can be traced to Bartlett as well as to Piaget. Procedures used in Cognitive Therapy such as identifying common themes in a patient's emotional reactions, narratives, and imagery are similar to the psychoanalytic method. Similarly, Beck's Cognitive Therapy incorporated behavioral methods to create cognitive change. More recently, it has borrowed emotive techniques from Gestalt and other experiential therapies to alter cognitions.

When Cognitive Therapy was first developed, it stood in contrast to the two prevailing modalities of the day: psychoanalysis and behavior modification. In many respects, it was the bridge between them, for it provided a structured, focused, active therapy which considers the client's inner world.

Beck's work can also be appreciated as part of the self-help movement begun in the 1960s and 1970s. By engaging the client as a co-investigator, Beck demystified much of the process of therapy. As therapy progressed, clients were to assume greater responsibility for homework assignments and were explicitly taught to 'be their own therapists'.

As self-help books proliferated, Cognitive Therapy became known to the public through the works of David Burns (1980, 1985) and Gary Emery (1984), among others. Later, Beck's book on couples' therapy, *Love Is Never Enough* (1988b), described for the general public the Cognitive Therapy view of distressed relationships. Through such books, people could learn what to expect in psychotherapy and could teach themselves how to resolve some of their difficulties.

Theoretical Importance

As Arnold Lazarus (1979) wrote years ago, Beck's work shifted the emphasis away from the behavior part of the behavior–cognition–emotion triumvirate to the cognitive domain. At this point, the field of cognitive therapy in general and Beck's work in particular have generated several areas of theoretical pursuit. One has taken the phenomenological approach and combined it with evolutionary epistemology to advocate a constructivist framework as the unifying perspective for the cognitive therapies (Guidano and Liotti, 1985). This perspective differs from Beck's in many regards, but clearly owes its debt to Beck's scientific approach to the study of mental constructs or schemas, his emphasis on collaboration with the client, and his notion of clients arriving at new perspectives themselves, rather than having them imposed by the therapist.

A second theoretical pursuit currently emphasizes the role of emotion in psychological functioning. The study of affect is ascending in both the social and biological sciences (R. Lazarus, 1991), and for some cognitive theorists it commands much attention. Emotion is incorporated into cognitive theories as a source of information about the self in interaction with the environment

(L.S. Greenberg and Safran, 1984, 1987; Safran and Greenberg, 1986, 1987). It is also an action tendency which helps motivate potentially adaptive behavior (Safran and Greenberg, 1982a). Safran and his associates are the foremost proponents of using emotion in cognitive therapy and in theorizing about its role. They also argue in favor of the inclusion of motivation in a comprehensive model of psychology. Cognitive Therapy has traditionally rejected motivational concepts because of a tendency to equate them with drive metapsychology. It is argued that motivation now be reconceptualized and integrated into a new model (Safran and Greenberg, 1988). Like Guidano, Liotti, Mahoney and other constructivists, Safran and Greenberg are also interested in the evolutionary adaptiveness of behaviors and cognitive organization.

Safran and Segal (1990; Segal, 1988) have focused on the schema concept, particularly self-schemas and interpersonal schemas. Safran and Segal's (1990) book discusses many of the perceived shortcomings of Beck's Cognitive Therapy, such as lack of attention to affect and the therapeutic relationship, and attempts to rectify them in a new approach to therapy.

Interestingly, many of these criticisms about the lack of attention to traditional process variables come from psychoanalysis and newer, constructivist cognitive therapies. While they lack clear procedural guidelines as yet, these constructivist approaches resemble psychoanalysis in regard to techniques (such as 'streaming'), a more passive role for the therapist, and a growth and exploration orientation rather than a change orientation.

A third theoretical pursuit is the connection between psychotherapy and cognitive science. Cognitive–behavior therapy has been criticized for being too separate from basic science: that is, relying too much on hypothetical constructs like schemas (Hawkins et al., 1992). Beck's Cognitive Therapy shows a great deal of promise empirically, but some say the theory would benefit from a greater use of findings from cognitive psychology (Power, 1987). In addition, it is argued that cognitive psychology provides a framework and a vocabulary for the reconciliation of disparate psychotherapies, such as psychoanalysis and behavior therapy (Goldfried and Hayes, 1989a; Power, 1987; Safran and Greenberg, 1988).

While Beck's theory is not derived from cognitive science, it has been influenced by it. In contrast to critics, Hollon and Garber (1990) argue that Cognitive Therapy has been heavily influenced by research in basic social and cognitive psychology. They state,

Conceptually, it has drawn from cognitive theories of emotion to explain negative affective states, has adapted schema theory and the concept of heuristic information processing to explain conservatism in the face of contradictory evidence, has adopted the distinction between automatic and deliberate information processing, and has turned to attribution theory to organize the domain of specific beliefs. (Hollon and Garber, 1990: 69)

There are links between cognitive science and Cognitive Therapy which could be further developed. Beck's notions of cognitive vulnerability, information processing in various mood states, and the level of consciousness reflected in 'automatic thoughts' have research implications in cognitive science.

Clinical Influence

Cognitive Therapy as a Cognitive–behavior Therapy
As part of the general field of cognitive–behavior therapies, Beck's Cognitive Therapy has had enormous impact on how psycho-therapy is practiced today. Albert Ellis (1991) recently enumerated the therapeutic areas influenced by cognitive–behavior therapies, including self-help groups, bibliotherapy with self-help materials, stress management, sex therapy, couples' therapy, and school programs. The role of cognitions in psychological distress proliferates the pop psychology literature and appears in books covering a great range of topics, from relationships (for instance DeAngelis, 1992) to work issues (for example Bernstein and Rozen, 1989).

Because cognitive–behavior therapies are structured and didactic, they can be applied to groups in business and educational settings. Ellis advocates the use of cognitive–behavior therapy in schools in order to promote education in emotional health. Knaus (1974) has applied RET to the elementary school setting. Judy Beck concurs that Cognitive Therapy is helpful in educational settings and conducts workshops with school counselors on how to apply cognitive techniques in their work with students, teachers, and supervisors.

Beck's Cognitive Therapy, in particular, has been empirically tested and its effectiveness has made cognitive strategies appealing to practitioners of other modalities. Many cognitive techniques, whether labeled 'cognitive restructuring,' 'rational responding' or 'challenging automatic thoughts,' are borrowed by those using psychodynamic, existential–humanistic or transactional analysis models (A. Ellis, 1991). Beck (1987b) argues that other therapies may, in fact, produce change through cognitive restructuring.

Beck's Contributions to Psychotherapy Process

Contributions which are distinctly Beck's are now well integrated into the mainstream of assessment, treatment, and clinical research. His focus on current experience and the products of consciousness shifted the emphasis in psychotherapy to focus on the moment. Although Beck's own work with personality disorders now includes more attention to childhood memories, he provided a balance to the conceptualization of clinical problems. Moreover, he devised ways to intervene in the here-and-now to deal with those problems, however longstanding. Ruth Greenberg believes that it is Beck's ability to focus on the moment, to ask what someone's experience is right now, that will remain a part of therapeutic technique, regardless of one's persuasion.

Beck's technique of Socratic dialogue, of posing questions to uncover meanings and to examine evidence in support of or contradictory of existing beliefs, is now incorporated into other therapies. The adoption of this manner of working with clients reflects a greater collaboration with clients for gathering data and making changes. It has appeal to other modalities because it provides structure to the process of therapy without being overly directive or prescriptive with a client.

On the other hand, many insight-oriented therapists, dissatisfied with insight as a sufficient goal of therapy, want more direction and are eager to learn methods of change. They are attracted to Cognitive Therapy for the cognitive and behavioral intervention strategies it provides. Beck's therapy is a very active and structured form of therapy which appreciates broader dynamic issues. This combination of insight and action has changed our perception of therapy from both analytic and behavior modification models.

Beck's Contributions to Case Conceptualization

Cognitive variables, such as typical underlying assumptions or types of cognitive distortions, are commonly being included in descriptions of personality styles or syndromes like anxiety disorders. Thus, Beck's concept of cognitive profiles and his hypothesis of specificity are often used to describe psychological problems, regardless of the therapeutic modality to be used in treating them.

In addition, Beck's focus on cognitions rather than on diagnoses *per se* in case conceptualization allows greater flexibility in understanding cases and a greater range of points of intervention. Diagnoses are certainly vital and necessary, but are merely descriptive of overt behaviors or symptoms. Problems arise when patients are labeled as their diagnosis, or when a diagnosis is overgeneralized to draw unwarranted conclusions about the patient, including the etiology and dynamics of a disorder. Beck provides cognitive profiles of themes or beliefs common to a diagnosis, but also emphasizes the idiographic and idiosyncratic nature of underlying cognitions. This approach prevents a unitary or reductionistic explanation of symptoms or behavior. It also allows access to the cognitions influencing the observed behavior, thereby providing ways to intervene in an often complex constellation of symptoms.

Mechanisms of Change

Beck's collaborative empiricism changed the nature of the therapeutic relationship to one which encourages the client to play an increasingly active role, one that is highly compatible with the current consumer orientation to psychotherapy. The empirical testing of beliefs changed how psychotherapy is practiced in several ways. First, in Cognitive Therapy therapeutic change is presumed *not* to be due to rational or philosophic disputation, to historical insight, to a secure relationship with a therapist, or to new behaviors prescribed by a therapist. It is presumed to be due to the confrontation of old beliefs with disconfirmatory evidence gathered and evaluated by the client. Second, new perspectives and attitudes are developed by the client as a consequence of his or her own investigations; they are not substitute cognitions recommended by the therapist. Third, collaborative empiricism has adapted behavioral techniques for cognitive purposes. For example, the strategy of self-monitoring was extended to include thoughts, which could be modified in the situation. The behavioral technique of homework became a forum for experiments which tested the veridicality or function of beliefs. This use of homework made what happened between therapy sessions as important as what went on within therapy sessions.

Clinical Applications of Beck's Model

The demonstrated efficacy of Cognitive Therapy for the treatment of depression and anxiety disorders has led to further applications of the model to diverse problem areas and populations, both clinical and nonclinical. Current areas of clinical research and application include schizophrenia (Perris, 1989), eating disorders (Garner and Bemis, 1982), marital distress (Dattilio and Padesky, 1990; Epstein and Baucom, 1989), drug abuse (Beck et al., in press; Beck, Wright and Newman, 1992; Woody et al., 1984), and inpatient treatment of depression (Miller, Norman and Keitner, 1989; Wright et al., 1993). Cognitive Therapy strategies are appearing unexpectedly in such resources as Ross' (1989) book on multiple personality disorder.

James Pretzer endorses the applicability of Beck's model across a wide range of problems and says that modification of details of the model is sufficient to treat many disorders. For this reason, Cognitive Therapy is likely to have longevity. These newer applications await empirical support, but preliminary findings (for example Miller, Norman and Keitner, 1989; Miller et al., 1989) are promising.

Pretzer foresees three possibilities for the future of Beck's model. One, that he believes in, is the maintenance of Beck's model with adjustments appropriate to various clinical syndromes. A second possibility is the transformation of Cognitive Therapy into an offshoot; for example, he cites 'cognitive analytic therapy,' a combination of Cognitive Therapy and object relations therapy. [Anthony Ryle (Ryle and Cowmeadow, 1992) terms his therapy Cognitive Analytic Therapy.] Pretzer says, 'Actually, in Cognitive Therapy of Personality Disorders we're doing what they're talking about without having to get into all kinds of obscure theoretical gymnastics.' A third possibility, which Pretzer sees as less likely, is that an assortment of different offshoots of Cognitive Therapy will be developed. Thus, Cognitive Therapy would become splintered like the psychoanalytic schools.

Jeffrey Young has developed an offshoot of Cognitive Therapy called Schema-Focused Cognitive Therapy (Young, 1990; Young and Klosko, 1993; Young and Lindeman, 1992). Schema-Focused Cognitive Therapy differs from Beck's approach to treating personality disorders in several ways. First, Young expands Beck's model to incorporate the concepts of schema maintenance, schema avoidance, and schema compensation to describe how schemas function in a self-perpetuating manner. Second, Young identifies 16 'early maladaptive schemas' by content. Beck, in contrast, defines schemas as cognitive structures, the contents of which, one presumes, are more variable than Young's description. Early maladaptive schemas, however, are not on par with Beck's notion of underlying assumptions. According to Young, underlying assumptions are conditional ('If I can be perfect, then I am worthwhile'), but early maladaptive schemas are absolute ('I am worthless'). Finally, Schema-Focused Cognitive Therapy provides specific guidelines for working directly on schemas, employing emotive techniques as well as cognitive and behavioral ones. Young's approach differs from Beck's in the order of therapeutic interventions used. Beck's approach is to begin with more peripheral tasks while building a relationship with the client.

Pretzer and Fleming (1989), for example, recommend starting with interventions which do not require extensive self-disclosure on the part of the patient and initially using more behavioral than verbal interventions.

In contrast, Young sees the order of interventions in reverse of Beck's model. He uses emotive techniques much earlier in therapy to identify and trigger schemas in order to work directly on them. Then he uses interpersonal techniques within the therapeutic relationship followed by cognitive and behavioral techniques. Beck's model employs behavioral and cognitive techniques much sooner in therapy.

Young believes that the trend for psychotherapy integration is powerful. Thus, he predicts that Cognitive Therapy as it is currently practiced will continue to be distinctive and to be applied to many disorders for another decade. Then, following this period, Cognitive Therapy will be integrated with other models, including popular twelve-step programs like Alcoholics Anonymous and inner-child work like John Bradshaw's (1990).

In the meantime, Young sees Cognitive Therapy as being particularly important in the current era of health care cost containment. He says, 'A lot of the focus on treatment from the point of view of financial containment is going to focus primarily on symptoms and on immediate life crisis improvement. Short-term therapy is still very useful for that. I think to the degree that there continues to be the emphasis on alleviation of symptoms to get the person back to functioning rather than looking at their overall life happiness and satisfaction, the original Cognitive Therapy will play an important role in treatment. There are still very few people who can do it. There's a long way to go before the field of practice even catches up and integrates what's already available in Cognitive Therapy.'

Influence on Health Care Policy

Beck demonstrated that short-term psychotherapy can work. Research examining relapse rates of depressed patients successfully treated with Cognitive Therapy supports the contention that psychotherapy can provide stable improvement and reduce the risk of relapse (Blackburn et al., 1986; Evans et al., 1992; Kovacs et al., 1981; Shea et al., 1992; Simons et al., 1986).

Such findings obviously can affect health care policy in the United States, for efficacious treatments will be recommended by managed care systems and paid for by insurance companies and government programs. As an effective short-term therapy,

Cognitive Therapy is likely to dominate in a socio-economic climate which values shorter treatment and demonstrated efficacy.

Research Influence

The Use of Clinical Populations

Beck's research in cognitive theory and therapy gave credibility and validity to the cognitive movement in psychology, for it substantiated theories and models using clinical populations. Much of the psychological research had been done using college students. Beck's work with samples drawn from patient populations produced findings which bolstered the cognitive movement significantly.

Suicide Research

Beck's research has resulted in a nomenclature for suicidal behaviors as well as scales for assessing depression, suicide risk, and hopelessness. His work in the area of suicide has led to a reconceptualization of suicide risk as a continuous variable, from brief and fleeting ideation to overt self-destructive behavior. The emergence of hopelessness as a key psychological risk factor in the etiology of suicide has directed clinical efforts toward ameliorating that variable through both Cognitive Therapy (Rush et al., 1982) and problem-solving training (Patsiokas and Clum, 1985). His assessment scales for suicide risk are used in a variety of settings worldwide, regardless of the orientation of the medical or psychotherapeutic staff. These scales, particularly the Beck Depression Inventory, have also been used in hundreds of research studies.

In addition, Beck and others have identified cognitive characteristics of suicidal individuals (Weishaar and Beck, 1990, 1992). Cognitive differences have been found to exist between suicidal and nonsuicidal persons even when level of depression and degree of psychopathology are controlled. Moreover, these cognitive characteristics persist between suicidal crises and may predispose the individual to future suicidality.

These findings change the way we conduct therapy with suicidal individuals. The traditional manner of responding to suicide risk is to treat each crisis and then return to the work that was interrupted by the suicidal emergency (T. Ellis, 1987). Instead, we now know that the cognitive characteristics which increase suicide risk, such as poor problem-solving skills or dichotomous thinking, must be addressed systematically and directly throughout the course of therapy, not just at the time of crisis.

Generating Research

Beck has worked at generating empirical findings and at developing an overarching theory of psychotherapy. By example, he has encouraged other orientations to specify therapeutic procedures and to operationalize them for empirical testing. Beck's hypotheses have generated a plethora of research studies concerning treatment efficacy, therapeutic process, and conceptual models. Some of these studies have been conducted by Beck's associates, but many have been conducted by research institutes and individuals who are not especially cognitive in orientation. Perhaps because Beck has been explicit about how Cognitive Therapy is conducted, his work has been more exposed to scrutiny and criticism than less codified approaches. Nevertheless, such scrutiny has led to constructive psychotherapy research and theoretical advances. In less than 30 years, Cognitive Therapy research has developed a model of depression and a corresponding therapy, tested the therapy's efficacy, made new applications of the therapeutic model, and now is returning to the viability of the theory.

Associates say that Beck has worked hard to foster the research endeavors of his students. As a consequence, research in cognitive theory and Cognitive Therapy outcome studies have proliferated. Beck's former students are working on theoretical constructs, clinical applications of Beck's model, and newer forms of cognitive therapy.

Shaw and Segal (1988) identify three current research areas for Cognitive Therapy: (1) the viability of the model, including variables which would enhance its explanatory and predictive capacities; (2) the ways in which cognitive and personality variables interact with stressful life events in the etiology of depression; and (3) the identification of those at risk for relapse.

The viability of the existing model pertains to the extent to which therapeutic change is explained by currrent cognitive theory. Hollon and Garber (1990) pinpoint five pertinent issues related to the model. First, it is not clear whether Cognitive Therapy works by altering existing schemas or by developing compensatory skills. Second, it is not known whether depressed individuals differ from nondepressed persons in the way they process information or just in the content of their thoughts and images. A third question is whether Cognitive Therapy works by teaching depressed persons to think like nondepressed persons or by some other mechanism. Fourth, it is unclear whether different classes of cognition play different roles in the etiology, maintenance, and treatment of depression. For example, causal attributions may play a dominant role in the etiology and prevention of depression, whereas negative expectations may play a more important role in the maintenance and treatment of depression. Last, it is unknown how idiosyncratic beliefs and meaning systems are established. They are only presumed to be derived from life experience. This area, the authors say, will require interdisciplinary research among clinical, social cognitive, and developmental psychologists. Biological psychiatry may also be involved in understanding the relationship between early life experience and subsequent vulnerability to depression. Dr David Kupfer of the University of Pittsburgh says, 'Early emotional stressors may affect neuron development, which can lead to a depression when you are under great stress decades later' (Goleman, 1992: C 13).

Another area of research concerns the preventive aspects of Cognitive Therapy. A number of studies suggest that Cognitive Therapy reduces risk for relapse to depression (Hollon and Garber, 1990; Evans et al., 1992; Shea et al., 1992). Building on these findings that Cognitive Therapy appears effective in secondary prevention (among those who have had an episode of depression), Drs Hollon and Seligman and associates at the University of Pennsylvania will study whether Cognitive Therapy can actually prevent the onset of a first episode of depression among young people making the transition to college. This sample of first-year college students is entering a major life change and a percentage can anticipate difficulties. Investigators, says Hollon, 'will try to give them at the outset the kinds of skills and capacities that you hope to provide clinical samples with Cognitive Therapy and see if that is effective in reducing the rate of depression in that group of normal individuals.' Dr Seligman, the principal investigator of the study, is proposing a similar project with school-age children.

The Future of Psychotherapy

In a recent article, Beck and Haaga (1992) predict five trends in psychotherapy: (1) psychotherapy will confront the issue of specificity versus nonspecificity at several levels of analysis; (2) psychotherapy will respond to continued pressure for research and accountability; (3) psychotherapy will make greater connections with basic psychological science; (4) delivery systems for psychotherapeutic knowledge will become more diverse; and (5) different systems of psychotherapy will continue to influence one another. They discuss the future of Cognitive Therapy in regard to how it articulates with each of these areas.

Specificity

The debate between the principles of specificity and nonspecificity occurs in three areas. The first is whether patients are best served by a primary diagnosis representing a discrete pattern of symptoms or by more general traits or psychological predispositions. A second area is whether it is possible or even desirable to match presenting problems with interventions aimed at a particular channel (affect, behavior, or cognition). A third area concerns cognitive correlates of psychological well-being: are they general or particular to each situation? Bandura's (1986) social cognitive theory emphasizes the situation- or task-specificity of self-efficacy expectations. Yet, other research findings, such as dispositional optimism (Scheier and Carver, 1987) and balances between positive and negative thinking (Schwartz and Garamoni, 1989), suggest more generic cognitive factors in psychological functioning.

Beck introduced specific cognitive profiles of personality disorders (Beck, Freeman and Associates, 1990) and other diagnoses (Beck and Weishaar, 1989b; Clark, Beck and Stewart, 1990). Yet, he supports a model proposed by Ingram and Kendall (1987; Ingram, 1990) which proposes that some cognitive factors (such as excessive self-focused attention) are common across diagnoses and others (such as cognitive themes of loss in depression and threat in anxiety) differentiate disorders.

Research and Accountability

As long as mental health services are provided as part of a health care model as opposed to a personal growth model, psychotherapy will operate with the pressure of accountability and cost containment. In addition to this socio-economic context, public awareness of psychological disorders and the trend toward a consumer view of health care require accountability by service providers.

As mentioned above, the short-term, structured and focused nature of Cognitive Therapy makes it economically efficient. Moreover, its demonstrated efficacy supports its selection as a treatment for depression and anxiety disorders. Beck and Haaga (1992) predict increased research on newer applications of Cognitive Therapy as well as refinements of the cognitive model to explain mechanisms of therapeutic change.

Beck says, 'I think there will be a consolidation of the therapies. Cognitive Therapy is the integrative therapy; it's the one that's closest to the advances of psychology itself, whether it's cognitive psychology or social psychology. I think ten years from now it should be the predominant therapy. By then it probably will have absorbed behavior therapy. And by then, I think, because of sociological forces, the psychodynamic approaches will be less powerful and less popular.'

Connections with Cognitive Science

Traditional comparative outcome studies and psychotherapy process research are time-consuming ways in which to study how to help people change. Haaga and Davison (1989) argue that these methods are insufficient. Research in cognitive psychology and social psychology could elucidate how people originate and modify affect-laden beliefs, especially those about the self and relationships (Beck and Haaga, 1992). This point is also made by Power (1987) and by Hollon and Garber (1990).

Disseminating Psychotherapeutic Knowledge

Beck and Haaga also predict continuing diversification of the ways in which people receive psychotherapeutic knowledge. Self-help groups and bibliotherapy will continue to be important alternatives of exposing people to therapy. Cognitive Therapy will also continue to change by becoming longer-term for more difficult problems and perhaps by becoming more oriented towards personal growth and self-exploration, following the constructivist movement. These changes in Cognitive Therapy will have to gain both theoretical and empirical support.

The Movement for Psychotherapy Integration

Within the field of cognitive therapy the dominant trend is to expand the conceptual model to include emotion, developmental factors, and nonconscious cognitive processes, and to place greater emphasis on the therapeutic relationship as a vehicle for change.

Outside cognitive therapy, yet inclusive of it, is the movement towards psychotherapy integration. The history of the psychotherapy integration movement is well-documented by Arnkoff and Glass (1992). They cite three trends in psychotherapy in the 1970s which contributed to a growing interest in eclectic and integrative therapy: (1) a general dissatisfaction clinically with any single school; (2) the failure of any one school to dominate outcome research for all disorders; and (3) the need for accountability and responsiveness to third-party payments.

Paul Wachtel (1977) and Marvin Goldfried (1980b) are recognized as being the primary initiators of the modern integrationist movement. Wachtel's book *Psychoanalysis and Behavior Therapy: Toward an Integration* describes the use of behavioral strategies such as homework and imaginal exposure to aid clients' explorations of dynamic themes. Both Wachtel, trained in analytic therapy, and Goldfried, originally trained in psychodynamic psychotherapy and later a behavior therapist, employed principles from behavior therapy and psychodynamic psychotherapy in their private practices (Arnkoff and Glass, 1992). Recently, Goldfried (1992) wrote of the personal dilemma he experienced years earlier of trying to teach students in clinical demonstrations using only behavioral interventions. Thus, the movement towards psychotherapy integration gained momentum as a consequence of the search for clinical tools and unifying principles of psychotherapy.

It should be pointed out that Arnold Lazarus (1981, 1985) developed Multimodal Therapy based on 'technical eclecticism,' the use of empirically valid techniques, to address any of seven areas: behavior, affect, sensation, imagery, cognition, interpersonal relationships, and biological functioning. Multimodal Therapy employs techniques from various therapies (such as Rogerian reflection, Gestalt empty chair exercises), but does not integrate these therapies at a theoretical level.

It should also be noted that the integrationist movement does not assume equivalence of therapies (Goldfried and Hayes, 1989a, 1989b). However, treatment efficacy may be increased by employing a clinically flexible approach. For example, one might incorporate Gestalt techniques into Cognitive Therapy to treat a depressed patient who has made little progress with less emotional techniques (Arnkoff, 1981; Haaga, 1986).

Just as Cognitive Therapy is influenced by other orientations to incorporate interpersonal theories and psychodynamic foci such as the therapeutic relationship and unconscious processes, so too does Cognitive Therapy influence psychotherapy integration. Albert Ellis (1991) has argued that most integrative therapies are heavily cognitive–behavioral. Arnold Lazarus uses primarily cognitive and behavioral interventions in Multimodal Therapy because of their demonstrated efficacy (Arnkoff and Glass, 1992).

Beck and Haaga (1992) see three contributions Cognitive Therapy makes to psychotherapy integration. The first is that any model of psychopathology and psychotherapy will have to consider the role of cognitive processing. The second is that Cognitive Therapy's use of a range of therapeutic techniques from different modalities demonstrates how techniques can be integrated. The third contribution is the conceptualization of the therapeutic relationship as collaborative empiricism, which requires the therapist to work with the patient to arrive at personally meaningful evaluations of negative assumptions, rather than suggesting substitute cognitions.

Alford and Norcross (1991) cite Cognitive Therapy along with

RET and Multimodal Therapy as having integrative components. 'Cognition is a bridge across diverse orientations and Beck's cognitive therapy is one exemplar in which this has occurred' (Alford and Norcross, 1991: 187). They go on to say that Cognitive Therapy emphasizes a common factors approach, which acknowledges common elements in different therapy orientations, but reformulates these factors into the language of Beck's model. In addition, Cognitive Therapy is theoretically integrative in an historical sense and maintains a stance of collaboration rather than confrontation with contemporary models.

Beck believes that Cognitive Therapy can serve as *the* integrative psychotherapy because of its blend of techniques and its cohesive theory (Beck, 1991b). He maintains that other schools of psychotherapy offer little to add to the explanatory power or empirical validity of Cognitive Therapy. Recent changes in his theory have come, he says, not so much from other systems of psychotherapy, but from cognitive psychology, social psychology, and evolutionary biology (Beck, 1991b). He credits Mahoney (1981) and Weimer (1979) with his reconsideration of nonconscious cognitive processing. Beck currently regards cognition as comprised of parallel systems which vary greatly in their mode of operation and the accessibility of their content (Beck, 1991b; Beck, Freeman and Associates, 1990).

The Continuing Evolution of Beck's Cognitive Therapy

Beck has been devoting increased attention to the evolutionary origins of depression, anxiety, and personality. He corresponds with ethologists and primatologists about social behavior of nonhuman primates. He also maintains correspondence with psychiatrists, anthropologists and others interested in the relevance of evolutionary biology to psychotherapy. Beck is especially drawn to the work of Darwin (1872) for concepts of adaptation and evolutionary survival principles. The evolutionary significance of various syndromes places greater emphasis on biology and how it interacts with psychology than has been previously considered by psychotherapy. Implications for clinical interventions have yet to be explored.

It is interesting to note that shortly before his death in 1990, Bowlby completed a psychobiography of Darwin (Bowlby, 1991) which discusses Darwin's chronic anxiety and how it compelled his prolific scholarship. Beck has commonalities with both Bowlby and Darwin.

Both Bowlby and Beck rejected much of psychoanalytic theory.

In his classic three-volume series, *Attachment and Loss* (1969–1980), Bowlby attempted to create a theory of human development that was consistent with Darwinian theory, particularly the concept that attachment and dependence on parents and others by children are normal and not neurotic, as Freud proposed (Sulloway, 1991).

Beck modified his own model of depression to recognize the importance of Bowlby's attachment theory (Beck, 1987a). He also uses concepts from Darwinian theory to explain the existence of depression (Beck 1987a), anxiety (Beck, 1991a; Beck, Emery and Greenberg, 1985), and personality disorders (Beck, Freeman and Associates, 1990).

It is striking that Beck has much in common with Bowlby's description of Darwin's intellectual style. Darwin is described as having reverence for the opinions of others, but being quite capable of challenging authority and thinking for himself. In addition, Darwin had such respect for negative evidence that there were few objections to his theory that he had not already anticipated and attempted to answer. Finally, Darwin was able to enlist other scientists as fellow collaborators in his own research projects. While it is not argued here that Beck's similarities to Darwin are derived from unstable attachments in childhood, their common traits are noteworthy, as are the links among Darwin and his devotees, Bowlby and Beck.

Now in his seventies, Aaron Beck continues to be a prolific writer and researcher, still involved in the training of therapists and in the dissemination of the cognitive model. He says he does not know the limits of Cognitive Therapy in terms of its applications, that he is still surprised when he learns of new problems treated with Cognitive Therapy. Thus, Beck sees Cognitive Therapy as still being full of promise. The researcher in him, however, is continually testing that promise.

A Select Bibliography of the Works of Aaron T. Beck

(in chronological order)

Beck, A.T. (1961) 'A systematic investigation of depression', *Comprehensive Psychiatry*, 2(3): 163–170.

Beck, A.T., Ward, C.H., Mendelson, M., Mock, J. and Erbaugh, J. (1961) 'An inventory for measuring depression', *Archives of General Psychiatry*, 4: 561–571.

Beck, A.T. and Ward, C.H. (1961) 'Dreams of depressed patients: Characteristic themes in manifest content', *Archives of General Psychiatry*, 5: 462–467.

Beck, A.T. (1963) 'Thinking and depression: 1. Idiosyncratic content and cognitive distortions', *Archives of General Psychiatry*, 9: 324–333.

Beck, A.T. (1964) 'Thinking and depression: 2. Theory and therapy', *Archives of General Psychiatry*, 10: 561–571.

Beck, A.T. (1967) *Depression: Clinical, Experimental, and Theoretical Aspects.* New York: Harper and Row.

Beck, A.T. (1970) 'Cognitive Therapy: Nature and relation to behavior therapy', *Behavior Therapy*, 1(2): 184–200.

Beck, A.T., Davis, J.H., Frederick, C.J., Perlin, S., Pokorny, A.D., Schulman, R.E., Seiden, R.H. and Wittlin, B.J. (1973) 'Classification and nomenclature', in H.L.P. Resnik and B.C. Hathorne (eds), *Suicide Prevention in the Seventies.* Washington, DC: US Government Printing Office. pp. 7–12.

Beck, A.T., Laude, R. and Bohnert, M. (1974) 'Ideation components of anxiety neurosis', *Archives of General Psychiatry*, 31: 319–325.

Beck, A.T., Weissman, A., Lester, D. and Trexler, L. (1974) 'The measurement of pessimism: The hopelessness scale', *Journal of Consulting and Clinical Psychology*, 42(6): 861–865.

Beck, A.T., Kovacs, M. and Weissman, A. (1975) 'Hopelessness and suicidal behavior: An overview', *Journal of the American Medical Association*, 234: 1146–1149.

Beck, A.T. (1976) *Cognitive Therapy and the Emotional Disorders.* New York: New American Library.

Rush, A.J., Beck, A.T., Kovacs, M. and Hollon, S.D. (1977) 'Comparative efficacy of cognitive therapy and pharmacotherapy in the treatment of depressed out-patients', *Cognitive Therapy and Research*, 1(1): 7–37.

Beck, A.T., Kovacs, M. and Weissman, A. (1979) 'Assessment of suicidal intention: The scale for suicidal ideation', *Journal of Consulting and Clinical Psychology*, 47(2): 343–352.

Beck, A.T., Rush, A.J., Shaw, B.F. and Emery, G. (1979) *Cognitive Therapy of Depression.* New York: The Guilford Press. Also published in Chichester, England: John Wiley & Sons Ltd, 1980.

Kovacs, M., Rush, A.J., Beck, A.T. and Hollon, S.D. (1981) 'Depressed out-patients treated with cognitive therapy or pharmacotherapy: a one year follow-up', *Archives of General Psychiatry*, 38: 33–39.

Beck, A.T. (1983) 'Cognitive therapy of depression: New perspectives', in P. Clayton and J. Barrett (eds), *Treatment of Depression: Old Controversies and New Approaches*. New York: Raven Press. pp. 265–284.

Beck, A.T. and Emery, G. with Greenberg, R.L. (1985) *Anxiety Disorders and Phobias: A Cognitive Perspective*. New York: Basic Books.

Beck, A.T., Steer, R.A., Kovacs, M. and Garrison, B. (1985) 'Hopelessness and eventual suicide: A ten-year prospective study of patients hospitalized with suicidal ideation', *American Journal of Psychiatry*, 142(5): 559–563.

Beck, A.T. (1987) 'Cognitive models of depression', *The Journal of Cognitive Psychotherapy: An International Quarterly*, 1(1): 5–37.

Beck, A.T. (1988) *Love is Never Enough*. New York: Harper and Row.

Beck, A.T., Freeman, A. and Associates (1990) *Cognitive Therapy of Personality Disorders*. New York: The Guilford Press.

Beck, A.T., Brown, G., Berchick, R.J., Stewart, B. and Steer, R.A. (1990) 'Relationship between hopelessness and ultimate suicide: A replication with psychiatric outpatients', *American Journal of Psychiatry*, 147: 190–195.

Beck, A.T. (1991) 'Cognitive therapy: A 30-year retrospective', *American Psychologist*, 46(4): 368–375.

Beck, A.T. (1991) 'Cognitive therapy as the integrative therapy: Comments on Alford and Norcross', *Journal of Psychotherapy Integration*, 1: 191–198.

References

Abramson, L.Y., Metalsky, G.I. and Alloy, L.B. (1989) 'Hopelessness depression: A theory-based subtype of depression', *Psychological Review*, 96 (2): 358–372.

Abramson, L.Y., Seligman, M.E.P. and Teasdale, J.D. (1978) 'Learned helplessness in humans: Critique and reformulation', *Abnormal Psychology*, 87: 49–74.

Adler, A. (1927) *Understanding Human Nature*. New York: Garden City.

Alford, B.A. and Carr, S.M. (1992) 'Cognition and classical conditioning in panic disorder: A Beckian integrative perspective', *the Behavior Therapist*, 15 (6): 143–147.

Alford, B.A. and Norcross, J.C. (1991) 'Cognitive Therapy as integrative therapy', *Journal of Psychotherapy Integration*, 1: 175–190.

Alloy, L.B. and Abramson, L.Y. (1979) 'Judgment of contingency in depressed and non-depressed students: Sadder but wiser?', *Journal of Experimental Psychology: General*, 108: 441–485.

American Psychologist, (1990) 'Distinguished Scientific Award for the Applications of Psychology: 1989', 45(4): 458–460.

Arnkoff, D.B. (1981) 'Flexibility in practicing cognitive therapy', in G. Emery, S.D. Hollon and R.C. Bedrosian (eds), *New Directions in Cognitive Therapy*. New York: The Guilford Press. pp. 203–223.

Arnkoff, D.B. and Glass, C.R. (1992) 'Cognitive therapy and psychotherapy integration', in D.K. Freedheim (ed.), *History of Psychotherapy: A Century of Change*. Washington, DC: American Psychological Association. pp. 657–694.

Baars, B.J. (1986) *The Cognitive Revolution in Psychology*. New York: The Guilford Press.

Bandura, A. (1969) *Principles of Behavior Modification*. New York: Holt, Rinehart & Winston.

Bandura, A. (1971) 'Vicarious and self-reinforcement processes', in R. Glaser (ed.), *The Nature of Reinforcement*. New York: Academic Press. pp. 228–278.

Bandura, A. (1974) 'Behavior theory and the models of man', *American Psychologist*, 29: 859–869.

Bandura, A. (1977a) 'Self-efficacy: Toward a unifying theory of behavioral change', *Psychological Review*, 84: 191–215.

Bandura, A. (1977b) *Social Learning Theory*. Englewood Cliffs, New Jersey: Prentice-Hall.

Bandura, A. (1986) *Social Foundations of Thought and Action: A Social Cognitive Theory*. Englewood Cliffs, New Jersey: Prentice-Hall.

Barnett, P.A. and Gotlib, I.H. (1988) 'Psychosocial functioning and depression: Distinguishing among antecedents, concomitants, and consequences', *Psychological Bulletin*, 104 (1): 97–126.

Baron, J., Baron, J.H., Barber, J.P. and Nolen-Hoeksema, S. (1990) 'Rational thinking as a goal of therapy', *Journal of Cognitive Psychotherapy: An International Quarterly*, 4 (3), 293–302.

Bartlett, F.C. (1932) *Remembering*. New York: Columbia University Press.

Baucom, D.H. (1985) 'Enhancing behavioral marital therapy with cognitive restructuring and emotional expressiveness training', paper presented at the 19th Annual Convention of the Association for Advancement of Behavior Therapy, Houston, November 1985.

Baucom, D.H. (1989) 'The role of cognitions in behavioral marital therapy: Current status and future directions', *the Behavior Therapist*, 12, (1), 3–6.

Baucom, D.H. and Lester, G.W. (1986) 'The usefulness of cognitive restructuring as an adjunct to behavioral marital therapy', *Behavior Therapy*, 17: 385–403.

Baucom, D.H., Sayers, S.L. and Sher, T.G. (1990) 'Supplementing behavioral marital therapy with cognitive restructuring and emotional expressiveness training: An outcome investigation', *Journal of Consulting and Clinical Psychology*, 58: 636–645.

Beck, A.T. (1963) 'Thinking and depression: I. Idiosyncratic content and cognitive distortions', *Archives of General Psychiatry*, 9: 324–333.

Beck, A.T. (1964) 'Thinking and depression: II. Theory and therapy', *Archives of General Psychiatry*, 10: 561–571.

Beck, A.T. (1967) *Depression: Clinical, Experimental, and Theoretical Aspects* New York: Harper and Row. Republished as *Depression: Causes and Treatment*. Philadelphia: University of Pennsylvania Press, 1972.

Beck, A.T. (1970a) 'Cognitive therapy: Nature and relation to behavior therapy', *Behavior Therapy*, 1: 184–200.

Beck, A.T. (1970b) 'The role of fantasies in psychotherapy and psychopathology', *Journal of Nervous and Mental Disease*, 150: 3–17.

Beck, A.T. (1976) *Cognitive Therapy and the Emotional Disorders*. New York: New American Library.

Beck, A.T. (1983) 'Cognitive therapy of depression: New perspectives', in P.J. Clayton and J.E. Barrett (eds), *Treatment of Depression: Old Controversies and New Approaches*. New York: Raven Press. pp. 265–284.

Beck, A.T. (1984) 'Cognition and therapy: Letter to the editor', *Archives of General Psychiatry*, 41: 1112–1114.

Beck, A.T. (1985) 'Cognitive therapy, behavior therapy, psychoanalysis and pharmacotherapy: A cognitive continuum', in M.J. Mahoney and A. Freeman (eds), *Cognition and Psychotherapy*. New York: Plenum Press. pp. 325–347.

Beck, A.T. (1987a) 'Cognitive models of depression', *Journal of Cognitive Psychotherapy, An International Quarterly*, 1 (1): 5–37.

Beck, A.T. (1987b) 'Cognitive therapy', in J. Zeig (ed.), *Evolution of Psychotherapy*. New York: Brunner/Mazel. pp. 149–163.

Beck, A.T. (1988a) 'Cognitive approaches to panic disorder: Theory and therapy', in S. Rachman and J. Maser (eds), *Panic: Psychological Perspectives*. Hillside, New Jersey: Erlbaum. pp. 91–110.

Beck, A.T. (1988b) *Love is Never Enough*. New York: Harper and Row.

Beck, A.T (1991a) 'Cognitive Therapy: A 30-year retrospective', *American Psychologist*, 46 (4): 368–375.

Beck, A.T. (1991b) 'Cognitive therapy as the integrative therapy: Comments on Alford and Norcross', *Journal of Psychotherapy Integration*, 1: 191–198.

Beck, A.T. and Greenberg, R. (1988) 'Cognitive therapy of panic disorder', in A.J. Frances and R.E. Hales (eds), *Review of Psychiatry, Vol. 7*. Washington, DC: American Psychiatric Press. pp. 571–583.

Beck, A.T. and Haaga, D. (1992) 'The future of cognitive therapy', *Psychotherapy*, 29 (1): 34–38.

Beck, A.T. and Mahoney, M.J. (1979) 'Schools of thought: A comment on Wolpe's "Cognition and causation in behavior and its therapy"', *American Psychologist*, 34 (1): 93–98.

Beck, A.T. and Steer, R.A. (1987) *Manual for the Revised Beck Depression Inventory*. San Antonio, TX: Psychological Corporation.

Beck, A.T. and Stewart, B. (1989) 'The self-concept as a risk factor in patients who kill themselves', Unpublished manuscript, Philadelphia, PA, University of Pennsylvania.

Beck, A.T. and Weishaar, M.E. (1989a) 'Cognitive Therapy', in R.J. Corsini and D. Wedding (eds), *Current Psychotherapies*. Itasca, IL: F.E. Peacock Publishers, Inc. pp. 285–320.

Beck, A.T. and Weishaar, M.E. (1989b) 'Cognitive therapy', in A. Freeman, K.M. Simon, L.E. Beutler and H. Arkowitz (eds), *Comprehensive Handbook of Cognitive Therapy*. New York: Plenum Press. pp. 21–36.

Beck, A.T. and Young, J.E. (1985) 'Depression', in D.H. Barlow (ed.), *Clinical Handbook of Psychological Disorders*. New York: The Guilford Press. pp. 206–244.

Beck, A.T. and Emery, G. with Greenberg, R.L. (1985) *Anxiety Disorders and Phobias: A Cognitive Perspective*. New York: Basic Books.

Beck, A.T., Epstein, N. and Harrison, R. (1983) 'Cognition, attitudes and personality dimensions in depression', *British Journal of Cognitive Psychotherapy*, 1: 1–16.

Beck, A.T., Freeman, A. and Associates (1990) *Cognitive Therapy of Personality Disorders*. New York: The Guilford Press.

Beck, A.T., Kovacs, M. and Weissman, A. (1979) 'Assessment of suicidal intention: The scale for suicide ideation', *Journal of Consulting and Clinical Psychology*, 47 (2): 343–352.

Beck, A.T., Laude, R. and Bohnert, M. (1974) 'Ideation components of anxiety neurosis', *Archives of General Psychiatry*, 31: 456–459.

Beck, A.T., Lester, D. and Albert, N. (1973) 'Suicidal wishes and symptoms of depression', *Psychological Reports*, 33: 770.

Beck, A.T., Schuyler, D. and Herman, I. (1974) 'Development of Suicidal Intent Scales', in A.T. Beck, H.C.P. Resnik and D.J. Lettieri (eds). *The Prediction of Suicide*. Bowie, MD: Charles Press. pp. 45–56.

Beck, A.T., Wright, F.D. and Newman, C.F. (1992) 'Cocaine abuse', in A. Freeman and F.M. Dattilio (eds), *Comprehensive Casebook of Cognitive Therapy*. New York: Plenum Press. pp. 185–192.

Beck, A.T., Ward, C.H., Mendelson, M., Mock, J. and Erbaugh, J. (1961) 'An inventory for measuring depression', *Archives of General Psychiatry*, 4: 561–571.

Beck, A.T., Davis, J.H., Frederick, C.J., Perlin, S., Pokorny, A.D., Schulman, R.E., Seiden, R.H. and Wittlin, B.J. (1973) 'Classification and nomenclature', in H.C.P. Resnik and B.C. Hathorne (eds), *Suicide Prevention in the Seventies* (DHEW Publication No. HSM 72-9054 pp. 7–12). Washington, DC: US Government Printing Office.

Beck, A.T., Weissman, A., Lester, D. and Trexler, L. (1974) 'The measurement of pessimism: The hopelessness scale', *Journal of Consulting and Clinical Psychology*, 42 (16): 861–865.

Beck, A.T., Rush, A.J., Shaw, B.F. and Emery, G. (1979) *Cognitive Therapy of Depression*. New York: The Guilford Press.

Beck, A.T., Steer, R.A., Kovacs, M. and Garrison, B. (1985) 'Hopelessness and eventual suicide: A ten-year prospective study of patients hospitalized with suicidal ideation', *American Journal of Psychiatry*, 142 (5): 559–563.

Beck, A.T., Riskind, J.H., Brown, G. and Sherrod, A. (1986, June) 'A comparison of likelihood estimates for imagined positive and negative outcomes in anxiety and depression', paper presented at the Annual Meeting of the Society for Psychotherapy Research, Wellesley, MA.

Beck, A.T., Brown, G., Steer, R.A., Eidelson, J.I. and Riskind, J.H. (1987) 'Differentiating anxiety and depression: A test of the cognitive content-specificity hypothesis', *Journal of Abnormal Psychology*, 96: 179–183.

Beck, A.T., Brown, G., Berchick, R.J., Stewart, B.L. and Steer, R.A. (1990a) 'Relationship between hopelessness and ultimate suicide: A replication with psychiatric outpatients', *American Journal of Psychiatry*, 147 (2): 190–195.

Beck, A.T., Steer, R.A., Epstein, N. and Brown, G. (1990b) 'The Beck Self-Concept Test', *Psychological Assessment: A Journal of Consulting and Clinical Psychology*, 2 (2): 191–197.

Beck, A.T., Wright, F.D., Newman, C.F. and Liese, B.S. (in press) *Cognitive Therapy of Substance Abuse*. New York: The Guilford Press.

Beidel, D.C. and Turner, S.M. (1986) 'A critique of the theoretical bases of cognitive–behavioral theories and therapy', *Clinical Psychology Review*, 6: 177–197.

Bernstein, A.J. and Rozen, S.C. (1989) *Dinosaur Brains: Dealing with All Those Impossible People at Work*. New York: John Wiley & Sons.

Bjorklund, D.F. and Green, B.L. (1992) 'The adaptive nature of cognitive immaturity', *American Psychologist*, 47 (1): 46–54.

Blackburn, I.M. and Bishop, S. (1983) 'Changes in cognition with pharmacotherapy and cognitive therapy', *British Journal of Psychiatry*, 143: 609–617.

Blackburn, I.M., Eunson, K.M. and Bishop, S. (1986) 'A two-year naturalistic follow-up of depressed patients treated with cognitive therapy, pharmacotherapy and a combination of both', *Journal of Affective Disorders*, 10: 67–75.

Blackburn, I.M., Roxborough, H.M., Muir, W.J., Glabus, M. and Blackwood, D.H.R. (1990) 'Perceptual and psychological dysfunction in depression', *Psychological Medicine*, 20: 95–103.

Bower, G.H. (1981) 'Mood and memory', *American Psychologist*, 36: 129–148.

Bowlby, J. (1969) *Attachment and Loss: Volume I: Attachment*. New York: Basic Books. Second edition (1982) London: Hogarth Press.

Bowlby, J. (1973) *Attachment and Loss: Volume II: Separation, Anxiety, and Anger*. New York: Basic Books.

Bowlby, J. (1977) 'The making and breaking of affectional bonds', *British Journal of Psychiatry*, 130: 201–210.

Bowlby, J. (1979) *The Making and Breaking of Affectional Bonds*. London: Tavistock.

Bowlby, J. (1980) *Attachment and Loss: Volume III: Loss, Sadness, and Depression*. New York: Basic Books.

Bowlby, J. (1991) *Charles Darwin: A New Life*. New York: Norton.

Bradley, B.P. and Mathews, A. (1988) 'Memory bias in recovered clinical depressives', *Cognition and Emotion*, 2: 235–245.

Bradshaw, J. (1990) *Homecoming: Reclaiming and Championing Your Inner Child*. New York: Bantam.

Breslow, R., Kocsis, J. and Belkin, B. (1981) 'Contribution of the depressive perspective to memory function in depression', *American Journal of Psychiatry*, 138: 227–230.

Brewin, C.R. (1989) 'Cognitive change processes in psychotherapy', *Psychological Review*, 96 (3): 379–394.

Brown, G. and Beck, A.T. (1989) 'The role of imperatives in psychotherapy: A reply to Ellis', *Cognitive Therapy and Research*, 13 (4): 315–321.

Bry, B.H. (1991) 'B.F. Skinner for behavior therapists', *the Behavior Therapist*, 14 (1): 9–10.

Burns, D. (1980) *Feeling Good: The New Mood Therapy*. New York: New American Library.

Burns, D.D. (1985) *Intimate Connections: The Clinically Proven Program for Making Close Friends and Finding a Loving Partner*. New York: New American Library.

Butler, G. and Mathews, A. (1983) 'Cognitive processes in anxiety', *Advances in Behaviour Research and Therapy*, 5: 51–62.

Butler, G., Fennel, M., Robson, P. and Gilder, M. (1991) 'A comparison of behavior therapy and cognitive therapy in the treatment of generalized anxiety disorder', *Journal of Consulting and Clinical Psychology*, 59: 167–175.

Caire, J.B. (1992) 'Daily record of dysfunctional thoughts: A better way of dealing with emotion', *the Behavior Therapist*, 15 (7): 162–164.

Carnegie, D. (1948) *How to Stop Worrying and Start Living*. New York: Simon and Schuster.

Clark, D.A., Beck, A.T. and Brown, G. (1989) 'Cognitive mediation in general psychiatric outpatients: A test of the content-specificity hypothesis', *Journal of Personality and Social Psychology*, 56: 958–964.

Clark, D.A., Beck, A.T. and Stewart, B. (1990) 'Cognitive specificity and positive-negative affectivity: Complementary or contradictory views on anxiety and depression', *Journal of Abnormal Psychology*, 99: 148–155.

Clark, D.M. (1986) 'A cognitive approach to panic', *Behaviour Research and Therapy*, 24: 461–470.

Clark, D.M. and Beck, A.T. (1988) 'Cognitive approaches', in C.G. Last and M. Hersen (eds), *Handbook of Anxiety Disorders*. New York: Pergamon. pp. 362–385.

Clark, D.M. and Teasdale, J.D. (1982) 'Diurnal variation in clinical depression and accessibility of memories of positive and negative experiences', *Journal of Abnormal Psychology*, 91: 87–95.

Clark, D.M., Salkovskis, P.M. and Chalkley, A.J. (1985) 'Respiratory control as a treatment for panic attacks', *Journal of Behavior Therapy and Experimental Psychiatry*, 16: 23–30.

Coue, E. (1922) *The Practice of Autosuggestion*. New York: Doubleday.

Coyne, J.L. and Gotlib, I.H. (1983) 'The role of cognition in depression: A critical appraisal', *Psychological Bulletin*, 94: 472–505.

Coyne, J.C. and Gotlib, I. (1986) 'Studying the role of cognition in depression: Well-trodden paths and cul-de-sacs', *Cognitive Therapy and Research*. 10 (6): 695–705.

Craighead, W.E. (1990) 'There's a place for us: All of us', *Behavior Therapy*, 21: 3–23.

Darwin, C.R. (1872) *The Expression of the Emotions in Man and Animals*. London: John Murray.

Dattilio, F.M. and Padesky, C.A. (1990) *Cognitive Therapy with Couples*. Sarasota, FL: Professional Resource Exchange, Inc.

Davey, G. (1987) 'An integration of human and animal models of Pavlovian conditioning: Association, cognitions and attributions', in G. Davey (ed.), *Cognitive Processes and Pavlovian Conditioning in Humans*. New York: John Wiley. pp. 83–114.

Davison, G.C. (1980) 'And now for something completely different: Cognition and little r', in M.J. Mahoney (ed.), *Psychotherapy Process: Current Issues and Future Directions*. New York: Plenum Press. pp. 203–209.

DeAngelis, B. (1992) *Are You the One for Me?* New York: Delacorte Press.

Dember, W.N. (1974) 'Motivation and the cognitive revolution', *American Psychologist*, 29: 161–168.

DeMonbreun, B.G. and Craighead, W.E. (1977) 'Distortion of perception and recall of positive and neutral feedback in depression', *Cognitive Therapy and Research*, 1: 311–329.

Diffily, A. (1991) 'Father and child: Tim Beck and his uncommon common sense', *Penn Medicine*, 4: 20–27.

Dobson, K.S. (ed.), (1988) *Handbook of Cognitive–Behavioral Therapies*. New York: The Guilford Press.

Dobson, K.S. (1989) 'A meta-analysis of the efficacy of cognitive therapy for depression', *Journal of Consulting and Clinical Psychology*, 57 (3): 414–419.

Dobson, K.S. and Block, L. (1988) 'Historical and philosophical bases of the cognitive–behavioral therapies', in K.S. Dobson (ed.), *Handbook of Cognitive–Behavioral Therapies*. New York: The Guilford Press. pp. 3–38.

Dryden, W. and Ellis, A. (1986) 'Rational–emotive therapy (RET)', in W. Dryden and W. Golden (eds), *Cognitive–Behavioural Approaches to Psychotherapy*. London: Harper and Row. pp. 129–168.

Dryden, W. and Ellis, A. (1988) 'Rational–emotive therapy', in K.S. Dobson (ed.), *Handbook of Cognitive–Behavioral Therapies*. New York: The Guilford Press. pp. 214–271.

Dryden, W. and Golden, W. (eds) (1986) *Cognitive–Behavioural Approaches to Psychotherapy*. London: Harper and Row.

DuBois, P. (1905) *The Psychic Treatment of Nervous Disorders (The Psychoneuroses and Their Moral Treatment)*, S.E. Jelliffe and W.A. White (ed. and trans.). New York: Funk & Wagnalls. Original work published in 1904.

Dunbar, G.C. and Lishman, W.A. (1984) 'Depression, recognition-memory and hedonic tone: A signal detection analysis', *British Journal of Psychiatry*, 144: 376–382.

Dyck, M.J. and Stewart, B.L. (1991) 'Cognitive vulnerability to depression', *Journal of Cognitive Psychotherapy: An International Quarterly*, 5 (2): 115–129.

Dykman, B.M., Abramson, L.Y., Alloy, L.B. and Hartlage, S. (1989) 'Processing of ambiguous and unambiguous feedback by depressed and non-depressed college students: Schematic bases and their implications for depressive realism', *Journal of Personality and Social Psychology*, 56: 431–445.

D'Zurilla, T.J. and Goldfried, M.R. (1971) 'Problem-solving and behavior modification', *Journal of Abnormal Psychology*, 78: 107–126.

Edwards, D.A. (1989) 'Cognitive restructuring through guided imagery: Lessons from Gestalt Therapy', in A. Freeman, K.M. Simon, L. Beutler and H. Arkowitz (eds), *Comprehensive Handbook of Cognitive Therapy*. New York: Plenum Press. pp. 283–297.

Edwards, D.A. (1990) 'Cognitive therapy and the restructuring of early memories through guided imagery', *Journal of Cognitive Psychotherapy: An International Quarterly*, 4 (1): 33–50.

Ehlers, A. (1991) 'Cognitive factors in panic attacks: Symptom probability and sensitivity', *Journal of Cognitive Psychotherapy: An International Quarterly*, 5 (3): 157–173.

Ehlers, A., Margraf, J., Roth, W.T., Taylor, C.B. and Birbaumer, N. (1988) 'Anxiety induced by false heart rate feedback in patients' panic disorder', *Behaviour Research and Therapy*, 26: 1–11.

Elkin, I., Shea, M.T., Watkins, J.T., Imber, S., Sotsky, S.M., Collins, J.F., Glass, D.R., Pilkonis, P.A., Leber, W.R., Docherty, J.P., Fiester, S.J. and Parloff, M.B. (1989) 'National Institute of Mental Health Treatment of Depression Collaborative Research Program: General effectiveness of treatments', *Archives of General Psychiatry*, 46: 971–983.

Ellis, A. (1955) 'New approaches to psychotherapy techniques', Brandon, VT: *Journal of Clinical Psychology Monograph Supplement Vol. 11*.

Ellis, A. (1962) *Reason and Emotion in Psychotherapy*. Seacaucus, New Jersey: Lyle Stuart.

Ellis, A. (1973) 'Are cognitive behavior therapy and rational therapy synonymous?', *Rational Living*, 8: 8–11.

Ellis, A. (1980) 'Rational–emotive therapy and cognitive behavior therapy: Similarities and differences', *Cognitive Therapy and Research*, 4: 325–340.

Ellis, A. (1987) 'A sadly neglected cognitive element in depression', *Cognitive Therapy and Research*, 11: 121–146.

Ellis, A. (1989) 'The history of cognition in psychotherapy', in A. Freeman, K.M. Simon, L.E. Beutler and H. Arkowitz (eds), *Comprehensive Handbook of Cognitive Therapy*. New York: Plenum. pp. 5–19.

Ellis, A. (1990) 'Is Rational–emotive therapy (RET) "rationalist" or "constructivist"?', in A. Ellis and W. Dryden, *The Essential Albert Ellis: Seminal Writings on Psychotherapy*. New York: Springer. pp. 114–141.

Ellis, A. (1991, August) 'The future of cognitive–behavioral and rational–emotive therapy', paper presented at the annual convention of the American Psychological Association, San Francisco.

Ellis, A. and Harper, R.A. (1961) *A Guide to Rational Living*. Englewood Cliffs, New Jersey: Prentice-Hall.

Ellis, A., Young, J. and Lockwood, G. (1987) 'Cognitive Therapy and Rational-emotive therapy: A dialogue', *Journal of Cognitive Psychotherapy*, 1 (4): 205–255.

Ellis, T.E. (1987) 'A cognitive approach to treating the suicidal client', in P.A. Keller and L.G. Ritt (eds), *Innovations in Clinical Practice: A Sourcebook*. Sarasota, FL: Professional Resource Exchange. pp. 93–107.

Emery, G. (1984) *Own Your Own Life*. New York: Signet.

Emery, G., Hollon, S. and Bedrosian, R. (eds) (1981) *New Directions in Cognitive Therapy*. New York: The Guilford Press.

Emmelkamp, P.M.G., VanLinden vanden Heuvell, C., Ruplan, M., Sanderman, R., Scholing, A. and Stroink, F. (1988) 'Cognitive and behavioral interventions: A comparative evaluation with clinically distressed couples', *Journal of Family Psychology*, 1: 365–377.

Epstein, N. and Baucom, D.H. (1989) 'Cognitive–behavioral marital therapy', in A. Freeman, K.M. Simon, L.E. Beutler and H. Arkowitz (eds), *Comprehensive Handbook of Cognitive Therapy*. New York: Plenum. pp. 491–513.

Epstein, N., Pretzer, J. and Fleming, B. (November 1982) 'Cognitive therapy and communication training: comparison of effects with distressed couples', Paper presented at the 16th Annual Convention of the Association for Advancement of Behavior Therapy, Los Angeles.

Erwin, E. (1992) 'Current philosophical issues in the scientific evaluation of behavior therapy: Theory and outcome', *Behavior Therapy*, 23: 151–171.

Evans, M.D., Hollon, S.D., DeRubeis, R.J., Piasecki, J.M., Grove, W.M., Garvey, M.J. and Tuason, V.B. (1992) 'Differential relapse following cognitive therapy and pharmacotherapy for depression', *Archives of General Psychiatry*, 49: 802–808.

Frank, J.D. (1985) 'Therapeutic components shared by all psychotherapies', in M.J. Mahoney and A. Freeman (eds), *Cognition and Psychotherapy*. New York: Plenum Press. pp. 49–79.

Freeman, A. (1981) 'Dreams and images in cognitive therapy', in G. Emery, S.D. Hollon and R.C. Bedrosian (eds), *New Directions in Cognitive Therapy*. New York: The Guilford Press. pp. 224–238.

Freeman, A. (ed.), (1983) *Cognitive Therapy With Couples and Groups*. New York: Plenum.

Freeman, A., Simon, K.M., Beutler, L.E. and Arkowitz, H. (eds) (1989) *Comprehensive Handbook of Cognitive Therapy*. New York: Plenum Press.

Garner, D.M. and Bemis, K.M. (1982) 'A cognitive–behavioral approach to anorexia nervosa', *Cognitive Therapy and Research*, 6: 123–150.

Gilson, M. (1983) 'Depression as measured by perceptual dominance in binocular rivalry'. PhD dissertation, Georgia State University. (University Microfilms No: AAD 83-27351).

Goldfried, M.R. (1971) 'Systematic desensitization as training in self-control', *Journal of Consulting and Clinical Psychology*, 37: 228–234.

Goldfried, M.R. (1980a) 'Psychotherapy as coping skills training', in M.J. Mahoney (ed.), *Psychotherapy Process: Current Issues and Future Directions*. New York: Plenum Press. pp. 89–119.

Goldfried, M.R. (1980b) 'Toward the delineation of therapeutic change principles', *American Psychologist*, 35 (11): 991–999.

Goldfried, M.R. (1988) ' A comment on therapeutic change: A response', *Journal of Cognitive Psychotherapy: An International Quarterly*, 2 (2): 89–93.

Goldfried, M.R. (1992) 'Psychotherapy integration: A mid-life for behavior therapy', *the Behavior Therapist*, 15 (2): 38–42.

Goldfried, M.R. and Hayes, A.M. (1989a) 'Can contributions from other orientations complement behavior therapy?', *the Behavior Therapist*, 12 (3): 57–60.

Goldfried, M.R. and Hayes, A.M. (1989b) 'Another look at Goldfried and Hayes', *the Behavior Therapist*, 12 (8): 174–175.

Goldfried, M.R., DeCanteceo, E.T. and Weinberg, L. (1974) 'Systematic rational restructuring as a self-control technique', *Behavior Therapy*, 5: 247–254.

Goleman, D. (1992) 'A rising cost of modernity: Depression', *New York Times*, December 8. pp. C1, C13.

Gotlib, I.H. (1981) 'Self-reinforcement and recall: Differential deficits in depressed and non-depressed psychiatric inpatients', *Journal of Abnormal Psychology*, 98: 9–13.

Gotlib, I.H. (1983) 'Perception and recall of interpersonal feedback: Negative bias in depression', *Cognitive Therapy and Research*, 7: 399–412.

Greenberg, L.S. and Safran, J.D. (1984) 'Integrating affect and cognition: A perspective on the process of therapeutic changes', *Cognitive Therapy and Research*, 8: 559–578.

Greenberg, L.S. and Safran, J.D. (1987) *Emotion in Psychotherapy*. New York: The Guilford Press.

Greenberg, L.S., Safran, J. and Rice, L. (1989) 'Experiential therapy: Its relation to cognitive therapy', in A. Freeman, K.M. Simon, L.E. Beutler and H. Arkowitz (eds), *Comprehensive Handbook of Cognitive Therapy*. New York: Plenum. pp. 169–187.

Greenberg, M.S. and Beck, A.T (1989) 'Depression versus anxiety: A test of the content specificity hypothesis', *Journal of Abnormal Psychology*, 98: 9–13.

Guidano, V.F. (1987) *Complexity of the Self: A Developmental Approach to Psychopathology and Therapy*. New York: The Guilford Press.

Guidano, V.F. (1991) *The Self in Process: Toward a Post-Rationalist Cognitive Therapy*. New York: The Guilford Press.

Guidano, V.F. and Liotti, G. (1983) *Cognitive Processes and Emotional Disorders*. New York: The Guilford Press.

Guidano, V.F. and Liotti, G. (1985) 'A constructivist foundation for cognitive therapy', in M.J. Mahoney and A. Freeman (eds), *Cognition and Psychotherapy*. New York: Plenum. pp. 101–142.

Haaga, D.A.F. (1986) 'A review of the common principles approach to integration of psychotherapies', *Cognitive Therapy and Research*, 10 (5): 527–538.

Haaga, D.A.F. and Davison, G.C. (1989) 'Slow progress in rational–emotive therapy outcome research: Etiology and treatment', *Cognitive Therapy and Research*, 13: 493–508.

Haaga, D.A.F., Dyck, M.J. and Ernst, D. (1991) 'Empirical status of cognitive theory of depression', *Psychological Bulletin*, 110 (2): 215–236.

Hammen, C., Ellicott, A. and Gitlin, M. (1989) 'Vulnerability to specific life events and prediction of course of disorder in unipolar depressed patients', *Canadian Journal of Behavioural Science*, 21: 377–388.

Hammen, C., Ellicott, A., Gitlin, M. and Jamison, K.R. (1989) 'Sociotropy/ autonomy and vulnerability to specific life events in patients with unipolar depression and bipolar disorders', *Journal of Abnormal Psychology*, 98: 1147–1159.

Hawkins, R.P. (1989, November) 'Can behavior therapy be saved from triviality? Toward an integrated science-technology of behavior', in A.W. Staats (Chair), AABT/ABA/Division 25: 'Inadequate organizational structure for the new challenge?' Symposium presented at the Annual Conference of the Association for Advancement of Behavior Therapy, Washington, DC.

Hawkins, R.P., Kashden, J., Hansen, D.J. and Sadd, D.L. (1992) 'The increasing reference to "cognitive" variables in behavior therapy: A 20-year empirical analysis', *the Behavior Therapist*, 15 (5): 115–118.

Hollon, S.D. and Beck, A.T. (1979) 'Cognitive therapy for depression', in P.C. Kendall and S.D. Hollon (eds), *Cognitive-Behavioral Intervention: Theory, Research and Procedures*. New York: Academic Press. pp. 153–203.

Hollon, S.D. and Garber, J. (1990) 'Cognitive therapy for depression: A social cognitive perspective', *Personality and Social Psychology Bulletin*, 16 (1): 58–73.

Hollon, S.D. and Kriss, M.R. (1984) 'Cognitive factors in clinical research and practice', *Clinical Psychology Review*, 4: 35–76.

Hollon, S.D. and Najavits, L. (1988) 'Review of empirical studies on cognitive therapy', in A.J. Frances and R.E. Hales (eds), *Review of Psychiatry, Vol. 7*. Washington, DC: American Psychiatric Press. pp. 643–666.

Hollon, S.D., DeRubeis, R.J, Evans, M.D., Weimer, M.J., Garvey, M.J., Grove,

W.M. and Tuason, V.B. (1992) 'Cognitive therapy and pharmacotherapy for depression', *Archives of General Psychiatry*, 49: 774–781.

Homme, L.E. (1965) 'Perspectives in psychology XXIV. Control of coverants, the operants of the mind', *Psychological Record*, 15: 501–511.

Horney, K. (1950) *Neurosis and Human Growth*. New York: Norton.

Horvitz, E.F. (1990) 'Harry S. Beck and other Jewish printers', *Rhode Island Jewish Historical Notes*, Vol. 10(4): 494–502.

Houts, A.C. and Follette, W.C. (1992) 'Philosophical and theoretical issues in behavior therapy', *Behavior Therapy*, 23: 145–149.

Huber, C.H. and Milstein, B. (1985) 'Cognitive restructuring and collaborative set in couples' work', *American Journal of Family Therapy*, 13: 17–27.

Ingram, R.E. (1990) 'Self-focused attention in clinical disorders: Review and a conceptual model', *Psychological Bulletin*, 107: 156–176.

Ingram, R.E. and Kendall, P.C. (1987) 'The cognitive side of anxiety', *Cognitive Therapy and Research*, 11: 523–536.

Kanfer, F.H. (1970) 'Self-regulation: Research issues and speculation', in C. Neuringer and L.L. Michael (eds), *Behavior Modification in Clinical Psychology*, New York: Appleton-Century-Crofts. pp. 178–220.

Kanfer, F.H. (1971) 'The maintenance of behavior by self-generated stimuli and reinforcement', in A. Jacobs and L.B. Sachs (eds), *The Psychology of Private Events: Perspectives on Covert Response System*. New York: Academic Press. pp. 39–59.

Kanfer, F.H. and Karoly, P. (1972) 'Self-control: A behavioristic excursion into the lion's den', *Behavior Therapy*, 3: 398–416.

Karasu, T.B. (1990) 'Toward a clinical model of psychotherapy for depression, I: Systematic comparison of three psychotherapies', *American Journal of Psychiatry*, 147 (2): 133–147.

Kelly, G. (1955) *The Psychology of Personal Constructs* (2 vols). New York: Norton.

Kendall, P.C. and Bemis, K.M. (1983) 'Thought and action in psychotherapy: The cognitive–behavioral approaches', in M. Hersch, A.E. Kazdin and A.S. Bellack (eds), *The Clinical Psychology Handbook*. New York: Pergamon. pp. 565–592.

Knaus, W. (1974) *Rational-Emotive Education: A Manual for Elementary School Teachers*. New York: Institute for Rational Living.

Kovacs, M. and Beck, A.T. (1978) 'Maladaptive cognitive structures in depression', *American Journal of Psychiatry*, 135: 525–533.

Kovacs, M., Rush, A.J., Beck, A.T. and Hollon, S.D. (1981) 'Depressed outpatients treated with cognitive therapy or pharmacotherapy: A one-year follow-up', *Archives of General Psychiatry*, 38: 33–39.

Krantz, S.E. (1985) 'When depressive cognitions reflect negative realities', *Cognitive Therapy and Research*, 9 (6): 595–610.

Krantz, S. and Hammen, C. (1979) 'Assessment of cognitive bias in depression', *Journal of Abnormal Psychology*, 88: 611–619.

Last, C.G. and Blanchard, E.B. (1982) 'Classification of phobics versus fearful nonphobics: procedural and theoretical issues', *Behavioral Assessment*, 4: 195–210.

Lazarus, A.A. (1979) 'A matter of emphasis' (A comment on Wolpe's 'Cognition and causation in behavior and its therapy'), *American Psychologist*, 34 (1): 100.

Lazarus, A.A. (1981) *The Practice of Multimodal Therapy*. New York: McGraw-Hill.

Lazarus, A.A. (ed.) (1985) *Casebook of Multimodal Therapy*. New York: The Guilford Press.

Lazarus, R.S. (1966) *Psychological Stress and the Coping Process.* New York: McGraw-Hill.

Lazarus, R.S. (1980) 'Cognitive behavior therapy as psychodynamics revisited', in M.J. Mahoney (ed.), *Psychotherapy Process: Current Issues and Future Directions.* New York: Plenum Press. pp. 121–126.

Lazarus, R.S. (1982) 'Thoughts on the relation between emotion and cognition', *American Psychologist,* 37: 1019–1024.

Lazarus, R.S. (1984) 'On the primacy of cognition', *American Psychologist,* 39: 124–129.

Lazarus, R.S. (1991) 'Progress on a cognitive–motivational–relational theory of emotion', *American Psychologist,* 46 (8): 819–834.

Liotti, G. (1991) 'Patterns of attachments and the assessment of interpersonal schemata: Understanding and changing difficult patient–therapist relationships in cognitive psychotherapy', *Journal of Cognitive Psychotherapy: An International Quarterly,* 5 (2): 105–114.

Luria, A.R. (1961) *The Role of Speech in the Regulation of Normal and Abnormal Behavior.* New York: Liveright.

Mahoney, M.J. (1974) *Cognition and Behavior Modification.* Cambridge, MA: Ballinger.

Mahoney, M.J. (1977) 'Reflections on the cognitive–learning trend in psychotherapy', *American Psychologist,* 32: 5–13.

Mahoney, M.J. (1980) 'Psychotherapy and the structure of personal revolutions', in M.J. Mahoney (ed.), *Psychotherapy Process: Current Issues and Future Directions.* New York: Plenum Press. pp. 157–180.

Mahoney, M.J. (1981) 'Clinical psychology and scientific inquiry', *International Journal of Psychology,* 16: 157–274.

Mahoney, M.J. (1983) 'Stream of consciousness: A therapeutic application' (videotape). Bellefonte, PA: Personal Empowerment Program.

Mahoney, M.J. (1984) 'Behaviorism, cognitivism, and human change process' in M.A. Reda and M.J. Mahoney (eds), *Cognitive Psychotherapies: Recent Developments in Theory, Research, and Practice.* Cambridge, MA: Ballinger. pp. 3–30.

Mahoney, M.J. (1985a) 'Personal knowing process: Illustrating the interface among cognitive and clinical sciences', paper presented at the Eastern Association for Behavior Therapy. Los Angeles, CA.

Mahoney, M.J. (1985b) 'Reflections on the cognitive revolution', paper presented at the meeting of the Association for Advancement of Behavior Therapy. Houston, TX.

Mahoney, M.J. (1988) 'The cognitive sciences and psychotherapy: Patterns in a developing relationship', in K. Dobson (ed.), *Handbook of Cognitive–Behavioral Therapies.* New York: The Guilford Press. pp. 357–386.

Mahoney, M.J. (1990) *Human Change Processes: The Scientific Foundation of Psychotherapy.* New York: Basic Books.

Mahoney, M.J. and Arnkoff, D.B. (1978) 'Cognitive and self-control therapies', in Garfield, S.L. and Bergin, A.E. (eds), *Handbook of Psychotherapy and Behavior Change: An Empirical Analysis.* New York: John Wiley & Sons. pp. 689–722.

Mahoney, M.J. and Gabriel, T.J. (1987) 'Psychotherapy and the cognitive sciences: An evolving alliance', *Journal of Cognitive Psychotherapy: An International Quarterly,* 1 (1): 39–59.

Mahoney, M.J. and Gabriel, T.J. (1990) 'Essential tensions in psychology:

Longitudinal data on cognitive and behavioral ideologies', *Journal of Cognitive Psychotherapy: An International Quarterly*, 4: 5–21.

Margolin, G. and Weiss, R.L. (1978) 'Comparative evaluation of therapeutic components associated with behavioral marital treatments', *Journal of Consulting and Clinical Psychology*, 46: 1476–1786.

Markus, H. (1977) 'Self-schema and processing information about the self', *Journal of Personality and Social Psychology*, 35: 63–78.

Mayer, J.D. and Bower, G.H. (1985) 'Naturally occurring mood and learning: Comment on Hasher, Rose, Zacks, Sanft, and Doren', *Journal of Experimental Psychology*, 114: 396–403.

Meichenbaum, D. (1974) *Cognitive Behavior Modification*. Morristown, New Jersey: General Learning Press.

Meichenbaum, D. (1975a) 'Self-instructional methods', in F.H. Kanfer and A.P. Goldstein (eds), *Helping People Change*. New York: Pergamon Press.

Meichenbaum, D. (1975b) 'A self-instructional approach to stress management: A proposal for stress inoculation training', in J. Sarason and C.D. Speilberger (eds), *Stress and Anxiety*, Vol. 2. New York: Wiley.

Meichenbaum, D. (1977) *Cognitive Behavior Modification*. New York: Plenum Press.

Meichenbaum, D. (1985) *Stress Inoculation Training*. New York: Pergamon.

Meichenbaum, D. and Gilmore, J.B. (1984) 'The nature of unconscious processes: A cognitive–behavioral perspective', in K.S. Bowers and D. Meichenbaum (eds), *The Unconscious Reconsidered*. New York: John Wiley & Sons. pp. 273–298.

Meyers, A.W. and Craighead, W.E. (1984) 'Cognitive behavior therapy with children: A historical, conceptual and organizational overview', in A.W. Meyers and W.E. Craighead (eds), *Cognitive Behavior Therapy with Children*, New York: Plenum. pp. 1–17.

Miller, I.W., Norman, W.H. and Keitner, G.I. (1989) 'Cognitive–behavioral treatment of depressed inpatients: Six and twelve-month follow-up', *American Journal of Psychiatry*, 146: 1274–1279.

Miller, I.W., Norman, W.H., Keitner, G.I., Bishop, S.B. and Dow, M.G. (1989) 'Cognitive–behavioral treatment of depressed inpatients', *Behavior Therapy*, 20 (1): 25–47.

Mischel, W. (1974) 'Processes in delay of gratification', in L. Berkowitz (ed.), *Advances in Experimental Social Psychology (Vol. 7)*. New York: Academic Press. pp. 249–292.

Morton, J., Hammersly, R.H. and Bikerian, D.A. (1985) 'Headed records: A model for memory and its failures', *Cognition*, 20: 1–23.

Moscovitch, M. (1985) 'Memory from infancy to old age: implications', *Annals of the New York Academy of Sciences*, 444: 78–96.

Moshman, D. and Hoover, L.M. (1989) 'Rationality as a goal of psychotherapy', *Journal of Cognitive Psychotherapy: An International Quarterly*, 3 (1), 31–51.

Newman, C.F. (1991) 'Cognitive therapy and the facilitation of affect: Two case illustrations', *Journal of Cognitive Psychotherapy: An International Quarterly*, 5 (4): 305–316.

Nezu, A.M., Nezu, C.M. and Perri, M.G. (1989) *Problem-Solving Therapy for Depression: Theory, Research and Clinical Guidelines*. New York: John Wiley & Sons.

Padesky, C. (1990) 'Treating personality disorders: A cognitive approach',

Workshop presented by the Institute for the Advancement of Human Behavior, Washington, DC. November 16-17.

Patsiokas, A.T. and Clum, G.A. (1985) 'Effects of psychotherapeutic strategies in the treatment of suicide attempters', *Psychotherapy*, 22: 281-290.

Peale, N.V. (1960) *The Power of Positive Thinking*. Englewood Cliffs, New Jersey: Prentice Hall.

Perris, C. (1989) *Cognitive Therapy with Schizophrenic Patients*. New York: The Guilford Press and London: Cassell.

Persons, J.B. (1989) *Cognitive Therapy in Practice: A Case Formulation Approach*. New York: Norton.

Persons, J.B. (1990) 'Disputing irrational thoughts can be avoidance behavior: A case report', *the Behavior Therapist*, 13 (6): 132-133.

Peterson, D. and Seligman, M.E.P. (1985) 'The learned helplessness model of depression: Current status of theory and research', in E.E. Beckham and W.R. Leber (eds), *Handbook of Depression: Treatment, Assessment and Research*. Homewood, IL: Dorsey. pp. 914-939.

Piaget, J. (1926) *The Language and Thought of the Child*. New York: Harcourt, Brace.

Piaget, J. (1936/1952) *The Origin of Intelligence in Children*. New York: International Universities Press.

Powell, M. and Hemsley, D.R. (1984) 'Depression: A breakdown of perceptual defense?', *British Journal of Psychiatry*, 145: 358-362.

Power, M.J. (1987) 'Cognitive theories of depression', in H.J. Eysenck and I. Martin (eds), *Theoretical Foundation of Behavior Therapy*. New York: Plenum Press. pp. 235-255.

Power, M.J. (1989) 'Cognitive therapy: An outline of theory, practice and problems', *British Journal of Psychotherapy*, 5 (4): 544-556.

Power, M.J. (1991) 'Cognitive science and behavioural psychotherapy: Where behaviour was, there shall cognition be?', *Behavioural Psychotherapy*, 19: 20-41.

Power, M.J. and Champion, L.A. (1986) 'Cognitive approaches to depression: A theoretical critique', *British Journal of Clinical Psychology*, 25: 201-212.

Pretzer, J.L. (1983, August) 'Borderline personality disorder: Too complex for cognitive-behavioral approaches?', paper presented at the meeting of the American Psychological Association, Anaheim, CA (ERIC Document Reproduction Service. No. ed 243, 007).

Pretzer, J.L. (1985, November) 'Paranoid personality disorders: A cognitive view', paper presented at the meeting of the Association for Advancement of Behavior Therapy, Houston, TX.

Pretzer, J.L. (1989, June) 'Borderline Personality Disorder: Cognitive-Behavioral Perspectives', paper presented at the World Congress of Cognitive Therapy, Oxford, England.

Pretzer, J.L. (1990) 'Borderline personality disorder', in A.T. Beck, A. Freeman and Associates. *Cognitive Therapy of Personality Disorders*. New York: The Guilford Press. pp. 176-207.

Pretzer, J.L. and Fleming, B. (1989) 'Cognitive-behavioral treatment of personality disorders', *the Behavior Therapist*, 12: 105-109.

Rachlin, H. (1988) 'Molar behaviorism', in D.B. Fishman, F. Rotgers and C.M. Franks (eds), *Paradigms in Behavior Therapy: Present and Promise*. New York: Springer. pp. 77-105.

Raimy, V. (1980) 'A manual for cognitive therapy', in M.J. Mahoney (ed.),

Psychotherapy Process: Current Issues and Future Directions. New York: Plenum Press. pp. 153–156.

Reda, M.A. and Mahoney, M.J. (1984) (eds), *Cognitive Psychotherapies: Recent Developments in Theory, Research, and Practice.* Cambridge, MA: Ballinger.

Riskind, J.H. (1983, August) 'Misconception of the cognitive model of depression', paper presented at the 91st Annual Convention of the American Psychological Association, Anaheim, CA.

Riskind, J.H. and Rholes, W.S. (1984) 'Cognitive accessibility and the capacity of cognitions to predict future depression: A theoretical note', *Cognitive Therapy and Research*, 8: 1–12.

Robinson, S. and Birchwood, M. (1991) 'The relationship between catastrophic cognitions and the components of panic disorder', *Journal of Cognitive Psychotherapy: An International Quarterly*, 5 (3): 175–186.

Rogers, C.R. (1951) *Client-Centered Therapy: Its Current Practice, Implications, and Theory.* Boston: Houghton Mifflin.

Ross, C.A. (1989) *Multiple Personality Disorder: Diagnosis, Clinical Features, and Treatment.* New York: John Wiley & Sons.

Ross, P. (1990) 'Aaron Beck's not-so-odd behavior', *The Pennsylvania Gazette*, 89(3): 28–35, 46.

Rush, A.J., Weissenberger, J. and Eaves, G. (1986) 'Do thinking patterns predict depressive symptoms?', *Cognitive Therapy and Research*, 10: 225–236.

Rush, A.J., Beck, A.T., Kovacs, M. and Hollon, S.D. (1977) 'Comparative efficacy of cognitive therapy and pharmacotherapy in the treatment of depressed outpatients', *Cognitive Therapy and Research*, 1: 17–37.

Rush, A.J., Kovacs, M., Beck, A.T., Weissenberger, J. and Hollon, S.D. (1981) 'Differential effects of cognitive therapy and pharmacotherapy on depressive symptoms', *Journal of Affective Disorders*, 3: 221–229.

Rush, A.J., Beck, A.T., Kovacs, M., Weissenberger, J. and Hollon, S.D. (1982) 'Differential effects of cognitive therapy and pharmacotherapy on hopelessness and self-concept', *American Journal of Psychiatry*, 139 (7): 862–866.

Ryle, A. and Cowmeadow, P. (1992) 'Cognitive analytic therapy', in W. Dryden (ed.), *Integrative and Eclectic Therapy: A Handbook.* Buckingham: Open University Press. pp. 84–108.

Sacco, W.P. and Beck, A.T. (1985) 'Cognitive therapy of depression', in E.E. Beckham and W.R. Leber (eds), *Handbook of Depression: Treatment, Assessment and Research.* Homewood, IL: Dorsey Press. pp. 3–38.

Safran, J.D. (1984) 'Assessing the cognitive–interpersonal cycle', *Cognitive Therapy and Research*, 8 (4): 333–348.

Safran, J.D. (1986) 'A critical evaluation of the schema construct in psychotherapy research', paper presented at The Society for Psychotherapy Research Conference, Boston.

Safran, J.D. (1987) 'Toward an integration of cognitive and interpersonal approaches to psychotherapy', unpublished manuscript.

Safran, J. (1989, July) 'Emotion in cognitive therapy: An appraisal of recent conceptual and clinical developments', paper presented at The World Congress of Cognitive Therapy, Oxford, England.

Safran, J. (1990) 'Toward a refinement of cognitive therapy in light of interpersonal theory: I. Theory', *Clinical Psychology Review*, 10: 87–105.

Safran, J.D. and Greenberg, L.S. (1982a) 'Cognitive appraisal and reappraisal: Implications for clinical practice', *Cognitive Therapy and Research*, 6: 251–258.

Safran, J.D. and Greenberg, L.S. (1982b) 'Eliciting "hot cognitions" in cognitive therapy', Canadian Psychology, 23: 83-87.

Safran, J.D. and Greenberg, L.S. (1986) 'Hot cognition and psychotherapy process: An information processing/ecological perspective', in P.C. Kendall (ed.), Advances in Cognitive-behavioral Research and Therapy (Vol. 5), New York: Academic Press. pp. 143-177.

Safran, J.D. and Greenberg, L.S. (1987) 'Affect and the unconscious: A cognitive perspective', in R. Stern (ed.), Theories of the Unconscious. Hillsdale, New Jersey: The Analytic Press. pp. 191-212.

Safran, J.D. and Greenberg, L.S. (1988) 'Feeling, thinking and acting: A cognitive framework for psychotherapy integration', Journal of Cognitive Psychotherapy: An International Quarterly, 2 (2): 109-131.

Safran, J.D. and Segal, Z.V. (1990) Interpersonal Process in Cognitive Therapy. New York: Basic Books, Inc.

Safran, J.D., Vallis, T.M., Segal, Z.V. and Shaw, B.F. (1986) 'Assessment of core cognitive processes in cognitive therapy', Cognitive Therapy and Research, 10: 509-526.

Salkovskis, P.M. (1990) Transcript of an interview with A.T. Beck. November 3, 1990, 24th Annual Convention of the Association for Advancement of Behavior Therapy, San Francisco.

Salkovskis, P.M. and Clark, D.M. (1991) 'Cognitive therapy for panic attacks', Journal of Cognitive Psychotherapy: An International Quarterly, 5 (13): 215-226.

Salkovskis, P.M., Clark, D.M. and Hackmann A. (1990) 'Treatment of panic attacks using cognitive therapy without exposure', Behaviour Research and Therapy, 28: 51-61.

Salkovskis, P.M, Jones, D.R.O. and Clark, D.M. (1986) 'Respiratory control in the treatment of panic attacks: Replication and extension with concurrent measurement of behavior and p CO_2', British Journal of Psychiatry, 148: 526-532.

Scheier, M.F. and Carver, C.S. (1987) 'Dispositional optimism and physical well-being: The influence of generalized outcome expectancies on health', Journal of Personality, 55: 169-210.

Schwartz, R.M. and Garamoni, G.L. (1989) 'Cognitive balance and psychopathology: Evaluation of an information processing model of positive and negative states of mind', Clinical Psychology Review, 9: 271-294.

Segal, Z.V. (1988) 'Appraisal of the self-schema construct in cognitive models of depression', Psychological Bulletin, 103 (2): 147-162.

Segal, Z.V. and Shaw, B.F. (1986a) 'Cognition in depression: A reappraisal of Coyne and Gotlib's Critique', Cognitive Therapy and Research, 10 (6): 671-693.

Segal, Z.V. and Shaw, B.F. (1986b) 'When cul-de-sacs are more mentality than reality: A rejoinder to Coyne and Gotlib', Cognitive Therapy and Research, 10 (6): 707-714.

Segal, Z.V., Shaw, B.F., and Vella, D.D. (1989) 'Life stress and depression: A test of the congruency hypothesis for life event content and depressive subtype', Canadian Journal of Behavioural Science, 21: 389-400.

Segal, Z.V., Hood, J.E., Shaw, B.F. and Higgins, E.T. (1988) 'A structural analysis of the self-schema construct in major depression', Cognitive Therapy and Research, 12: 471-485.

Seligman, M.E.P. (1988) 'Competing theories of panic', in S. Rachman and J.D.

166 Aaron T. Beck

Maser (eds), *Panic: Psychological Perspectives*. Hillsdale, New Jersey: Lawrence Erlbaum Associates. pp. 321-329.

Shaw, B.F. (1977) 'Comparison of cognitive therapy and behavior therapy in the treatment of depression', *Journal of Consulting and Clinical Psychology*, 45: 543-551.

Shaw, B.F. (1979) 'The theoretical and experimental foundations of a cognitive model of depression', in P. Pliner, I. Spiegel and K. Blankstein (eds), *Perception of Emotion in Self and Others*. New York: Plenum. pp. 137-163.

Shaw, B.F. (1984) 'Specification of the training and evaluation of cognitive therapists for outcome studies', in J.B.W. Williams and R.L. Spitzer (eds), *Psychotherapy Research: Where Are We and Where Are We Going?* New York: The Guilford Press. pp. 173-189.

Shaw, B.F. (1988) 'The value of researching psychotherapy techniques: A response', *Journal of Cognitive Psychotherapy: An International Quarterly*, 2 (2): 83-87.

Shaw, B.F. and Segal, Z.V. (1988) 'Introduction to cognitive theory and therapy', in A.J. Frances and R.E. Hales (eds), *Review of Psychiatry, Vol. 7*. Washington, DC: American Psychiatric Press. pp. 538-553.

Shea, M.T., Elkin, I., Imber, S.D., Sotsky, S.M., Watkins, J.T., Collins, J.F., Pilkonis, P.A., Beckham, E., Glass, D.R., Dolan, R.T. and Parloff, M.B. (1992) 'Course of depressive symptoms over follow-up: Findings from the National Institute of Mental Health treatment of depression collaborative research program', *Archives of General Psychiatry*, 49: 782-787.

Shulman, B.H. (1988) 'Dissecting the elements of therapeutic change: A response', *Journal of Cognitive Psychotherapy: An International Quarterly*, 2 (2): 95-103.

Siddle, D.A.T. and Remington, B. (1987) 'Latent inhibition and human Pavlovian conditioning: Research and relevance', in G. Davey (ed.), *Cognitive Processes and Pavlovian Conditioning in Humans*. New York: John Wiley & Sons. pp. 115-146.

Simons, A.D., Garfield, S.L., Murphy, G.E (1984) 'The process of change in cognitive therapy and pharmacotherapy for depression', *Archives of General Psychiatry*, 41: 45-51.

Simons, A.D., Murphy, G.E., Levine, J.E. and Wetzel, R.D. (1986) 'Cognitive therapy and pharmacotherapy for depression: Sustained improvement over one year', *Archives of General Psychiatry*, 43: 43-49.

Skinner, B.F. (1977) 'Why I am not a cognitive psychologist', *Behaviorism*, 5: 1-10.

Skinner, B.F. (1988) 'Reply to Harnad', in A.C. Cataina and S. Harnard (eds), *The Selection of Behavior: The Operant Behaviorism of B.F. Skinner: Comments and Consequences*. Cambridge: Cambridge University Press. pp. 468-473.

Sokol, L., Beck, A.T. and Clark, D.A. (1989, June) 'A controlled treatment trial of cognitive therapy for panic disorder', paper presented at the World Congress of Cognitive Therapy. Oxford, England.

Sokol, L., Beck, A.T., Greenberg, R.L., Berchick, R.J. and Wright, E.D. (1989) 'Cognitive therapy of panic disorder: A non-pharmacological alternative', *Journal of Nervous and Mental Diseases*, 177: 711-716.

Spivack, G., Platt, J.J., Shure, M.B. (1976) 'The problem-solving approach to adjustment', San Francisco: Jossey-Bass.

Strupp, H.H. (1988) 'What is therapeutic change?' *Journal of Cognitive Psychotherapy: An International Quarterly*, 2 (2): 75-82.

Sulloway, F.J. (1991) 'Darwinian psychobiography', *New York Review of Books*, October 10: 29-32.

Szykula, S.A., Czajkowski, L., Laylander, J.A. and Sayger, T.V. (1989) '"Consciousness streaming". A single subject within session analysis of therapeutically relevant verbalizations', *Journal of Cognitive Psychotherapy: An International Quarterly*, 3 (4): 299–310.

Taylor, F.G. and Marshall, W.L. (1977) 'Experimental analysis of a cognitive-behavioral therapy for depression', *Cognitive Therapy and Research*, 1: 59–72.

Taylor, S.E. (1983) 'Adjustment to threatening events: A theory of cognitive adaptation', *American Psychologist*, 38 (11): 1161–1173.

Teasdale, J.D. and Fennell, M.J.V. (1982) 'Immediate effects on depression of cognitive therapy intervention', *Cognitive Therapy and Research*, 6: 343–352.

Thyer, B.A. (1992) 'The term "cognitive–behavior therapy" is redundant', *the Behavior Therapist*, 15 (5): 112.

Vallis, T.M., Shaw, B.F. and Dobson, K.S. (1986) 'The Cognitive Therapy Scale: Psychometric properties', *Journal of Consulting and Clinical Psychology*, 54: 381–385.

Vygotsky, L.S. (1962) *Thought and Language*. New York: John Wiley & Sons.

Wachtel, P.L. (1977) *Psychoanalysis and Behavior Therapy: Toward an Integration*. New York: Basic Books.

Weimer, W.B. (1979) *Notes on the Methodology of Scientific Research*. Hillsdale, New Jersey: Lawrence Erlbaum Associates.

Weishaar, M.E. and Beck, A.T. (1986) 'Cognitive therapy', in W. Dryden and W. Golden (eds), *Cognitive–Behavioural Approaches to Psychotherapy*. London: Harper and Row. pp. 61–91.

Weishaar, M.E. and Beck, A.T. (1990) 'Cognitive approaches to understanding and treating suicidal behavior', in S.J. Blumenthal and D.J. Kupfer (eds), *Suicide over the Life Cycle: Risk Factors, Assessment and Treatment of Suicidal Patients*. Washington, DC: American Psychiatric Press. pp. 469–498.

Weishaar, M.E. and Beck, A.T. (1992) 'Clinical and cognitive predictors of suicide', in R.W. Maris, A.L. Berman, J.T. Mattsberger and R.I. Yufit (eds), *Assessment and Prediction of Suicide*. New York: The Guilford Press. pp. 467–483.

Weissman, A.N. (1979) 'The Dysfunctional Attitude Scale: A validation study', PhD Dissertation, University of Pennsylvania.

Weissman, A. and Beck, A.T. (1978) 'Development and validation of the Dysfunctional Attitude Scale', paper presented at the Annual Convention of the Association for Advancement of Behavior Therapy, Chicago.

Wessler, R.L. (1986) 'Conceptualizing cognition in the cognitive–behavioural therapies', in W. Dryden and W. Golden (eds), *Cognitive–Behavioural Approaches to Psychotherapy*. London: Harper and Row. pp. 1–30.

Wilson, G.T. (1978) 'Cognitive behavior therapy: Paradigm shift or passing phase?', in J.P. Foreyt and D.P. Rathjen (eds), *Cognitive Behavior Therapy: Research and Application*. New York: Plenum. pp. 7–32

Wolpe, J. (1958) *Psychotherapy by Reciprocal Inhibition*. Stanford, CA: Stanford University Press

Wolpe, J. (1976a) 'Behavior therapy and its malcontents: I. Negation of its bases and psychodynamic fusionism', *Journal of Behavior Therapy and Experimental Psychiatry*, 7: 1–5.

Wolpe, J. (1976b) 'Behavior therapy and its malcontents: II. Multimodal eclecticism, cognitive exclusivism and "exposure" empiricism', *Journal of Behavior Therapy and Experimental Psychiatry*, 7: 109–116.

Wolpe, J. (1978) 'Cognition and causation in human behavior and its therapy', *American Psychologist*. 33: 437–446.

Wolpe, J. (1980) 'Cognitive behavior and its roles in psychotherapy: An integrative account', in M.J. Mahoney (ed.), *Psychotherapy Process: Current Issues and Future Directions*. New York: Plenum Press. pp. 185–201.

Wolpe, J. (1985) 'Requiem for an Institution', *the Behavior Therapist*, 8: 113.

Wolpe, J. (1989) 'The derailment of behavior therapy: A tale of conceptual misdirection', *Journal of Behavior Therapy and Experimental Psychiatry*, 20: 3–15.

Wolpe, J. and Rowan, V.C. (1988) 'Panic disorder: A product of classical conditioning' [Invited Essay], *Behaviour Research and Therapy*, 26 (6): 441–450.

Woody, G.E., McLellan, A.T., Luborsky, L., O'Brien, C.P., Blaine, J., Fox, S., Herman, I. and Beck, A.T. (1984) 'Severity of psychiatric symptoms as a predictor of benefits from psychotherapy: The Veterans Administration – Penn Study', *American Journal of Psychiatry*, 141: 1172–1177.

Wright, J.H. (1988) 'Cognitive therapy of depression', in A.J. Frances and R.E. Hales (eds), *Review of Psychiatry, Vol.7*. Washington, DC: American Psychiatric Press. pp. 554–570.

Wright, J.H., Thase, M., Beck, A.T. and Ludgate, J.W. (eds) (1993) *Cognitive Therapy with Inpatients: Developing a Cognitive Milieu*. New York: The Guilford Press.

Yapko, M.D. (1991) 'An interview with Aaron T. Beck, M.D.', *The Milton H. Erickson Foundation Newsletter*, 11 (2): 1, 8–12.

Young, J.E. (1982) 'Loneliness, depression and cognitive therapy: Theory and application', in L.A. Peplau and D. Perlman (eds), *Loneliness: A Source Book of Current Theory, Research and Therapy*. New York: John Wiley & Sons. pp. 388–389.

Young, J.E. (1990) *Cognitive Therapy for Personality Disorders: A Schema-Focused Approach*. Sarasota, FL: Professional Resource Exchange.

Young, J. and Beck, A.T. (1980) 'Cognitive therapy rating scale: rating manual'. Unpublished manuscript, Center for Cognitive Therapy, Philadelphia.

Young, J. and Klosko, J.S. (1993) *Reinventing Your Life: Smart Moves for Escaping Negative Life Patterns*. New York: Dutton.

Young, J.E. and Lindemann, M.D. (1992) 'An integrative schema-focused model for personality disorders', *Journal of Cognitive Psychotherapy: An International Quarterly*, 6 (1): 11–23.

Zajonc, R.B. (1980) 'Feeling and thinking: Preferences need no references', *American Psychologist*, 35: 151–175.

Zajonc, R.B. (1984) 'On the primacy of affect', *American Psychologist*, 39: 117–123.

Index